CONTENTS

INTRODUCTION

Higher English

Welcome to Essential SQA Exam Practice for Higher English. The purpose of this book is to help you develop your skills for the exam. It is written with you, the student, in mind. The book is focused on the exam and, by using sample papers, gives you plenty of hints and tips to not only help you pass, but pass well.

It will benefit you to work through all the exercises in this book. However, if you are short of time, think about the areas you need to work on the most. You can then focus your learning and/or revision on these particular areas. The first part of the book is structured so that you can 'dip in and out' of it, but covering all of them can only benefit you.

Structure of the book

This book is divided into two parts. Part one covers sample questions and advice on how to answer these. Part two consists of two full papers that you can use to practise on for your exam.

The first section of the book looks in detail at the two papers you will sit in the exam (see below for more detail) and the different types of questions you will have to answer. It gives you advice on how to answer questions on how to **identify** and **explain** information. It then shows you how to answer questions based on **techniques**, such as **word choice** and **sentence structure**. You are walked through how to deal with the **agreement/disagreement** question (the last question). Underneath each type of question there are examples of questions you may be asked, based on the four sample passages at the start of this section. You should attempt these questions and mark them according to the Answers to the Practice Questions at the end of the Practice Questions section. Make sure you attempt the question before looking at the answers! But also use the answers to learn.

The second section of the Practice Questions examines the Critical Reading paper and gives you advice on how to tackle the short questions and the 'ten-marker' for the Scottish Text. There are examples of different types of questions you might be asked for each of the most popular texts: *Men Should Weep*, *The Cone-Gatherers* and Carol Ann Duffy's poetry. You will find the answers to these at the end of the Practice Questions.

You are then given some essay writing advice and again, sample questions are offered. There are also some sample essays to help you understand what is required in this section. First though, here is an outline of the course and what you need to do to pass.

The course

The Higher English course aims to:

▶ provide you with the opportunity to develop listening, talking, reading and writing skills that will enable you to understand and use language
▶ develop your understanding of the complexities of language by studying a wide range of texts and building on your literacy skills
▶ develop high levels of analytical thinking and understanding of the impact of language.

Course assessment

The Higher English course assessment covers the following:

▶ Spoken language component – which is assessed in school or college. This does not count towards your final grade, but you must achieve the minimum requirements in it before you can get a final graded award
▶ your Portfolio of Writing; this is submitted in March or April for marking by SQA and counts for 30% of your final grade
▶ the exam you sit in May (70% of your overall mark); that is what this book is all about.

The exams

Reading for Understanding, Analysis and Evaluation

▶ Exam time: 1 hour 30 minutes
▶ Total marks: 30
▶ Weighting in final grade: 30%
▶ What you have to do: read two passages and answer questions about the ideas and use of language in them.

ESSENTIAL SQA EXAM PRACTICE

HIGHER ENGLISH

Practice Questions & Exam Papers

HODDER GIBSON
No.1 choice for students & teachers FOR OVER 100 YEARS

QUESTIONS & PAPERS

▶ Practise **40+ questions** covering every question type and topic

▶ Complete **2 practice papers** that mirror the real SQA exams

Judith Horne

HODDER GIBSON
AN HACHETTE UK COMPANY

Acknowledgements: please refer to page 165.

Every effort has been made to trace all copyright holders, but if any have been inadvertently overlooked, the Publishers will be pleased to make the necessary arrangements at the first opportunity.

Although every effort has been made to ensure that website addresses are correct at time of going to press, Hodder Gibson cannot be held responsible for the content of any website mentioned in this book. It is sometimes possible to find a relocated web page by typing in the address of the home page for a website in the URL window of your browser.

Hachette UK's policy is to use papers that are natural, renewable and recyclable products and made from wood grown in well-managed forests and other controlled sources. The logging and manufacturing processes are expected to conform to the environmental regulations of the country of origin.

Orders: please contact Hachette UK Distribution, Hely Hutchinson Centre, Milton Road, Didcot, Oxfordshire, OX11 7HH. Telephone: +44 (0)1235 827827. Email: education@hachette.co.uk Lines are open from 9 a.m. to 5 p.m., Monday to Friday. You can also order through our website: www.hoddereducation.co.uk. If you have queries or questions that aren't about an order, you can contact us at hoddergibson@hodder.co.uk

© Judith Horne 2019

First published in 2019 by

Hodder Gibson, an imprint of Hodder Education

An Hachette UK Company

50 Frederick Street

Edinburgh, EH2 1EX

Impression number   5   4   3

Year   2023

Typeset in India by Aptara Inc.

Printed and bound by CPI Group (UK) Ltd, Croydon CR0 4YY

A catalogue record for this title is available from the British Library.

ISBN: 978 1 510 4717 71

SCOTLAND EXCEL

We are an approved supplier on the Scotland Excel framework.

Find us on your school's procurement system as

Hachette UK Distribution Ltd or *Hodder & Stoughton Limited t/a Hodder Education.*

MIX

Paper | Supporting responsible forestry

FSC
www.fsc.org   FSC™ C104740

Critical Reading

▶ Exam time: 1 hour 30 minutes
▶ Total marks: 40
▶ Weighting in final grade: 40%
▶ What you have to do: Section 1: read an extract from one of the Scottish Texts and answer questions about it; Section 2: write an essay about a work of literature you have studied during your course.

General exam advice (more specific advice is offered later)

Reading for Understanding, Analysis and Evaluation

▶ Read Passage 1 before you attempt the questions!

Questions which ask for understanding (e.g. questions which say 'Identify ...' or 'Explain what ...', etc.)
▶ Keep your answers fairly short and pay attention to the number of marks available for the question. In most cases you get 1 mark for a basic comment and two for something that is more 'detailed' or 'insightful'. It is not always possible to gain 2 marks easily, so it is advisable to offer two different points for a 2-mark question.
▶ Use your own words as far as possible. This means you must not just copy chunks from the passage – you have to show that you understand what it means by rephrasing it in your own words.

Questions about language features (questions which say 'Analyse how ...')
▶ This type of question will ask you to comment on features such as: word choice, imagery, sentence structure, tone.
▶ You should pick out a relevant language feature and make a valid comment about its impact. Try to make your comments as specific as possible and avoid vague comments like 'It is a good word to use because it gives me a clear picture of what the writer is saying'. Remember that you will get no marks for just picking out a word or an image or a feature of sentence structure – it is the comment that counts.
Some hints:

▶ **Word choice**: pick a single word, or a small group of words, and then offer some connotations, i.e. what the word suggests.
▶ **Sentence structure**: don't just name the feature – try to explain what effect it achieves.
▶ **Imagery**: You can gain good marks if you try to explain what the image means literally (what the word/words really mean) and then go on to explain what the writer is trying to say by using that comparison, but you can also score marks by making a more basic comment.
▶ **Tone**: this is always difficult – a good tip is to imagine the sentence or paragraph being read out loud and try to spot how the words or the structure create a particular tone.

The last question
▶ Read the question first.
▶ Read Passage 2 before you attempt the question.
▶ Make sure you follow the instruction about whether you are looking for agreement or disagreement.
▶ When you start on Passage 2, you will already have answered several questions on Passage 1, so you should know its key ideas quite well. As you read Passage 2, try to spot important ideas in it which are similar or different (depending on the question). Highlighting ideas as you read is a good tip.
▶ Stick to **key ideas** and don't include trivial ones; you need to outline **three** relevant key ideas – your task is to decide what the most significant ones are.

Critical Reading

Section 1 – Scottish Text
The most important thing to remember here is that there are two very different types of question to be answered:

▶ three questions (for a total of 10 marks) which focus entirely on the extract
▶ one question (for 10 marks) which requires knowledge of the whole text (or of another poem or short story by the same writer).

The first type of question will nearly always ask you to use some of the same skills you use in the RUAE part of the exam, such as analysis of word choice, imagery and sentence structure. The golden rule, however, is always to read each question very carefully and do exactly as instructed, and to remember that as in RUAE there are no marks for just picking out a word or a feature – it is the comment that matters. While it is possible at Higher to score 2 marks for a really good comment, you should always try to make one comment for each mark available.

The second type of question requires you to identify common features (of theme and/or technique) in the extract and elsewhere in the writer's work. You can write a series of bullet points, or a table or a 'mini-essay', so choose the approach you feel more comfortable with.

A final bit of advice for the Scottish Text question: when you see the extract in the exam paper, don't get too confident just because you recognise it, because you certainly should recognise it if you've studied properly! And even if you've answered questions on that extract or that poem before, remember that the questions in the exam are likely to be different, so stay alert.

Finally, it might be useful to think about where things go wrong, so you can avoid them!

Common errors

▶ Not reading the passage carefully. Read the passages before attempting questions on them – for example, use highlighters, underline, notice language features.

▶ Not being clear enough in your answers. If you do not explain what you mean clearly, your examiner will not understand your points.

▶ Muddling up techniques. Be very clear what the different techniques (such as word choice and sentence structure) mean.

▶ In the essay, not answering the question. Use the words from the question in your answer.

▶ Not giving enough points in the answers. If the question is worth 4 marks, give four bullet points, unless you are fully confident you have gained 2 marks each for two points.

You can download a Revision Calendar to use as part of your studies from our website at www.hoddergibson.co.uk/ESEP-extras

Finally, good luck with your revision and all the best for the exam!

Practice Questions
Reading for Understanding, Analysis and Evaluation

Question type	Command word(s)	Approach	Practice questions in this book
Identify	Identify	Find and translate	1, 2
Explain	Explain how	Find and translate	3, 4
Link-type questions	Link/function/ development	Look for what comes before the section you are directed to, what comes after it and explain how they are related.	5, 6
Use of language	Use of language, word choice, sentence structure, tone, contrast, imagery	Identify techniques (these may be explicitly asked for or not) and then say how they answer the question.	7, 8
Word choice	Word choice, use of language	Find the words that answer the question and explain what the connotations are.	9, 10
Sentence structure	Sentence structure, use of language	Find the techniques of sentence structure that answer the question and explain why they are effective.	11, 12
Imagery	Imagery, use of language	Look for metaphors, similes or personification and explain what these mean literally and in the context of the passage/ question.	13, 14
Tone	Tone, use of language	Find the words that indicate the tone and explain how they do so.	15, 16
Contrast	Contrast, use of language	Identify both sides of the contrast and explain why they contrast, in relation to the question.	17, 18
Usefulness	Effectiveness, content, ideas, language	In relation to the question, pick examples of content, ideas or language and explain how these work.	19, 20
Comparison question	Agree or disagree	Read both passages carefully. A good way to approach this is to draw a grid outlining areas of agreement or disagreement (as appropriate); give quotes from each text to back up your 'areas' and explain why you picked these quotes.	21, 22

Critical Reading

Question type	Command word(s)	Approach	Practice questions in this book
Short questions	Explain, analyse how	Find the information in the text that answers the question. Quote and then explain in your own words why you have picked it.	23a), 23b), 24, 26, 27, 28, 30, 31, 32, 34, 35, 36, 38, 39, 40, 42, 43, 44
Ten-marker	Discuss how	Include: 2 marks' worth for commonality; two for extract and six for elsewhere	25, 29, 33, 37, 41, 45

Practice Papers

Reading for Understanding, Analysis and Evaluation

Question type	Command word(s)	Approach	Practice questions in this book Paper A	Paper B
Identify	Identify	Find and translate	7	1
Explain	Explain	Find and translate	1, 3a), 5	4a), 5
Link-type questions	Link/function/ development	Look for what comes before the section you are directed to, what comes after it and explain how they are related.		
Use of language	Use of language, word choice, sentence structure, tone, contrast, imagery	Identify techniques (these may be explicitly asked for or not) and then say how they answer the question.	2, 3b), 4, 6	2, 3, 7
Word choice	Word choice, use of language	Find the words that answer the question and explain what the connotations are.	2, 3b), 4, 6	2, 3, 7
Sentence structure	Sentence structure, use of language	Find the techniques of sentence structure that answer the question and explain why they are effective.	2, 3b), 4, 6	2, 3, 6
Imagery	Imagery, use of language	Look for metaphors, similes or personification and explain what these mean literally and in the context of the passage/ question.	2, 3b), 4	2, 3, 4b)

Question type	Command word(s)	Approach	Practice questions in this book	
			Paper A	Paper B
Tone	Tone, use of language	Find the words that indicate the tone and explain how they do so.	2, 3b), 4, 6	2, 3, 7
Contrast	Contrast, use of language	Identify both sides of the contrast and explain why they contrast, in relation to the question.	7	4a)
Usefulness	Effectiveness, content, ideas, language	In relation to the question, pick examples of content, ideas or language and explain how these work.	8	
Comparison question	Agree or disagree	Read both passages carefully. A good way to approach this is to draw a grid outlining areas of agreement or disagreement (as appropriate); give quotes from each text to back up your 'areas' and explain why you picked these quotes.	9	8

Critical Reading

Question type	Command word(s)	Approach	Practice questions in this book	
			Paper A	Paper B
Short questions	Explain, analyse how	Find the information in the text that answers the question. Quote and then explain in your own words why you have picked it.	1, 2, 3, 5a), 5b), 6, 8, 9, 10, 12, 13, 14, 16, 17, 18, 20, 21, 22, 24, 25, 26, 28, 29, 30, 32, 33, 34, 36, 37, 38, 40, 41, 42, 44, 45, 46	1, 2, 3, 5, 6, 7, 9, 10, 11, 13, 14, 15, 17, 18, 19, 21, 22, 23, 25, 26, 27, 29, 30, 31, 33, 34, 35, 37, 38, 39, 41, 42, 43, 45, 46, 47
Ten-marker	Discuss how	Include: 2 marks' worth for commonality; 2 for extract and 6 for elsewhere	4, 7, 11, 15, 19, 23, 27, 31, 35, 39, 43, 47	4, 8, 12, 16, 20, 24, 28, 32, 36, 40, 44, 48

Critical Essay marking guidance

	Marks 20–19	Marks 18–16	Marks 15–13	Marks 12–10	Marks 9–6	Marks 5–0
Knowledge and understanding The critical essay demonstrates:	thorough knowledge and understanding of the text perceptive selection of textual evidence to support line of argument which is fluently structured and expressed perceptive focus on the demands of the question	secure knowledge and understanding of the text detailed textual evidence to support line of thought which is coherently structured and expressed secure focus on the demands of the question	clear knowledge and understanding of the text clear textual evidence to support line of thought which is clearly structured and expressed clear focus on the demands of the question	adequate knowledge and understanding of the text adequate textual evidence to support line of thought which is adequately structured and expressed adequate focus on the demands of the question	limited evidence of knowledge and understanding of the text limited textual evidence to support line of thought which is structured and expressed in a limited way limited focus on the demands of the question	very little knowledge and understanding of the text very little textual evidence to support line of thought which shows very little structure or clarity of expression very little focus on the demands of the question
Analysis The critical essay demonstrates:	perceptive analysis of the effect of features of language/filmic techniques	detailed analysis of the effect of features of language/filmic techniques	clear analysis of the effect of features of language/filmic techniques	adequate analysis of the effect of features of language/filmic techniques	limited analysis of the effect of features of language/filmic techniques	very little analysis of features of language/filmic techniques
Evaluation The critical essay demonstrates:	committed evaluative stance with respect to the text and the task	engaged evaluative stance with respect to the text and the task	clear evaluative stance with respect to the text and the task	adequate evidence of an evaluative stance with respect to the text and the task	limited evidence of an evaluative stance with respect to the text and the task	very little evidence of an evaluative stance with respect to the text and the task
Technical accuracy The critical essay demonstrates:	few errors in spelling, grammar, sentence construction, punctuation and paragraphing the ability to be understood at first reading			significant number of errors in spelling, grammar, sentence construction, punctuation and paragraphing which impedes understanding		

Reading for Understanding, Analysis and Evaluation

Before reading the questions, make sure you are familiar with the passages. When answering the questions, make sure you return to the line numbers you are guided to find your answer. It is advisable to read passage one first and leave passage two until later. It is a good idea to highlight anything you notice of interest as you go, such as sentences structure, metaphors and contrast. Then answer the questions on passage one. When you are ready to move on, read the final question before reading passage two, so you have some idea of what you are looking for. Then, read passage two, highlighting areas of agreement or disagreement as you do. Finally, write your answer to the last question.

Paper A

The following two passages consider the problems of having too much choice.

Passage 1

From 'The Tyranny of Choice' by Ben Macintyre

In the first passage, Ben Macintyre reflects on some experiences on a holiday in Florida.

Last week, on holiday in Florida, I went to a supermarket near Fort Myers to buy some breakfast cereal with the children, and suffered the first of a series of choice overdoses. A vast canyon of cereals stretched to the horizon, a universe of flakes, crunchies, puffs and additives, an overflowing cornucopia of baffling breakfast options. The children whooped, and began grabbing at the boxes. A fight broke out over Trix, Froot Loops, Chex, or
5 Cheerios, and then another over the specific variety of Cheerios. The youngest wept bitterly when her heart's desire – some sort of sawdust in teddy bear shapes and radioactive pastels – was flatly rejected by the other two. As the debate raged, I counted 137 separate cereals, and 8 different combinations of variety pack. There are, I subsequently learnt, 275 different sorts of cereal available in the US. I made an executive decision. We would go to a restaurant for breakfast.

10 'With your pancakes or waffles do you want hash browns, grits, cheese grits, fried potatoes, syrup, maple or walnut, strawberry, cherry or blueberry topping?' said the waitress. 'With the coffee is that whole milk, organic, skimmed milk, half 'n' half, eggs well done, over-medium, over easy, scrambled, poached …?' 'Er, why don't you choose?' I suggested. She looked scandalised, horrified at this dereliction of the God-given duty to choose. No one had ever not chosen in her restaurant before. It was weird. It was un-American.

15 But it was the jeans rack, in the outlet store next door, that finally broke me. I wanted some normal blue jeans; what I was offered was relaxed fit, easy fit, slim fit, distressed, traditional cut, stone-washed, acid-washed, zipper, button, low-slung, classic, frayed, boot-leg, drainpipe, turn-up. 'Relaxed, or easy?' asked the saleswoman brightly. 'Neither,' I snarled, and left.

The tyranny of choice is not peculiar to America; it has taken root wherever choice is conflated, quite wrongly,
20 with freedom. Some Eastern European intellectuals in former Communist countries look back nostalgically at a time when so many choices, about food, clothing, housing, were made by others, or strictly limited, giving people time to concentrate on more useful activities, like thinking. Some choice is essential to the patina of life, but too much, according to the latest research, merely promotes anxiety, uncertainty, and even clinical depression.

25 We have become shackled to the demands of choice. Time, the commodity that should truly be ours to spend freely, is stolen by the years spent pondering what, in the vast, bogus and repetitive menu laid before us, we really want. And built into all these choices is a permanent and inescapable disappointment. When we choose one of the 275 sorts of cereal we inevitably harbour a suspicion that we cannot have chosen the best one. And so we quest, hopelessly, after some ideal thing that the advertisers insist is exactly right for us, just waiting to be
30 chosen.

Even when we believe we have made the right choice, we live in fear of post-payment trauma: people who have bought a new car subsequently enjoy watching advertisements for that car, but avoid information about rival makes.

The psychologist Barry Schwartz, in his book *The Paradox of Choice*, argues that the superabundance of choice
35   has become a crushing burden, as consumers are themselves consumed by the pressure to choose. A society
that prizes personal selection as an intrinsic virtue inevitably encourages what Schwartz labels 'maximisers',
those people who relentlessly hunt out the best, or best price, from the multiplicity of options, and discourages
'satisficers' (combining satisfaction and sacrifice), who simply go through the possibilities until they find
something acceptable. Maximisers are doomed to depression, to channel surf through life in the mistaken belief
40   that there is always something better on the other side; the satisficers make do, and are happier for it.

A plethora of choices can be self-defeating. One might expect that with, say, 57 varieties on offer, more
consumers would find contentment more often. Research has shown that the reverse is true. Offer buyers half a
dozen types of sausages, and they will probably choose one without difficulty; give them 100 choices, and they
are far more likely to buy nothing at all. A single item with a reduced price in a shop window will attract buyers;
45   but put two different items, equally marked down, in the same window, and buyers become uncertain, with a
substantial drop in sales.

Weighed down by choice, we postpone a choice of mate, delaying and searching, paralysed by the maximisers'
myth of Mr or Miss Right. We ponder and doubt and repeatedly take our life choices back to the vendor,
insisting that they are never quite the right fit.

50   But a revolution is brewing against the tyranny of choice. Internet shopping sets a template of purchases,
allowing one to choose, at a click, exactly what was chosen before. Another method of limiting choice is what
social scientists now call 'self-binding pre-commitment'. This used to be known as a shopping list. Or we could
simply choose not to waste any more time choosing but take the first acceptable thing we come across, and
then get on with something more important (i.e. just about anything). As the old proverb goes, 'No choice is
55   also a choice'; it is also a lot less confusing and time-consuming.

On the plane back from Florida the stewardess leant over and with real anguish admitted: 'There is no more
chicken or pasta, I'm afraid. Just the beef casserole.'

'That's fine,' I reassured her. 'We all have to make satisfices.'

https://www.thetimes.co.uk/article/its-a-tough-choice-of-course-but-maybe-this-is-the-one-to-read-first-6svsdfphvsp

Passage 2

Use this for the agreement/disagreement question (Question 21).

From 'Choose to Have Less Choice' by Tim Lott

In the second passage, Tim Lott explores the problem of too much choice.

Once, when I was suffering a fit of depression, I walked into a supermarket to buy a packet of washing powder. Confronted by a shelf full of different possibilities, I stood there for 15 minutes staring at them, then walked out without buying any washing powder at all.

5   I still feel echoes of that sensation of helplessness. If I just want to buy one item but discover that if I buy three of the items I will save myself half the item price, I find myself assailed by choice paralysis.

I hate making consumer choices at the best of times, because I have this uncomfortable suspicion that big companies are trying to gull me out of as much money as possible, using sophisticated techniques designed by people who are smarter than I am.

This issue of choice and complexity lies at the heart of the experience of being modern. It penetrates
10   commerce, politics and our personal lives. It may even be connected to the fact that there are higher levels of depression in society than ever before.

Choice oppresses us. Why? Because there are too many choices and they are often too complex for us to be confident that we are making the right one.

When you might have 200 potential choices to make of a particular style of camera, it is difficult to feel sure you
15   have chosen the right one – even if you spend an inordinate amount of time trying to make a rational decision. Or you may see the same model two weeks after you've bought it being sold more cheaply. When there was less choice and fewer types of camera, this kind of experience was rare. Our capacity for hindsight has become a means of punishing ourselves.

This complexity is not entirely accidental. Modern capitalism solves the dilemma of competition (for the
20   producer) through complexity. To try to choose a mortgage, or a pension, or a computer, requires a tremendous amount of application, so we become relatively easy to gull. Whether it is a power company or a loan company, we struggle to understand tariffs, terms and the small print. Exhausted, we just take a stab and hope for the best, or we succumb to inertia; choose what we have always chosen. Consumers are thrown back on simple cues that are advantageous to the producers, such as brand recognition.

25   This problem of choice and complexity is ubiquitous. It applies in medicine. If I am ill and asked to make a choice about treatment, I would often rather leave the choice to the doctor, if only because if the wrong choice is made, I am not going to feel nearly so bad about it. I had a prostate cancer scare recently, and I just wanted to be told what to do – not decide whether, say, I should choose an operation that would guarantee impotency in order to stave off a 5% chance of cancer. The burden of choice was too big.

30   In the personal realm, once, you stayed married for life. Now, if you are in an unhappy marriage you have to decide whether to stay or not. These may be all positive developments, but they come at a cost – the potential for regret.

So how should one react to complexity? Perhaps we should limit choice, not extend it. If you are shopping for food, go to supermarkets that are priced simply with a limited range, such as Aldi and Lidl. Recognise and
35   accept complexity – which means accepting that you can never be sure that you've made the right choice.

Above all, don't fall for the old trope of only wanting 'the best'. In his book The Paradox of Choice, Barry Schwartz calls such people 'maximisers' – people who are never happy, because they have expectations that can never be met, since in a world of complexity and unlimited choice there is always a better option. Be a 'satisficer' instead – people who are happy to say 'that's good enough', or 'it'll do'. As a consumer, and in life
40   generally, it's a pretty good formula. It'll do, anyway.

https://www.theguardian.com/commentisfree/2015/may/18/choose-less-choice-shopping-around

Paper B

The following two passages consider the issue of veganism and its impact on the environment.

Passage 1

From 'If you want to save the world, veganism isn't the answer' by Isabella Tree

In the first passage, Isabella Tree explains why going vegan may not be the best way to save the environment.

Veganism has rocketed in the UK over the past couple of years – from an estimated half a million people in 2016 to more than 3.5 million – 5% of our population – today. Influential documentaries such as Cowspiracy and What the Health have thrown a spotlight on the intensive meat and dairy industry, exposing the impacts on animal and human health and the wider environment.

5 But calls for us all to switch entirely to plant-based foods ignore one of the most powerful tools we have to mitigate these ills: grazing and browsing animals.

Rather than being seduced by exhortations to eat more products made from industrially grown soya, maize and grains, we should be encouraging sustainable forms of meat and dairy production based on traditional rotational systems, permanent pasture and conservation grazing. We should, at the very least, question the

10 ethics of driving up demand for crops that require high inputs of fertiliser, fungicides, pesticides and herbicides, while demonising sustainable forms of livestock farming that can restore soils and biodiversity, and sequester carbon.

In 2000, my husband and I turned our 1,400-hectare (3,500-acre) farm in West Sussex over to extensive grazing

15 using free-roaming herds of old English longhorn cattle, Tamworth pigs, Exmoor ponies and red and fallow deer as part of a rewilding project. For 17 years we had struggled to make our conventional arable and dairy business profitable, but on heavy Low Weald clay, we could never compete with farms on lighter soils. The decision turned our fortunes around. Now eco-tourism, rental of post-agricultural buildings, and 75 tonnes a year of organic, pasture-fed meat contribute to a profitable business. And since the animals live outside all year round, with plenty to eat, they do not require supplementary feeding and rarely need to see the vet.

20 The animals live in natural herds and wander wherever they please. They wallow in streams and water-meadows. They rest where they like (they disdain the open barns left for them as shelter) and eat what they like. The cattle and deer graze on wildflowers and grasses but they also browse among shrubs and trees. The pigs rootle for rhizomes and even dive for swan mussels in ponds. The way they graze, puddle and trample stimulates vegetation in different ways, which in turn creates opportunities for other species, including small mammals

25 and birds.

Crucially, because we don't dose them with avermectins (the anti-worming agents routinely fed to livestock in intensive systems) or antibiotics, their dung feeds earthworms, bacteria, fungi and invertebrates such as dung beetles, which pull the manure down into the earth. This is a vital process of ecosystem restoration, returning nutrients and structure to the soil. Soil loss is one of the greatest catastrophes facing the world today. A 2015

30 report from the UN Food and Agriculture Organization states that, globally, 25 to 40bn tonnes of topsoil are lost annually to erosion, thanks mainly to ploughing and intensive cropping. In the UK topsoil depletion is so severe that in 2014 the trade magazine Farmers Weekly announced we may have only 100 harvests left. Letting arable land lie fallow and returning it to grazed pasture for a period – as farmers used to, before artificial fertilisers and mechanisation made continuous cropping possible – is the only way to reverse that process, halt erosion and

35 rebuild soil, according to the UN Food and Agriculture Organisation. The grazing livestock not only provide farmers with an income, but the animals' dung, urine and even the way they graze, accelerates soil restoration. The key is to be organic, and keep livestock numbers low to prevent over-grazing.

Twenty years ago, our soils at the farm – severely degraded after decades of ploughing and chemical inputs – were almost biologically dead. Now we have fruiting fungi and orchids appearing in our former arable fields:

40 an indication that subterranean networks of mycorrhizal fungi are spreading. We have 19 types of earthworm – keystone species responsible for aerating, rotavating, fertilising, hydrating and even detoxifying the soil. We've found 23 species of dung beetle in a single cowpat, one of which – the violet dor beetle – hasn't been seen in Sussex for 50 years. Birds that feed on insects attracted by this nutritious dung are rocketing. The rootling of the pigs provides opportunities for native flora and shrubs to germinate, including sallow, and this has given rise

45 to the biggest colony of purple emperors in Britain, one of our rarest butterflies, which lays its eggs on sallow leaves.

Not only does this system of natural grazing aid the environment in terms of soil restoration, biodiversity, pollinating insects, water quality and flood mitigation – but it also it guarantees healthy lives for the animals, and they in turn produce meat that is healthy for us. In direct contrast to grain-fed and grain-finished meat
50 from intensive systems, wholly pasture-fed meat is high in beta carotene, calcium, selenium, magnesium and potassium and vitamins E and B, and conjugated linoleic acid (CLA) – a powerful anti-carcinogen. It is also high in the long-chain omega-3 fatty acid DHA, which is vital for human brain development but extremely difficult for vegans to obtain.

Much has been made of the methane emissions of livestock, but these are lower in biodiverse pasture systems
55 that include wild plants such as angelica, common fumitory, shepherd's purse and bird's-foot trefoil because they contain fumaric acid – a compound that, when added to the diet of lambs at the Rowett Institute in Aberdeen, reduced emissions of methane by 70%.

In the vegan equation, by contrast, the carbon cost of ploughing is rarely considered. Since the industrial revolution, according to a 2017 report in the science journal Nature, up to 70% of the carbon in our cultivated
60 soils has been lost to the atmosphere.

So there's a huge responsibility here: unless you're sourcing your vegan products specifically from organic, 'no-dig' systems, you are actively participating in the destruction of soil biota, promoting a system that deprives other species, including small mammals, birds and reptiles, of the conditions for life, and significantly contributing to climate change.

65 Our ecology evolved with large herbivores – with free-roaming herds of aurochs (the ancestral cow), tarpan (the original horse), elk, bear, bison, red deer, roe deer, wild boar and millions of beavers. They are species whose interactions with the environment sustain and promote life. Using herbivores as part of the farming cycle can go a long way towards making agriculture sustainable.

There's no question we should all be eating far less meat, and calls for an end to high-carbon, polluting,
70 unethical, intensive forms of grain-fed meat production are commendable. But if your concerns as a vegan are the environment, animal welfare and your own health, then it's no longer possible to pretend that these are all met simply by giving up meat and dairy. Counterintuitive as it may seem, adding the occasional organic, pasture-fed steak to your diet could be the right way to square the circle.

www.theguardian.com/commentisfree/2018/aug/25/veganism-intensively-farmed-meat-dairy-soya-maize

Passage 2

Use this for the agreement/disagreement question (Question 22).

From 'I make vegan cheese in Amsterdam. And no one here calls it faux' by Brad Vanstone

In the second passage, Brad Vanstone discusses why farmers and vegans should work in unison.

I know that in polarised, tribal Britain, my plant-based product would be dismissed. The Netherlands is more open-minded.

For environmental reasons I started following a plant-based diet in 2017. I found the transition surprisingly simple, the only stumbling block was cheese. So last year, I began making plant-based cheese at my home in
5 Amsterdam. After several months of experimenting, I was sufficiently encouraged with the results to launch my vegan cheese business.

My British grandparents were dairy farmers for more than 60 years, which is why I find the current them-against-us attitude among both vegans and non-vegans so unhelpful. My sister and I spent every school holiday on the dairy farm, and we treasure those memories dearly, although not the memories of my grandmother's cooking.
10 Anyone who has eaten cow's tongue or tried her assortment of watery soups would understand why. Our mornings started at 6am sharp. If you didn't make it out of bed in time, you missed breakfast. My grandparents taught us to love and care for all living beings. Their animals would live out long and comfortable lives in spacious Devon fields. Not every livestock farmer is evil, and not all farm animals are locked behind bars.

15 True, my diet now is in stark contrast with those early years, and my occupation seems at odds with my grandparents'. Like many of their peers, they began farming for noble reasons, to feed a nation recovering from the Second World War. But my change in diet and decision to launch a plant-based cheese company have also been motivated by a food-related crisis.

Ignoring the facts about the negative impact of animal products on the environment puts life as we know it at risk for future generations. We all need to examine what we eat, where it comes from and the impact of our
20 personal decisions. That doesn't have to mean going vegan tomorrow: maybe it starts with adjusting one meal a week to be animal-free, or even keeping an open mind to the possibility of doing so.

The tone of the debate around food, though, is an obstacle to progress. On one side, vegans vilify farmers; on the other, farmers offer blanket condemnation of plant-based products that are better for our health, as well as our planet.

25 Few topics offer a better example of the polarised nature of British society than the uproar surrounding the opening of La Fauxmagerie, the UK's first plant-based cheesemonger. Industry lobby group Dairy UK, which represents dairy farmers, has written to the store, citing an EU ruling that states that 'cheese', 'milk' and 'butter' can only refer to products derived from dairy.

The us-versus-them mentality is helping no one. Relaxing the adoption of dairy food names for plant-based
30 products would be a good place to begin cooling tempers. A big part of moving to a vegan diet is being able to view a plant-based burger as a burger, or plant-based milk as milk: it's worth noting that the 2013 EU law does not apply to almond milk or coconut milk.

Witnessing the dairy industry's action against La Fauxmagerie was disheartening. Consumers are more conscious of what they eat than they've ever been. Distinguishing between a plant-based product and its
35 dairy equivalent is easy for us. Time and energy would be much better spent trying these products first, before passing judgment. It's a matter of sticking to the food tests we have used since the dawn of time: taste, nutrition, appearance and smell.

The tribalised nature of debate generally in the UK is a major reason why I live in the Netherlands. Most Dutch people are honest and frank, but they are nearly always open to new opinions and reasoning.

40 Much of my cheese sales are at markets in Amsterdam. There's no hiding place there as you're met with people from all ages and walks of life, yet the energy I receive back is genuinely inspiring, with the majority of passersby curious to try something new.

If we are to survive as a species, we have to make drastic changes to the way we eat. It won't be an easy transition, but if we all keep an open mind and avoid passing judgment before trying new ideas, I believe we
45 can find common ground.

www.theguardian.com/commentisfree/2019/mar/06/vegan-cheese-mentality-netherlands-open-minded-food?CMP=Share_iOSApp_Other

Types of questions

Now you have read the passages, it is time to look at the questions.

There are different types of questions in the 'Reading for Understanding, Analysis and Evaluation' paper. These broadly fall into four types. Firstly, you are being assessed on how well you can put the information you are reading in the article into your own words. Secondly, you are being assessed on spotting and analysing techniques. Thirdly, you are being assessed on how well you can justify if the writer has been convincing or not in their argument and finally, how well you can identify and explain how the writers of the two passages agree, disagree or do both.

This section will look at these different types of questions, show you how to answer them and then give you two examples of questions based on the passages above. In the question papers, you will see that the process words (what you are being asked to do) are always the same. These have been made bold, so you can begin to learn and understand them.

Group 1: Questions that assess putting your information in your own words

Question type: identify

>> HOW TO ANSWER

'**Identify**' questions ask you to find information and put it in your own words. The question may start with the word '**identify**'. The numbers on the side will give you a guide as to how many points you need to **identify**. For example, if the marks awarded are 2, you would be advised to offer two points of information.

To approach the question, read the lines you are directed to carefully. Then look at the question and underline exactly what it is that the question is asking you to find (**identify**). Then, return to the passage and underline the information you can use to answer the question.

Your next job is to translate. Translate means take the information and put it in your own words. To make it clear, it is useful to quote the phrase you are going to use and then translate it. It is a good idea to bullet point the answer. If the question asks for two 'causes' of something, for example, you could bullet point (twice) as follows:

▶ Cause 1
▶ Quote (if necessary)
▶ Own words explaining why you picked the quote you did.

MARKS

1 Paper A, Passage 1. Read lines 25–30. **Identify** two problems with having too much choice. **2**

2 Paper B, Passage 1. Read lines 7–12. **Identify** two ways the writer believes people can grow 'sustainable forms of meat and dairy'. **2**

Answers can be found on page 31.

Question type: explain

>> HOW TO ANSWER

These questions are similar to **identify** questions, but you need to take the explanation a bit further. You need to **explain** (describe) how the information you have chosen answers the question. Again, the numbers at the side will give you an indication of how many points you need to make.

Top Tip!

In these questions, you are often awarded 1 mark for a straightforward point and 2 marks for a more detailed or insightful point. It is easier to gain lots of little marks than 2 marks, so unless you are running really short of time, it is a good idea to give the same amount of points as marks (i.e. if there are 4 marks awarded, give four points).

Top Tip!

These questions will often say 'in your own words' but you should always use your own words anyway! However, this can serve as a useful reminder, especially if you are under pressure.

Approach these questions in a similar way to **identify** ones. Read the question, underline important parts, read the lines you are directed to, underline what you will use for your answer and then write your answer.

Answer in bullet points following this structure:

▶ Explanation 1 (perhaps a quote)
▶ write the explanation in your own words

MARKS

3 Paper A, Passage 1. Read lines 34–40. Using your own words as far as possible, **explain** the way different types of people, according to Schwartz, react to choice.

4

4 Paper B, Passage 1. Read lines 26–37. **Explain** what farmers can do to reduce soil erosion.

2

Answers can be found on page 31.

Group 2: Questions that ask you to spot and analyse techniques

These questions ask you to find techniques (**links**, **word choice**, **sentence structure**, **imagery**, **tone** and **contrast**) and explain how they work in the context of the section you are directed to. Students often find it easy to spot the techniques, but harder to explain how they work. This is what we will address here.

Question type: link

 HOW TO ANSWER

These questions will not necessarily tell you they are looking for **links** (connections). You will need to work that out. Look for words like '**function**' or phrases like '**change in argument**' or '**moving the argument forward**'. **Links** are often **turning points** (where the text changes from talking about one topic and moves on to another).

It can be helpful to answer this question in a three-part structure, in bullet points, as follows:

▶ what the argument was about
▶ how the writer has used language to change/move/develop the argument
▶ what the argument is about now.

Top Tip!

To answer these questions, read the lines you are directed to. Then look at the information given before the lines and work out what the main thrust of the argument is in relation to the question. Then look at what comes after the link and work out what the main point is in this next part of the passage.

MARKS

5 Paper A, Passage 1. Read line 50. **Explain** the function of the sentence 'But … tyranny of choice'. **3**

6 Paper B, Passage 1. Read lines 1–6. **Explain** how the second paragraph develops the writer's argument. **2**

Answers can be found on page 32.

Question type: use of language

>> HOW TO ANSWER

Sometimes students panic when they see 'use of language' and are not sure what it means. Use of language is an 'umbrella' term for the techniques that are outlined below (such as **word choice**, **sentence structure**, **imagery**, **tone** and **contrast**). You are expected to draw on some of these techniques in order to answer the question.

Top Tip!

It will be useful to do the questions in this section after you have worked through all of the language technique questions listed below.

Top Tip!

As a rule of thumb, it is good to give four examples if the question is worth 4 marks and two if the question is worth 2. You can also get 2 marks for a 'detailed and insightful' comment.

To deal with these types of questions, pick the most obvious **language techniques** and explain how they answer the question. Use the following bullet point structure:

▶ Technique
▶ Quote/point
▶ Explanation

MARKS

7   Paper A, Passage 1. Read lines 41–46. **Analyse** how the writer uses **language** to emphasise that too much choice is problematic.   **4**

8   Paper B, Passage 1. Read lines 54–57. By referring to at least one example, **analyse** how the writer uses **language** to emphasise her point.   **2**

Answers can be found on pages 32–33.

⟩Hint!

Questions may ask about use of language, as above, or they may ask more specifically about techniques. If you are asked for two techniques in a question, make sure you cover them both, otherwise you cannot get full marks. For example, if you get asked about **word choice** and **sentence structure** and it is worth 4 marks, make sure you give at least one example for each.

Question type: word choice

≫ HOW TO ANSWER

This is probably the easiest analytical question. The chances of completing a Higher English paper without referring to word choice are minimal!

You answer this by finding the appropriate word, and then explaining the connotations (what the word makes you think of in relation to the context of the surrounding text) of that word in relation to the question. A good way to approach it is as follows:

▶ Technique (write **word choice** here)
▶ Word/words (keep this as short as possible – usually one word (or a small group of words) will do, otherwise it looks like you are 'hedging your bets'!
▶ Explain the connotations in relation to the question and the context in which the word appears in the sentence. Explain how the word works/is powerful.

Top Tip!

Although techniques have been dealt with separately in this section of the book, in the exam you will probably be offered a list of techniques to choose from. Often, word choice questions will form part of a list at the end of 'analyse how' questions.

Top Tip!

Word choice questions want you to look for the words the writer has selected for particular impact. Look for strong words that stand out, but do not pick words you do not understand! Often, there will be many options, so you should not be limited in choice.

MARKS

9 Paper A, Passage 1. Read lines 25–30. By referring to at least two examples, **analyse** how the writer's **word choice** conveys his negative attitude to choice.   **4**

10 Paper B, Passage 1. Read lines 20–25. By referring to at least two examples, **analyse** how the writer uses **word choice** to create an idyllic picture of the farm.   **4**

Answers can be found on page 33.

Question type: sentence structure

>> HOW TO ANSWER

Sentence structure often causes students issues, but this does not have to be the case. All you have to do is learn the basic techniques and how they work, then connect them to the meaning of the sentence(s).

You would answer the same way as above, only replace the technique you are using, so:

► Technique (list, for example)

► Quote or explain where it is (you need to choose what is most appropriate – you cannot quote great big sentences for example)

► Explain the function of the technique *in relation to the context of the sentence/sentences.*

The table below outlines the different '**sentence structure**' techniques that may appear in the text. It is unlikely you would be asked separately about these techniques, but you need to know them because these are the ones you draw on to answer the **sentence structure** questions.

Top Tip!

Sentence structure questions, like **word choice** ones, often come at the end of a 'use of language' question as part of a list, but they can also appear as a stand-alone question in their own right.

Technique	What to look for	Function	How to answer/ questions to ask
Repetition	Words or phrases that appear over and over again.	To emphasise a particular point	What is being repeated and why? Refer to the context of the text.
Parallel structuring	Parallel structuring is really just an advanced way of saying repetition, but it is more to do with structure, rather than just words. Structure means how the information is positioned. Sentences can repeat themselves in structure. It might be that several sentences start with the same word, or that the way the sentences are written follows a pattern. For example, 'They came, they saw, they conquered' follows a pattern of repetition.	For emphasis To build tension To build to a climax	What is being repeated and why? Make sure you cover what the words/phrases that are being repeated mean, as well as how they work.
Lists	Look for commas and semicolons. Lists can be three-part (where there are three items in a list) or longer. Lists may consist of words or phrases. If you see semicolons, the likelihood is it will be a list of phrases (but not always).	To show 'how many' there are (range or variety) To build to a climax	What is in the list and why would the writer put a list here?

Technique	What to look for	Function	How to answer/ questions to ask
Length	Sometimes sentences are either very long, or very short. You can identify these by looking for where the sentences start and end.	Short sentences are usually for impact Long sentences could be to emphasise a particular point and sometimes relate to the context of the sentence; for example, if a sentence is long and flowing and about a river, it could be that the river is also long and flowing	Why does the short sentence add impact? What is the relationship between the sentence and the context of the prose?
Colons	Colons are two dots like so (:)	To introduce a list For balance To explain a point To provide an explanation of what came before	What is the point of the colon? What does it do? How does it add to the meaning of the text?
Semicolons	Semicolons are a dot and a comma (;)	To separate phrases in a list To indicate a longer 'pause' in a sentence than a comma For balance	What is the purpose of the semicolon? How does it add to the meaning of the text?
Commas	,	Indicate a list Used as parenthesis (see below) To indicate phrases that are out of normal sequence	Why are the commas being used here? How does this help to clarify the meaning of the text?
Dashes	– or - -	A single dash is usually used to provide extra information A double dash is used as parenthesis (see below)	What is the information provided and what does it add to the meaning of the sentence?
Parentheses	Brackets (()) or dashes (–) or commas (,)	To provide additional information in a sentence; the information could be a sentence on its own, but it is put in parenthesis to clarify something	What is the information in the brackets and how does it help clarify the writer's point?
Questions	May be just one question or a series of questions	A question may or may not need an answer. If the answer is already known, then we call this a rhetorical question. If there is a series of questions, the aim is to provoke the reader to think	What are the questions that are being asked and why is the writer asking them?

Note: It is important not just to identify the function of the technique – so do not just say 'dashes add extra information'. Say what the extra information is and why it has been added to the sentence.

MARKS

11   Paper A, Passage 1. Read lines 10–14. By referring to at least one example, **analyse** how the writer uses **sentence structure** to emphasise his point.   2

12   Paper B, Passage 1. Read lines 38–53. By referring to at least two examples, **analyse** how the writer uses **sentence structure** to emphasise the benefits of her new way of farming.   4

Answers can be found on page 34.

Question type: imagery

>> HOW TO ANSWER

Imagery questions, again, usually fall under 'use of language questions' but can also be stand-alone questions or combined in a list with other techniques. **Imagery** questions will be expecting you to 'spot' some of the techniques in the table below. Basically, an **image** has a *literal root* and a *metaphorical use*. An **image** can be seen as a combination of the literal and the metaphorical. The writer has taken the 'literal' and used it in a 'metaphorical' way. For example, in the following sentence:

The classroom was a zoo.

The writer does not literally mean that the classroom was full of lions, tigers, monkeys and sharks. The writer means that the children were behaving in a wild manner, like wild animals. So, the literal root is a zoo 'picture' and the metaphorical picture is children being very noisy and chaotic like animals in a zoo.

You want to tackle this question with a 'just as … so' formula.
Use the following bullet point structure:

▶ Technique (metaphor, for example)
▶ Quote
▶ Explain the literal root and metaphorical image, using '**just as … so**'.

For example, you could say '**Just as** zoos are full of noisy and wild animals, **so** the children's behaviour was loud and unsettled'.

Use this structure for each of the image 'types'. See in the table below.

Top Tip!
Do not worry if you cannot remember the technique – just miss this bit out.

Imagery techniques

Technique	Explanation
Metaphor	When the writer claims something is something else, but does not use 'like' or 'as'. For example: *The classroom was a zoo.*
Simile	When the writer makes a comparison between two things, using 'like' or 'as'. For example: *The classroom was like a zoo.*
Personification	When the writer gives an inanimate object life-like qualities. For example: *The chairs fought back against the children.* Chairs cannot fight, so by giving them this characteristic the writer is bringing these objects alive.

MARKS

13   Paper A, Passage 1. Read lines 19–30. By referring to at least one example, **analyse** how the writer uses **imagery** to demonstrate his ideas about choice.   2

14   Paper B, Passage 1. Read lines 1–4. By referring to at least one example, **analyse** how **imagery** is used to emphasise the increase in the popularity of veganism.   2

Answers can be found on page 35.

Question type: tone

>> HOW TO ANSWER

Tone questions are very similar to word choice questions. They can appear on their own or as a 'use of language' question. **Tone** means 'what the prose sounds like'. So, if your teacher was praising the class for working hard, they would probably be speaking in an enthusiastic and celebratory tone. If the class had not done homework, the teacher may speak disappointedly or perhaps even in a **tone** of irritation!

Approach tone questions as follows:

▶ Technique (write **tone** here)
▶ Write the **tone**
▶ Write the words that tell you the **tone**
▶ Explain how you know this is the **tone**: for example, the repetition of 'on and on and on' suggests the teacher droned continuously, giving a tone of monotony.

Top Tip!

To answer **tone** questions, you need to understand what the sentences would sound like if you read them out loud. You get your answer from analysing **word choice** and **punctuation**.

MARKS

15 Paper A, Passage 1. Read lines 1–18. By referring to at least two examples, **analyse** how the writer's language creates a light-hearted **tone** in this part of the passage. — **4**

16 Paper B, Passage 1. Read lines 7–12. By referring to at least one example, **analyse** how the writer creates a **tone** of exasperation. — **2**

Answers can be found on pages 35–36.

Question type: contrast

>> HOW TO ANSWER

A **contrast** question will probably appear under a 'use of language' question. In this case, you use the structure below.

▶ Bullet point the technique (**contrast**)
▶ Explain what the **contrast** is
▶ Choose a quote for one side of the **contrast**
▶ Explain what this first quote means/what side of the **contrast** it refers to
▶ Choose a quote for the other side of the **contrast**
▶ Explain what this first quote means/what side of the **contrast** it refers to.

MARKS

17 Paper A, Passage 1. Read lines 41–46. **Analyse** how the writer uses **contrast** to develop his argument. — **2**

18 Paper B, Passage 1. Read lines 58–64. **Identify** the writer's main point of **contrast** in these lines. — **2**

Answers can be found on pages 36–37.

Hint!

You may also draw on the technique of onomatopoeia, which is when a word sounds like its noise (for example, 'bang') or alliteration (when words start with the same letter in a sequence). If you do so, modify the approaches outlined above.

Group 3: Has the writer been convincing enough?

Question type: usefulness

>> HOW TO ANSWER

This type of question usually appears at the end of the first passage, although that does not mean it may not appear elsewhere. The question often asks how effective the last paragraph has been in concluding the writer's argument. You may also find one on the first paragraph, asking how well the writer introduced the argument.

There are several ways to answer this type of question. However, you do need to pay attention to what you might be asked specifically to comment on. For example, you might be asked about **content**, **ideas** or **language**.

If you are asked about **content** or **ideas**, use the following formula:

▶ Allocate 1 mark to one point.

▶ Then write a heading 'effective conclusion: reason 1' (for example).

▶ Then say what point you have chosen and why it is effective. The easiest way to do this is to make links back to information or arguments that have come earlier in the article and explain what the link is that you are making.

▶ Then do the same for as many reasons as you need.

If you are asked about **language** (and note that you might be asked about both, in which case you allocate marks per point, as outlined above), follow the formula below.

▶ Write a heading 'effective conclusion: reason 1'.

▶ Find an example of **language**, such as **sentence structure** or **word choice**, and write it down.

▶ Explain why this example of language is useful/clear/interesting (in relation to the question).

▶ Then do the same for as many reasons as you need.

Top Tip!

If the question asks about ideas, content and language, make sure you write which one you are referring to.

You might think that the paragraph is not effective. This is not wrong, but it is probably more difficult to argue, so it is probably best to argue for effectiveness. Also, it is unlikely that any examiner would pick a terrible article for an exam paper, so the chances are it will be effective!

MARKS

19 Paper A, Passage 1. Read lines 50–58. **Evaluate** the effectiveness of these lines as a conclusion to the passage as a whole. In your answer you should refer to **ideas** and to **language.**   4

20 Paper B, Passage 1. Read lines 1–4. **Evaluate** the effectiveness of the writer's use of **language** in introducing her argument.   2

Answers can be found on pages 37–38.

Group 4: Identifying areas of agreement and/or disagreement

Question type: agreement/disagreement

≫ HOW TO ANSWER

This is the last question you have to do in the paper and by this stage, you might be feeling quite exhausted. But, actually, this question is not too difficult. It just seems so because it is worth 5 marks and you have more material to deal with.

What you have to do is read the second passage and then answer the question. The second passage will be related to the first one.

The first thing to do is to **look at the question** and work out if you are looking for areas of **agreement** (where the passages argue the same things), or **disagreement** (where the passages argue something different).

Top Tip!

Do this before you read the second passage, so you know what you are looking for.

Then, read the second passage. As you read, slowly and carefully, **highlight** any areas that match what you are being asked to do. This will make your job easier for the next stage.

Usually you will be asked to **identify** three areas of **agreement or disagreement**. The most effective way to do this is by drawing a table, as follows.

Area of agreement/disagreement	Passage 1	Passage 2
Write area 1 here.	Give a quote and explain why you picked it. How does it relate to area 1?	Give a quote and explain why you picked it. How does it relate to area 1?
Write area 2 here.	As above, but for area 2.	As above, but for area 2.
Write area 3 here.	As above, but for area 3.	As above, but for area 3.

It is important to explain clearly **why you have picked the example you have** to back up your 'area' otherwise the examiner will not understand. It is also important to make sure your areas are as different as possible. Areas that are too similar will not be awarded marks twice.

MARKS

21 Paper A, Passages 1 and 2. Look at both passages. Both writers express their views about choice. **Identify** three key areas on which they **agree**. You should support the points by referring to important ideas in both passages. You may answer this question in continuous prose or in a series of developed bullet points.

5

22 Paper B, Passages 1 and 2. Look at both passages. Both writers express their views about eating a vegan diet and modern-day farming. **Identify** three key areas on which they **disagree**. You should support the points by referring to important ideas in both passages. You may answer this question in continuous prose or in a series of developed bullet points.

5

Answers can be found on pages 38–39.

Critical Reading

Paper 2 of the exam is split into lots of different sections, but you only need to do two parts. Part 1 is the Scottish Text section. You need to find the questions that are based on the Scottish text that you have been studying in class. Remember that you cannot answer on the same genre in the essay question.

This section is worth 20 marks and is usually divided into four questions. The first three questions are short questions, asking about your understanding of the language used in the text you have chosen. These questions are usually worth 2, 3 or 4 marks. The fourth question is worth 10 marks and assesses your understanding of the text as a whole.

Group 1: Short questions on the Scottish Text

Question type: use of language questions and/or explain questions

>> HOW TO ANSWER

These questions are simply language questions like those outlined in the RUAE section above, but this time they are focused on the text you have been studying in class. They will usually have the words 'analyse how' in them. Sometimes, there may be a question asking you to 'explain' or 'evaluate'. Asking about techniques is more common in poetry questions and drama questions, although this can appear in prose questions too. You may also be asked about character or theme.

To answer these questions, use the techniques outlined in the section above. So, quote the 'language' you want to use and then explain how it answers the question (why you chose it). Make sure you use the marks as your guide, so if the question is worth 4 marks, it is advisable to give four points, even if the question says 'at least two'.

Top Tip!
To get full marks by answering with only two points, you would need to give two in-depth answers. It is much easier to pick up single marks than in-depth marks.

Group 2: The ten-marker

Question type: 'discuss how' questions

>> HOW TO ANSWER

This is the question that people always seem to fear, but actually, if you know what you are doing with this question it is quite straightforward. The question will always ask you to 'discuss how' the 'extract' or the text in front of you is related to a specific theme, character or technique in a book, short stories or poems you have studied by the same author.

Follow these steps:

▶ Write '**commonality**' as a heading – then explain how the question can be answered in relation to the extract and the rest of the text(s) you have studied. This part is worth 2 marks.

▶ Write '**extract**' as a heading – then look at the extract and identify two points, or one detailed and insightful point, using quotes and/or examples to answer the question. This part is worth 2 marks.

▶ Write '**elsewhere**' as a heading – show how the question connects to the rest of the text or poems/short stories. Do as above, where you give examples or quotes from the text that back up the ideas in the question. You need to write 6 marks' worth. You can make six small points, or three more detailed points to get your marks. Sometimes the question lends itself more easily to writing detailed points, but always write six if you are in doubt.

Top Tip!
Use headings and bullet points. Your three headings will be *commonality*, *extract* and *elsewhere*.

We will now look at some sample questions. Below, you will see six extracts on the most popular texts used in the Higher, with questions underneath. These mimic the structure of the paper.

Sample questions with extracts

Drama

From *Men Should Weep* by Ena Lamont Stewart

Example 1

In this extract from near the beginning of the play, Lily questions some of Maggie's assumptions.

	LILY:	Dae you think *you're* happy?
	MAGGIE:	Aye! I'm happy!
	LILY:	In this midden?
5	MAGGIE:	Ye canna help havin a midden o a hoose when there's kids under yer feet a day. I dae the best I can.
	LILY:	I ken ye do. I'd gie it up as hopeless. Nae hot water. Nae place tae dry the weans' clothes … nae money. If John wad gie hissel a shake …
	MAGGIE:	You leave John alane! He does his best for us.
10	LILY:	No much o a best. O.K. O.K. Keep yer wig on! Ye're that touchy ye'd think ye wis jist new merriet. I believe you still love him!
	MAGGIE:	Aye. I still love John. And whit's more, he loves me.
	LILY:	Ye ought to get yer photies took and send them tae the Sunday papers! 'Twenty-five years merriet and I still love ma husband. Is this a record?'
	MAGGIE:	I'm sorry for you, Lily. I'm right sorry for you.
15	LILY:	We're quits then.
	MAGGIE:	Servin dirty hulkin brutes o men in a Coocaddens pub.
	LILY:	Livin in a slum and slavin efter a useless man an his greetin weans.
	MAGGIE:	They're *my* weans! I'm workin for ma ain.
	LILY:	I'm *paid* for my work.
20	MAGGIE:	So'm I! No in wages – I'm paid wi love. (*Pause*) And when did you last have a man's airms roon ye?
	LILY:	*Men!* I'm wantin nae man's airms roon me. They're a dirty beasts.
	MAGGIE:	Lily, yer mind's twisted. You canna see a man as a man. Ye've got them a lumped thegither. You're daft!
	LILY:	You're *saft!* You think yer man's wonderful and yer weans is a angels. Look at Jenny …
25	MAGGIE:	(*instantly on the defensive*) There's naethin wrang wi Jenny!
	LILY:	No yet.

Questions

MARKS

23 a) Look at lines 1–15. By referring to at least two examples, **analyse** how aspects of Maggie's character are revealed in these lines.   **4**

23 b) Look at lines 1–15. By referring to at least one example, **analyse** how aspects of Lily's character are revealed in these lines.   **2**

24 Look at lines 16–26. By referring to at least two examples, **analyse** how the structure of these lines add to the developing argument.   **4**

25 By referring to this extract and to elsewhere in the play, **discuss** the way Lamont Stewart explores the role of men.   **10**

Example 2

Near the end of the play, Jenny comes home.

(JENNY *turns her back on* LILY.)

	JENNY:	Mammy, Bertie …
	MAGGIE:	Oh, Bertie's gettin on fine. Still in the hospital, but gettin on fine.
5	JENNY:	*(gently)* Mammy, I've been up. I've seen the Sister and the doctor. Mammy, you and ma daddy's got tae *dae* somthin! The Sister said she spoke tae ye, and the Lady Almoner, I seen her tae. Mammy, why d'you no listen tae them at the hospital?
	MAGGIE:	*(guilty and bewildered)* I dae … I try … but I get that excited. They hospitals make me feart and ma heid gets intae a kind o a buzz. When I'm oot the gate, I canna rightly think back on whit they said tae dae…
10	LILY:	Jenny, whit're ye getting at?
	JENNY:	Mammy seems to think they're letting Bertie hame; but they're no. *No here*. Nae tae this. Mammy, ye've tae see the Corporation for a Cooncil hoose.
	MAGGIE:	A Cooncil hoose! A Cooncil hoose! Yer daddy's been up tae that lot till he's seeck scunnert. Ye've tae wait yer turn in the queue.
15	JENNY:	But if they kent aboot Bertie –
	LILY:	Is this whit brought ye back, Jenny?
	JENNY:	It's whit gied me the courage taw come. Least – it was ma daddy's face … in the water; *(more to herself than the others)* there wis lights shimmerin on the blackness … it kind o slinks alang slow, a river, in the night. I was meanin tae let it tak me alang wi it.
20	(MAGGIE *gives a gasp.*)	

Questions

MARKS

26 Look at lines 1–8. **Analyse** how language and stage directions are used to reveal the characters' emotions about the Bertie situation.   **4**

27 Look at lines 9–14. **Analyse** how language is used to create a sense that argument is building between Jenny and Maggie.   **4**

28 Look at lines 15–20. **Analyse** how language is used to reveal the more complex aspects of Jenny's character.   **2**

29 By referring to this extract and to elsewhere in the play, **discuss** how Lamont Stewart explores the theme of poverty.   **10**

Prose
From *The Cone-Gatherers* by Robin Jenkins
Example 1

In this extract from Chapter 1, Duror is secretly watching the cone-gatherers.

Hidden among the spruces at the edge of the ride, near enough to catch the smell of larch off the cones and to be struck by some of those thrown, stood Duror the gamekeeper, in an icy sweat of hatred, with his gun aimed all the time at the feebleminded hunchback grovelling over the rabbit. To pull the trigger, requiring far less force than to break a rabbit's neck, and then to hear simultaneously the clean report of the gun and the last obscene
5   squeal of the killed dwarf would have been for him, he thought, release too, from the noose of disgust and despair drawn, these past few days, so much tighter.

He had waited over an hour there to see them pass. Every minute had been a purgatory of humiliation: it was as if he was in their service, forced to wait upon them as upon his masters. Yet he hated and despised them far more powerfully than ever he had liked and respected Sir Colin and Lady Runcie-Campbell. While waiting, he
10 had imagined them in the darkness missing their footing in the tall tree and coming crashing down through the sea of branches to lie dead on the ground. So passionate had been his visualising of that scene, he seemed himself to be standing on the floor of a fantastic sea, with an owl and a herd of roe-deer flitting by quiet as fish, while the yellow ferns and bronzen brackens at his feet gleamed like seaweed, and the spruce trees swayed above him like submarine monsters.

15 He could have named, item by item, leaf and fruit and branch, the overspreading tree of revulsion in him; but he could not tell the force which made it grow, any more than he could have explained the life in himself, or in the dying rabbit, or in any of the trees about him.

This wood had always been his stronghold and sanctuary; there were many places secret to him where he had been able to fortify his sanity and hope. But now the wood was invaded and defiled; its cleansing and reviving
20 virtues were gone. Into it had crept this hunchback, himself one of nature's freaks, whose abject acceptance of nature, like the whining prostrations of a heathen in front of an idol, had made acceptance no longer possible for Duror himself. He was humpbacked, with one shoulder higher than the other; he had no neck, and on the misshapen lump of his body sat a face so beautiful and guileless as to be a diabolical joke.

Questions

MARKS

30 Look at lines 1–6. **Analyse** how the language in these lines conveys Duror's loathing for Calum.   **2**

31 Look at lines 7–14. By referring to at least two examples, **analyse** how the writer makes the reader aware of Duror's disturbed state of mind.   **4**

32 Look at lines 15–23. By referring to at least two examples, **analyse** how the imagery in these lines gives insight into Duror's feelings.   **4**

33 By referring to this extract and to elsewhere in the novel, **discuss** the conflict between Duror and the cone-gatherers.   **10**

Example 2

In this extract from the last chapter, Mr Tulloch tries to persuade the cone-gatherers to help Roderick down from the tree.

"There's a boy up a tree," he roared. "You, and your brother, have to come and fetch him down. The mistress sent me for you. Now what could be simpler than that?"

Neil shook his head. "I can hear you." He said, in agitation. "I am not deaf. We will not go."

5 Graham clapped both hands to his head. "God Almighty," he cried, "all you've to do is climb a tree and help to bring the boy down. You've climbed dozens of trees as high as yon. I've seen you do it. Your brother up there could climb to the moon if there was a tree high enough."

"We are not her servants," said Neil.

On another occasion, Graham would have admired such irrelevancy: it was a conversational ruse he often adopted. Here it was abhorrent.

10 "Would you save a life?" he cried. "Would you sit there and let the lad fall and break his neck?"

"There are other men besides us, if we are men in her eyes. I tell you," went on Neil, with passion, crushing a cone in his fist, "she cannot one day treat us lower than dogs, and next day order us to do her bidding. We will starve first. If she wishes our help, let her come and ask for it."

"The mistress! Are you daft? Don't you know she owns all this estate, or at least her man does, and everybody
15 knows she's the brains and the heart of the partnership? You can't expect her to come like a byremaid and say, 'please!'"

"I expect nothing of her. Let her expect nothing of us."

Graham gave a jump of rage; yet he was impressed: such thrawness he had never encountered before in a sober man.

20 "Listen to me," he said. "Save the boy, and you name your price. I have no authority for saying that, mind you, but the boy's the heir and she loves him, and if you were to save him, she'd show you gratitude like a queen."

"I love my brother."

Graham shot up both hands to clutch God out of His sky for creating such stupidity. Then he saw; he went down on one knee beside Neil.

Questions

34 Look at lines 1–7. **Analyse** how the language in these lines conveys Neil's determination that he will not save Roderick. — **2**

35 Look at lines 8–17. By referring to at least two examples, **analyse** how the theme of inequality is explored in these lines. — **4**

36 Look at lines 18–24. By referring to at least two examples, **analyse** how these lines show Graham's desperation. — **4**

37 By referring to this extract and to elsewhere in the novel, **discuss** how Neil's character is developed. — **10**

Poetry
From *War Photographer* by Carol Ann Duffy

He has a job to do. Solutions slop in trays
beneath his hands which did not tremble then
though seem to now. Rural England. Home again
to ordinary pain which simple weather can dispel,
5   to fields which don't explode beneath the feet
of running children in a nightmare heat.

Something is happening. A stranger's features
faintly start to twist before his eyes,
a half-formed ghost. He remembers the cries
10   of this man's wife, how he sought approval
without words to do what someone must
and how the blood stained into foreign dust.

A hundred agonies in black-and-white
from which his editor will pick out five or six
15   for Sunday's supplement. The reader's eyeballs prick
with tears between the bath and pre-lunch beers.
From the aeroplane he stares impassively at where
he earns his living and they do not care.

Questions

MARKS

38 Look at lines 1–6. By referring to at least two examples, **analyse** how the poet contrasts the photographer's home with the war zones he photographs. — **4**

39 Look at lines 7–12. **Analyse** how the horror of the war zone is conveyed. — **2**

40 Look at lines 13–18. By referring to at least two examples, **analyse** how the poet conveys the attitude of other people to his photographs. — **4**

41 By referring to this poem and to at least one other poem by Duffy, **discuss** how she explores the emotions of the characters in her poems. — **10**

The Way My Mother Speaks by Carol Ann Duffy

I say her phrases to myself

in my head

or under the shallows of my breath,

restful shapes moving.

5   *The day and ever. The day and ever.*

The train this slow evening

goes down England

browsing for the right sky,

too blue swapped for a cool grey.

10   For miles I have been saying

What like is it

the way I say things when I think.

Nothing is silent. Nothing is not silent.

What like is it.

15   Only tonight

I am happy and sad

like a child

who stood at the end of summer

and dipped a net

20   in a green, erotic pond. *The day*

and ever. The day and ever.

I am homesick, free, in love

with the way my mother speaks.

Questions

		MARKS
42	Look at lines 1–5. By referring to at least one example, **analyse** how language is used to create a soothing tone.	2
43	Look at lines 6–14. By referring to at least two examples, **analyse** how the poet uses contrast to emphasise change.	4
44	Look at lines 15–23. By referring to at least two examples, **analyse** how the poet demonstrates she is 'happy and sad'.	4
45	By referring to this poem and to at least one other poem, **discuss** how journeys are a central concern in Duffy's poetry.	10

Question type: The essay question

≫ HOW TO ANSWER

The essay question is out of 20 marks. You will see that this part of the paper has six sections. You must not answer on the same genre that you used in Part One of the exam.

The six sections are: drama, prose fiction, prose non-fiction, poetry, film and television drama, and language. If you are using a play, answer on drama; a novel or short story, answer on prose fiction; articles or 'factual' stories use prose non-fiction.

The questions are deliberately broad so they can encapsulate most texts. The table below summarises the different types of questions that have come up in previous years.

Top Tip!

Once you know which section you are going to do, read through all the questions and pick the one you think is most suitable for your text and your strengths.

Genre	Question type
Drama	character, theme, structure
Prose fiction	character, theme, structure, setting, techniques
Prose non-fiction	how thinking is challenged, theme, structure, techniques
Poetry	character, theme, structure, setting, techniques
Film and television drama	character, structure, setting, techniques
Language	the different ways people use language in society

Once you have chosen your question, break it down so you can understand exactly what you are being asked to do. Look at the **second line of the question**. Here you will be asked something like 'By referring to appropriate techniques, discuss how …' and the second line often ends with **'text as a whole'**. Your job is to work out how you are going to answer this question. A big mistake people make is just writing about the text. You want to do more than that. You want to create an argument. To achieve this, make sure you do exactly what the question is asking you to do.

Your next job is to make a plan. You can use a spider-gram or arrange around headings, but you do need to think about what you are going to do before you do it. This will avoid you 'running out of steam' halfway down the first page!

Planning, and breaking down the question, should take no more than 10 minutes. You should then write your essay, having a very brief introduction and then creating your argument through several clear paragraphs. At the start of every paragraph, make sure you include a sentence that relates back to what you are doing and what you are moving on to do – these are linking statements, like you learned about in Paper 1. Make sure you also include evidence. Evidence can be quotes, or examples from the text. Only use evidence that is appropriate to the question. Add a quick conclusion, restating what your discussion has been about.

Never ever use a pre-prepared answer for this part of the exam. You can go in with an idea of what you might write about if there is a question on setting, for example, but you don't know what the question will be exactly, so you cannot pre-plan.

The trick to do well here is to know your text very well. Reading it once will not suffice. You need to know the details and nuances of the text. You will have been studying it over a period of time in class and the examiners expect you will have more than just a 'rough idea' of what is going on in your texts.

Top Tip!

Plan your essay around the questions. So, if it says outline a scene, that is what you must do first. If it asks 'how your understanding is important to the text as a whole' it means you might need to look at the theme (central concerns) or plotline (or both)! Much depends on the question.

You are being assessed on the following:

▶ how well you know and understand your text
▶ how well you answer and stick to the point of the question
▶ how well you engage with the powerful techniques used in the text
▶ how engaged you are with the text: can you feel empathy with the characters or main concern?
▶ how well your spelling, punctuation and grammar allow the essay to be understood.

The marking is holistic. This means that the examiner will give you an 'overall' mark, by looking at how well you have achieved the bullet points above.

 Hints!

→ **Do not rely on essays you have done in class**, and do not 'regurgitate' these in the exam. The trick is to come to the exam with lots of ideas and thoughts about at least one of the texts you have studied and use these to tackle **the question you choose from the exam paper**.

→ **Be relevant to the question all the time** – not just in the first and last paragraphs.

→ **Show you have thought about and understood the central concerns of the text**, i.e. what it is 'about' – the ideas and themes the writer is exploring in the text.

→ In poetry and drama essays, you are expected to **quote from the text**, but never fall into the trap of learning a handful of quotations and forcing them all into the essay regardless of the question you are answering. In essays on a prose text, quotation is less important; you can also show your knowledge by referring in detail to what happens in key sections of the novel or the short story.

→ **Refer to techniques, but don't just name them**. The idea is to demonstrate your understanding of how various literary techniques work within a text, by referring to them in support of a key idea which is relevant to the question. Don't structure your whole essay around a list of techniques.

Sample essays

Sample essay on drama

Imagine you were faced with the following question:

Choose a play where two characters are very different in personality or behaviour or attitude. By referring to appropriate techniques, explain how the dramatist makes you aware of this difference and discuss how this contributes to your appreciation of the play as a whole.

A good play to choose for this question would be *A Streetcar Named Desire* by Tennessee Williams. Note the use of the word **or** in the question. You do not want to do all of the 'differences' so concentrate on one of them. Note that there are many different ways to tackle questions like these and this is just one suggestion. It is good to have your own ideas! You could write something like the following:

> *A Streetcar Named Desire* by Tennessee Williams is a play where two characters display very different attitudes. These two characters are Blanche Dubois and Stanley Kowalski. This essay will describe these differences and explain why these are important to understanding the key concerns of fragility, class and gender relationships in 1940s New Orleans.
>
> Blanche Dubois, destitute and alone, arrives at her sister's apartment in the French Quarter, where the play is set, and is horrified by what she sees. She has not seen her sister in a long time and was not aware of the conditions she was living in with her husband, Stanley. Her sister's flat is very small and the area has 'an atmosphere of decay'. This is in direct contrast to Blanche's own old home, which was 'a great big place with white columns'. This difference in class leads to tension between Stanley and Blanche. Blanche's attitude to Stanley is that he is someone beneath her, whereas Stanley sees Blanche as someone who thinks she is too refined to be living with them. Straightaway, this tension engages the audience's attention.

As the play progresses, the audience see that Stanley is a down-to-earth, sometimes violent character, who has no time for 'dame Blanche' (who is constantly bathing and decorating his flat). In Scene Three, Stanley hits Stella and the sisters have to escape to Eunice's (the upstairs neighbour) for safety. The next day, Stella and Stanley have made up and continue as if nothing has happened. Blanche is horrified by this, as her attitude is that unrefined behaviour is not appropriate and, as the audience sees Stanley off-stage, lets her sister know exactly what she thinks of Stanley – 'a survivor of the stone-age'.

The tension in the play builds as Blanche becomes involved with Stanley's friend, Mitch. Blanche sees Mitch as a way to escape her perilous situation – if she marries Mitch, she can escape the claustrophobic apartment and her desperate situation. This highlights many women's plight during this time. Men were often their only way to gain financial security. Blanche, because of her history, believes that she needs to create a persona in order to 'catch' Mitch and get him to marry her. She won't let him see her in the light (a symbol for the truth) in case he notices her age and doesn't tell him the details of her 'sordid past'. It is all going mostly to plan until Stanley finds out that Blanche had been told to leave Laurel for sleeping with many men and had been fired from her teaching job for getting involved with a student. We, as an audience, feel some sympathy here for Blanche, and realise that her baths have been a symbol for her desperation to cleanse herself of her past. We also feel sorry for Mitch, who has been 'tricked' by Blanche's schemes. Stanley, disgusted by Blanche's 'lies and conceit and tricks' reveals all to Stella and to Mitch (to 'rescue' him from Blanche). This difference in attitude to loyalty and honesty leads to the end of Mitch and Blanche's relationship and builds to the climax of the play, Scene Ten.

In Scene Ten, Williams cleverly removes Stella from the set. She is away having her baby and Blanche and Stanley are alone. Initially, Stanley is in a fine mood, but this quickly degenerates as Blanche addresses him as 'swine'. The staging allows for the audience to anticipate the tension, as 'lurid reflections' appear on the walls of the stage and the locomotive (representing desire) frightens Blanche and foreshadows the crisis to come. The suggestion is that Stanley rapes Blanche, highlighting the twist in the play: Blanche, initially with the attitude she has power to attract men, has been crushed by that attitude, as Stanley gains power, reverts to the caveman and claims 'we've had this date since the beginning'. It is interesting that in the end, both become disloyal: only Stanley's disloyalty is not believed, which is an indication of gender inequalities of the time.

Overall, these two characters have attitudes that are very different. Blanche believes in refinement and manipulation to survive, whereas Stanley believes in taking what he wants and living day to day. Williams teaches us that lies and manipulation are dangerous, but also that we should not be quick to judge. Just because Blanche told lies and tricked people, circumstance, gender and class all played a part in her desperate situation.

Sample essay on poetry

Imagine you were faced with the following essay question:

Choose a poem which makes you feel sympathy for a character or place or situation. With reference to appropriate techniques, discuss how the poet's presentation of the character or place or situation makes you feel sympathy and contributes to your appreciation of the poem as a whole.

A good example to choose here could be *Assisi* by Norman MacCaig. Make sure you choose character **or** place **or** situation. You could write an answer as follows:

A poem which makes me feel great sympathy for a character is *Assisi* by Norman MacCaig. The central concern of *Assisi* is the hypocrisy of the church. The poem is a 'snapshot' in time where the poet describes the horror of a deformed beggar, obviously starving, who is ignored by those passing by, because they are more interested in looking at the grand structure of the church. This essay will demonstrate why the reader does and should have sympathy for the beggar.

The first reason we should have sympathy for the beggar is because a great irony is presented between the elaborate nature of the church and the tiny, deformed stature of the beggar. We learn that the church has 'three tiers' and beautiful paintings by 'Giotto'. This contrasts dramatically with the beggar sitting outside who has 'tiny twisted legs' and is 'slumped like a half-filled sack'. These two quotes build up a picture of a beggar with legs that do not function correctly, emphasised by the alliteration of 'tiny, twisted', and a back that cannot straighten, emphasised by the simile 'half-filled sack'. What we see here is a human being in pain and bent over, possibly in shame as well as deformity. When we compare this to the beauty of the church, the key concern of the lack of humanity we have towards others is brought to light.

Next, we should feel sympathy because very few people visiting the church seem to be paying this beggar any attention. 'Tourists, clucking contendingly' run after the priest. They are metaphorically compared to hens, onomatopoetically clacking away among themselves and ignoring the irony of the beggar's situation. This irony is further built on because of the anger we feel from reading the end of stanza one. St Francis, who the church was built 'in honour' of, was a 'brother of the poor'. He believed in helping those less fortunate. We question, as a reader, how just it is to build a church which must have cost a lot of money, when St Francis would rather it was spent on those like the poor, unfortunate beggar.

Finally, the end reveals to us how our sympathies may lead us to misjudge our preconceptions of those less fortunate than ourselves. The poet does this by again building up the contrast between the beggar's physicality: his 'lopsided mouth' and his eyes that 'wept pus' and his beautiful voice, which is 'as sweet as a child's when she speaks to her mother'. We learn that the voice of the beggar is almost mystical and this is not what we would expect when looking at his deformities. The central concern here is that we should not be quick to judge human beings just because of their image.

All in all, this poem teaches us, by feeling sympathy for the beggar, that it is our human duty to avoid prejudice and help those in need. The power of this message is unquestionable and it is a poem that stays with us, even after we close the page.

Below you will find examples of essay questions from each genre. The marking guidance can be found on page x.

Part A – Drama

1   Choose a play in which a central character's behaviour is at times irrational **or** unstable **or** obsessive.

    By referring to appropriate techniques, describe the nature of the character's behaviour and discuss how this behaviour contributes to your appreciation of the play as a whole.

2   Choose a play which explores one of the following ideas: the power of love; the nature of heroism; the impact of self-delusion; the burden of responsibility.

    By referring to appropriate techniques, discuss how the dramatist explores the idea and how it contributes to your appreciation of the play as a whole.

3   Choose from a play a scene which causes you to see a character in a new light.

    By referring to appropriate techniques, explain how the scene causes this and discuss how it contributes to your understanding of the character in the play as a whole.

Part B – Prose Fiction

4   Choose a novel **or** short story in which a central character's behaviour is at times unwise **or** foolish **or** misguided.

By referring to appropriate techniques, explain how the character's behaviour is made apparent and discuss how this contributes to your appreciation of the text as a whole.

5   Choose a novel **or** short story which explores a theme of social **or** political **or** moral importance.

By referring to appropriate techniques, explain how the writer explores the theme and discuss how this exploration adds to your appreciation of the text as a whole.

6   Choose a novel **or** short story in which symbolism plays an important part.

By referring to appropriate techniques, discuss how the writer's use of symbolism adds to your understanding of the text as a whole.

Part C – Prose Non-Fiction

7   Choose a non-fiction text which presents difficult **or** challenging ideas in an accessible way.

By referring to appropriate techniques, explain briefly what is difficult **or** challenging about the writer's ideas and discuss how she or he presents them in an accessible way.

8   Choose a non-fiction text which you find to be inspirational **or** moving.

By referring to appropriate techniques, explain how the writer evokes this response and discuss why you find the text inspirational **or** moving.

9   Choose a non-fiction text which is structured in a particularly effective way.

By referring to appropriate techniques, discuss how the structure enhances your understanding of the text as a whole.

Part D – Poetry

10 Choose a poem in which the prevailing mood is sombre **or** unsettling **or** disturbing.

With reference to appropriate techniques, explain how the poet creates this mood and discuss how it enhances your appreciation of the poem as a whole.

11 Choose a poem which makes use of vivid imagery **or** word choice.

With reference to appropriate techniques, discuss how the poet's use of imagery **or** word choice contributes to your appreciation of the poem as a whole.

12 Choose a poem in which the personality of the speaker **or** of another character is revealed as the poem progresses.

With reference to appropriate techniques, discuss how the personality is revealed and how this contributes to your appreciation of the poem as a whole.

Part E – Film and Television Drama

13   Choose a film **or** television drama* in which the true nature of a central character is gradually revealed to the audience.

With reference to appropriate techniques, explain how the film **or** programme makers present the gradual revelation and discuss how this adds to your appreciation of the film **or** television drama as a whole.

14   Choose a film **or** television drama in which one sequence is crucial to your understanding of an important theme.

With reference to appropriate techniques, discuss why the sequence is so important to your understanding of the theme.

15   Choose a film **or** television drama which is set in a particular period of history and explores significant concerns of life at that time.

With reference to appropriate techniques, explain how the film **or** programme makers explore significant concerns of life during that period and how these contribute to your appreciation of the film **or** television drama as a whole.

* 'Television drama' includes a single play, a series or a serial.

ANSWERS TO PRACTICE QUESTIONS

Question number	Question text	Marks available	Commentary, hints and tips
1	Read lines 25–30. **Identify** two problems with having too much choice. No marks for straight lifts from the passage. 1 mark for each point from the 'Commentary, hints and tips' column.	2	Possible answers include: ▶ Problem 1 – time: we spend too much time deciding what we want which means we have less time to do more important things. ▶ Problem 2 – being unhappy: 'constant disappointment' – because of the extent of choice, we worry we could have chosen something better.
2	Read lines 7–12. **Identify** two ways the writer believes people can grow 'sustainable forms of meat and dairy'. No marks for straight lifts from the passage. 1 mark for each point from the 'Commentary, hints and tips' column (up to a maximum of 2).	2	Possible answers include: ▶ Way 1 – use farmland in circular (old) ways: 'traditional rotational system'. ▶ Way 2 – don't involve all fields in rotation and let crops grow as they will: 'permanent pasture'. ▶ Way 3 – use animals to help with land maintenance: 'conservation grazing'.
3	Read lines 34–40. Using your own words as far as possible, **explain** the way different types of people, according to Schwartz, react to choice. For full marks, different types of people should be dealt with. No marks for straight lifts from the passage. 2 marks may be awarded for detailed/insightful comment. 1 mark for more basic comment. (Marks may be awarded 2+2 or 2+1+1 or 1+1+1+1.)	4	Possible answers include: ▶ the 'maximiser' believes it is possible to find the ideal choice; spends time and energy looking for it and worries that they have not made the right choice ▶ the 'satisficer' accepts that this is not possible and chooses quickly, accepts that the choice might not be ideal, lives with his/her choice and is content.
4	Read lines 26–37. **Explain** what farmers can do to reduce soil erosion. No marks for straight lifts from the passage. 1 mark for each point from the 'Commentary, hints and tips' column.	2	Possible answers include: ▶ 'let arable land lie fallow' – allow the fields to rest periodically ▶ 'return ... grazed pasture' – let animals live in fields as naturally as possible, which helps the soil recover.

Question number	Question text	Marks available	Commentary, hints and tips
5	Read line 50. **Explain** the function of the sentence 'But … tyranny of choice'. For full marks you should show understanding of the key point: the writer changes from discussing too much choice to limiting that choice. 2 marks may be awarded for detailed/insightful comment supported by appropriate use of reference/quotation; 1 mark for more basic comment; 0 marks for reference alone.	3	Possible answers include: ▸ Before the 'but' the writer is discussing the problems with having too much choice, even in our romantic relationships. ▸ The 'but' sentence is a link sentence, which moves the argument from discussing too much choice to how we can rebel against it. ▸ The second paragraph tells us how we can rebel, i.e. using pre-set lists and item selections online.
6	Read lines 1–6. **Explain** how the second paragraph develops the writer's argument. For full marks you should show understanding of the key point: the writer changes from discussing why veganism is exploding as a reaction against intensive farming to what can be done about it. 2 marks may be awarded for detailed/insightful comment supported by appropriate use of reference/quotation; 1 mark for more basic comment; 0 marks for reference alone.	2	Possible answers include: ▸ The second paragraph, signalled by the use of 'but', explains that becoming vegan because you are against intensive farming is a problem that can be solved by allowing animals to be farmed in more traditional ways, which contrasts with paragraph one.
7	Read lines 41–46. **Analyse** how the writer uses language to emphasise that too much choice is problematic. For full marks there should be comments on at least two examples. 2 marks may be awarded for detailed/insightful comment plus quotation/reference; 1 mark for more basic comment plus quotation/reference; 0 marks for quotation/reference alone. (Marks may be awarded 2+2 or 2+1+1 or 1+1+1+1.)	4	Possible answers include: **Word choice**: ▸ 'self-defeating' suggests that too much choice offers the opposite of what we think it should ▸ 'uncertain' suggests people are not sure what to do. **Contrast**: ▸ 'contentment' vs. 'reverse' shows that instead of us being happy with lots of choice the opposite is the case ▸ half a dozen vs. 100 – numbers emphasise the ludicrous nature of the statement. **Sentence structure**: ▸ emphatic nature of first sentence emphasises the problem with too much choice ▸ semicolons (balanced nature of sentences): 'offer buyers … choose 1' then 'offer 100' 'buy nothing' and 'single item' … 'two different items' emphasises the issue with giving people too much choice in shops – the more you are offered, the harder it is to choose.

Question number	Question text	Marks available	Commentary, hints and tips
8	Read lines 54–57. By referring to at least one example, **analyse** how the writer uses language to emphasise her point. For full marks there should be comments on at least one example. 2 marks may be awarded for detailed/insightful comment plus quotation/reference; 1 mark for more basic comment plus quotation/reference; 0 marks for quotation/reference alone. (Marks may be awarded 2+1 or 1+1.)	2	Possible answers include: ▶ Structure of 'much … but' emphasises the difference between what vegans say about methane production and what biodiverse pasture systems show. ▶ List of plants makes biodiverse pasture seem idyllic (not what we would expect of methane omissions). ▶ Dash – after the dash we are introduced to explanation of fumaric acid, emphasising that biodiversity can reduce methane omissions. ▶ Use of statistics emphasises the extent of the reduction.
9	Read lines 25–30. By referring to at least two examples, analyse how the writer's **word choice** conveys his negative attitude to choice. For full marks there should be comments on at least two examples. 2 marks may be awarded for detailed/insightful comment plus quotation/reference; 1 mark for more basic comment plus quotation/reference; 0 marks for quotation/reference alone. (Marks may be awarded 2+2 or 2+1+1 or 1+1+1+1.)	4	Possible answers include: ▶ 'shackled' suggests we are bound, imprisoned, have no control ▶ 'demands' suggests that choice imposes on us, insists we behave in a certain way ▶ 'stolen' suggests that something (time) is being taken from us illegally, without our knowledge or permission ▶ 'inescapable disappointment' suggests we are pulled from happiness to despair when we struggle with decisions ▶ 'harbour a suspicion' just as a boat berths in a harbour, doubt lingers at the back of our minds ▶ 'quest' suggests the unending nature of the search for perfection ▶ 'hopelessly' suggests we will never get what we want.
10	Read lines 20–25. By referring to at least two examples, analyse how the writer uses **word choice** to create an idyllic picture of the farm. For full marks there should be comments on at least two examples. 2 marks may be awarded for detailed/insightful comment plus quotation/reference; 1 mark for more basic comment plus quotation/reference; 0 marks for quotation/reference alone. (Marks may be awarded 2+2 or 2+1+1 or 1+1+1+1.)	4	Possible answers include: ▶ 'Natural herds' suggests there are no 'breeding programmes' ▶ 'wander' suggests walking about, happily, with no purpose ▶ 'wallow' suggests they roll about where they please ▶ 'streams and water meadows/wildflowers and grasses' makes the farmland seem picturesque and tranquil ▶ 'rest' suggests sleeping/relaxing ▶ 'graze' suggests they eat as and when they please ▶ 'browse' suggests they take their time as they graze ▶ 'even dive' suggests the pigs are graceful ▶ 'puddle' suggests they are childlike in their walking.

Question number	Question text	Marks available	Commentary, hints and tips
11	Read lines 10–14. By referring to at least one example, analyse how the writer uses **sentence structure** to emphasise his point. For full marks there should be comments on at least one example. 2 marks may be awarded for detailed/insightful comment plus quotation/reference; 1 mark for more basic comment plus quotation/reference; 0 marks for quotation/reference alone. (Marks may be awarded 2 or 1+1.)	2	Possible answers include: ▶ The lists of choices offered in the restaurant are almost ridiculously long, mocking the absurdity of the choice (and perhaps the waitress's skill in memorising them). ▶ The repetition of the lists and structure of the sentences further emphasises this. ▶ The ellipsis suggests the list could be even longer. ▶ The short sentence in reply, in comparison to the long sentence, emphasises the writer's despair. ▶ The short nature of the last three sentences emphasises the waitress's shock, showing how embedded choice has become in American culture.
12	Read lines 38–53. By referring to at least two examples, analyse how the writer uses **sentence structure** to emphasise the benefits of her new way of farming. For full marks there should be comments on at least two examples. 2 marks may be awarded for detailed/insightful comment plus quotation/reference; 1 mark for more basic comment plus quotation/reference; 0 marks for quotation/reference alone. (Marks may be awarded 2+2 or 2+1+1 or 1+1+1+1.)	4	Possible answers include: ▶ Structure of 'twenty … now' emphasises the difference in the farm's fields. ▶ Parenthesis in line 38 emphasises the problems with the farm. ▶ Colon in line 39 adds information to show the contrast in the labyrinthian quality of land now compared to then. ▶ Dash in line 40 explains why it is useful to have 19 different types of earthworm. ▶ List in line 41 emphasises all the different things the earthworms do to develop the land. ▶ Repetition of 'we have' emphasises the amount of benefits from farming this way. ▶ Parenthesis in line 43 gives the name of the special beetle, which emphasises its special nature. ▶ Parenthesis 'one of our rarest butterflies' again emphasises how this new farming attracts new species. ▶ 'not only … but' builds and emphasises the importance of healthy animals for healthy meat. ▶ The list (lines 46–47) emphasises the number of benefits of natural grazing. ▶ The dash (line 47), emphasises the turn in thought – not only is it good for animals, it is good for humans. ▶ Use of contrast in lines 49–51 emphasises how rich in minerals and vitamins natural grazing meat is. ▶ List in lines 50–51 emphasises the amount of vitamins and minerals in naturally grazed animal meat. ▶ The dash explains why CLA is so useful and leads to the climax of the sentence. ▶ The contrast and use of 'but' in the final sentence emphasises the writer's point that we need the mineral to work our brains, but vegans find it hard to get.

Question number	Question text	Marks available	Commentary, hints and tips
13	Read lines 19–30. By referring to at least one example, analyse how the writer uses **imagery** to demonstrate his ideas about choice. For full marks there should be comments on at least one example. 2 marks may be awarded for detailed/insightful comment plus quotation/reference; 1 mark for more basic comment plus quotation/reference; 0 marks for quotation/reference alone. (Marks may be awarded 2 or 1+1.)	2	Possible answers include: ▶ 'tyranny': Just as a tyrannical government rules over a population powerfully, so does the amount of choice offered in modern-day capitalism. ▶ Just as a plant/tree 'takes root' and is difficult to move, so too has out-of-control choice in modern capitalist states. ▶ Just as a 'patina' is a gloss or shine, so too is 'some choice' in the fabric of what makes us enjoy being human. ▶ Just as a prisoner can be 'shackled' to a post, we too are stuck in this desire for choice. ▶ Just as a 'quest' is a journey in order to achieve a specific outcome, so too is there a journey to find the 'ideal item', which is impossible to achieve.
14	Read lines 1–4. By referring to at least one example, analyse how **imagery** is used to emphasise the increase in the popularity of veganism. For full marks there should be comments on at least one example. 2 marks may be awarded for detailed/insightful comment plus quotation/reference; 1 mark for more basic comment plus quotation/reference; 0 marks for quotation/reference alone. (Marks may be awarded 2 or 1+1.)	2	Possible answers include: ▶ Just as a rocket takes off extremely quickly into the sky, so has veganism. ▶ Just as a spotlight is a light on an actor on a stage, so is the shift from being naive to being informed about farming.
15	Read lines 1–18. By referring to at least two examples, analyse how the writer's language creates a light-hearted **tone** in this part of the passage. For full marks there should be comments on at least two examples. 2 marks may be awarded for detailed/insightful comment plus quotation/reference. 1 mark for more basic comment plus quotation/reference. 0 marks for quotation/reference alone.	4	Possible answers include: ▶ The exaggeration in the imagery of 'A vast canyon' suggests that ordinary supermarket shelves resembled a huge, imposing natural feature. ▶ The exaggeration in 'a universe of flakes, crunchies …' compares something fairly trivial with the entirety of creation. ▶ 'Cornucopia' suggests a bounteous profusion of beauty and riches but is used to describe the very mundane 'breakfast options'. ▶ The list of brand names 'Trix, Froot Loops, Chex, or Cheerios' sounds fairly childish, and is made more infantile by the addition of 'and then another over the specific variety of Cheerios'. ▶ 'Wept bitterly … her heart's desire' attaches high emotion to a dispute over breakfast cereal.

Question number	Question text	Marks available	Commentary, hints and tips
15 (continued)	(Marks may be awarded 2+2 or 2+1+1 or 1+1+1+1.)		▶ Mocking description of 'some sort of sawdust in teddy bear shapes and radioactive pastels' shows a contempt for the gaudy packaging and unhealthy content. ▶ The two short simple sentences 'I made an executive decision. We would go to a restaurant for breakfast' after the lengthy, list-like descriptions and high emotions are tongue-in-cheek, deliberately downbeat. ▶ The lists of choices offered in the restaurant are almost ridiculously long, mocking the absurdity of the choice (and perhaps the waitress's skill in memorising them). ▶ Description of the waitress's reaction ('scandalised … dereliction of the God-given duty … weird … un-American') uses words usually associated with profound concepts, suggests he felt bemused at such a strong reaction. ▶ List of choices in jeans store is amusingly long and detailed. ▶ The question 'Relaxed, or easy?' refers to styles of jeans, but he turns it into a comment on his own state of mind: 'Neither'.
16	Read lines 7–12. By referring to at least one example, analyse how the writer creates a **tone** of exasperation. For full marks there should be comments on at least one example. 2 marks may be awarded for detailed/insightful comment plus quotation/reference; 1 mark for more basic comment plus quotation/reference; 0 marks for quotation/reference alone. (Marks may be awarded 2 or 1+1.)	2	Possible answers include: ▶ 'seduced' suggests, in her opinion, the promotion of vegan products is ill-informed ▶ 'at the very least' suggests that surely vegans should be taking into account their impact on the environment in becoming vegan, especially if they are arguing becoming vegan for environmental reasons ▶ 'driving up demand' has connotations of driving one mad/there is no stopping it ▶ 'demonising': just as a demon is something evil that embeds itself within someone, sustainable farming is being classified as evil along with the rest of farmers (such as the writer).
17	Read lines 41–46. Analyse how the writer uses **contrast** to develop his argument. For full marks a clear contrast should be identified. 2 marks may be awarded for detailed/insightful comment plus quotation/reference; 1 mark for more basic comment plus quotation/reference; 0 marks for quotation/reference alone. (Marks may be awarded 2 or 1+1.)	2	Possible answers include: **Contrast:** ▶ 'Contentment' vs. 'reverse' shows that instead of us being happy with lots of choice the opposite is the case. ▶ Half a dozen vs. 100 – numbers emphasise the difficulty of choosing when faced with too much. ▶ 'Offer buyers … choose 1' then 'offer 100 … buy nothing': parallel structure emphasises (via hyperbole) writer's point that if people see many items, they will struggle to choose. ▶ 'Single item' … 'two different items' emphasises the point that too much choice leads to fewer sales.

Question number	Question text	Marks available	Commentary, hints and tips
18	Read lines 58–64. Identify the writer's main point of **contrast** in these lines. For full marks a clear contrast should be identified. 2 marks may be awarded for detailed/insightful comment plus quotation/reference; 1 mark for more basic comment plus quotation/reference; 0 marks for quotation/reference alone. (Marks may be awarded 2 or 1+1.)	2	Possible answers include: ▶ Main point of contrast (and irony) is that vegans are trying to save the planet by eating more alternative food, but ploughing land for plants produces a lot of carbon too. ▶ The writer suggests that vegans should be getting their food from organic farming because if they don't they are reducing wildlife and adding to climate issues.
19	Read lines 50–58. Evaluate the effectiveness of these lines as a conclusion to the passage as a whole. In your answer you should refer to ideas and to language. 2 marks may be awarded for detailed/insightful comment plus quotation/reference; 1 mark for more basic comment (plus quotation/reference for language points); 0 marks for quotation/reference alone. (Marks may be awarded 2+2, 2+1+1 or 1+1+1+1.)	4	Possible answers include: **Ideas:** ▶ introduces the idea that a change might be coming – acts as a counterbalance to the problems outlined in the passage ▶ specific examples of solutions (internet, shopping list) provide a positive way forward ▶ offers definite advice: don't agonise over it ▶ supports/reinforces the 'satisficer' idea from earlier ▶ the stewardess's 'real anguish' at there being no choice recalls the idea that for some, choice is hugely important ▶ his relief at not having to make a choice supports his argument that making choices can be stressful ▶ the joke in 'We all have to make satisifices' picks up on the term from Schwartz's book. **Language:** ▶ 'But …' suggests a turning point, that perhaps there is an answer ▶ 'revolution is brewing' suggests people are preparing to rise up against an unfair, evil force ▶ 'tyranny of choice' reinforces his argument that choice is an oppressive, undemocratic imposition ▶ the tongue-in-cheek explanation of 'self-binding pre-commitment' as 'This used to be known as a shopping list' mocks the social scientists' jargon and is in keeping with the light-hearted tone at the start ▶ the parenthetical '(i.e. just about anything)' shows his low opinion of the time spent on unnecessary choice ▶ the tone in the final line where he shows relief at not having to make a choice and makes a private joke about 'satisfices' matches the light-hearted tone at the start.
20	Read lines 1–4. Evaluate the effectiveness of the writer's use of language in introducing her argument.	2	Possible answers include: Effective because it draws attention to the increase in veganism via:

Question number	Question text	Marks available	Commentary, hints and tips
20 (continued)	1 mark for more basic comment (plus quotation/ reference for language points). 0 marks for quotation/ reference alone. (Marks may be awarded 2 or 1+1.)		**Imagery:** ▸ just as a rocket takes off extremely quickly into the sky, so has veganism ▸ just as a spotlight is a light on an actor on a stage, so is the shift from being naive to being informed about farming **Use of statistics:** ▸ emphasises how the number of vegans has multiplied substantially in recent years **Sentence structure:** ▸ use of parenthesis justifies the writer's argument that veganism has increased dramatically ▸ 'exposing' suggests revealing the truth of the dairy industry **Article structure:** ▸ sets up the argument for the turning point introduced in the next paragraph ▸ suggests the passage will be about the benefits of veganism on farming and it's not (so could argue therefore that it is not effective).

Question 21

See answers to generic guidance (in paper answers in Part 2) for further information.

	Area of agreement	Passage 1	Passage 2
1	the extent of choice	too much of it everywhere; it pervades many areas of modern life	is embedded in consumer choice, in financial matters, in personal affairs
2	principal problem	it dominates us, weighs us down, is 'tyrannical'	it is 'oppressive'
3	psychological impact	causes mental strain, family arguments, loss of control	causes depression, mental 'paralysis'
4	effect on decision-making	makes confident decision-making almost impossible; leads to fear/ worry that the wrong decision has been made	leads to a lingering concern that the wrong choice has been made, 'the burden of choice'; the perfect choice is illusory
5	the role of business/commerce	it is driven by/is a tool of modern business methods and advertising	modern business employs complexity of choice as a method of diverting attention from competition; sense that consumers are being cheated, tricked
6	response to Schwartz's book	sympathises with the 'satisficer' over the 'maximiser', who is 'doomed …'	condemns 'maximisers', who are 'never happy'; supports 'satisficers'
7	suggested solution	don't agonise over choice, make an early decision and live with it	don't even try for 'the best'; accept what 'will do'

Question 22

	Area of disagreement	Passage 1	Passage 2
1	Plant-based diets impact on the environment	Plant-based diets do not have to have this impact if we change to environmentally friendly farming.	Author follows a plant-based diet because he believes meat and dairy farming damages the environment.
2	Vegans vs. non-vegans	There is a war: vegans do not understand that their diet impacts on the environment too.	There should not be a 'war' between them.
3	The change in farming	'Conventional' farming is moving over to more environmentally friendly farming.	'Traditional' farming was part of life post-war and now is less so.
4	Meat consumption	We should eat some meat at least ('pasture-fed steak').	We should all be reducing our meat consumption and considering veganism.
5	The future	If we farm environmentally, we can reduce the damage (encouraging sustainable forms of meat and dairy production).	If we keep eating meat, the environmental impact could be catastrophic (risk for future generations).
6	The extent of the changes that are required	We need to adjust the way we farm rather than give up meat and dairy (last paragraph).	Changes need to be extreme and far-reaching ('drastic changes').
7	Farmers vs. vegans	Vegans have to 'bend' and eat meat occasionally.	There can be a solution.

Drama – *Men Should Weep* by Ena Lamont Stewart

Example 1

Question number		Question text	Marks available	Commentary, hints and tips
23	a)	Look at lines 1–15. By referring to at least two examples, analyse how aspects of Maggie's character are revealed in these lines. 2 marks may be awarded for detailed/insightful comment plus quotation/reference; 1 mark for more basic comment plus quotation/reference; 0 marks for quotation/reference alone. (Marks may be awarded 2+2, 2+1+1 or 1+1+1+1.)	4	Possible answers include: ▶ defensive of her role: 'Ye canna help …', 'I dae the best I can' ▶ defensive of her family: 'You leave John alane', 'He does his best for us' ▶ sentimental: 'I still love John. And whit's more, he loves me' ▶ self-deluding: 'Aye! I'm happy!', 'I'm sorry for you, Lily.'
	b)	Look at lines 1–15. By referring to at least one example, analyse how aspects of Lily's character are revealed in these lines.	2	Possible answers include: ▶ she speaks her mind, not afraid to be negative: 'midden', 'No much o a best', 'nae' repeated ▶ quick to placate, conciliate: 'O.K. O.K. …'

Question number	Question text	Marks available	Commentary, hints and tips
23 b) *(continued)*	2 marks may be awarded for detailed/insightful comment plus quotation/reference; 1 mark for more basic comment plus quotation/ reference; 0 marks for quotation/reference alone. (Marks may be awarded 1+1 or 2.)		▸ sense of humour: 'photies to the Sunday papers … Is this a record?'
24	Look at lines 16–26. By referring to at least two examples, analyse how the structure of these lines add to the developing argument. 2 marks may be awarded for detailed/insightful comment plus quotation/reference; 1 mark for more basic comment plus quotation/ reference; 0 marks for quotation/reference alone. (Marks may be awarded 2+2, 2+1+1 or 1+1+1+1.)	**4**	Possible answers include: ▸ the key ideas are: the back and forth, tennis-match-style, balanced nature of the exchanges, and the way each pair of lines is linked to the next by a word or an idea, e.g.: balance: 'Servin …' – 'Livin …'; 'in a Coocaddens pub' – 'in a slum'; 'brutes o men' – 'a useless man' ▸ link: 'weans' ▸ balance: 'his greetin weans' – 'They're *my* weans!' ▸ link: 'workin … work' ▸ balance: '*paid* for my work' – 'paid wi love' ▸ link: 'airms roon ye/me' ▸ balance 'a man's …' – '*Men!*' ▸ link: 'They're a dirty beasts' – 'a lumped thegither' ▸ balance: 'You're daft!' – 'You're *saft!*'
25	By referring to this extract and to elsewhere in the play, discuss the way Lamont Stewart explores the role of men. You can answer in bullet points in this final question, or write a number of linked statements.	**10**	You can gain up to 2 marks for identifying elements of commonality as identified in the question, i.e. how Lamont Stewart explores the role of men. A further 2 marks can be achieved for reference to the extract given. 6 additional marks can be gained for discussion of similar references to at least one other part of the text. In practice this means: Identification of commonality (1+1), e.g. men are portrayed as lazy or unmotivated (1) and rely on women for their survival. (1) From the extract: 2 marks for detailed/insightful comment plus quotation/reference; 1 mark for more basic comment plus quotation/reference; 0 marks for quotation alone. For example, John is portrayed as lazy by Lily 'gie hissel a shake' (1) and the men in the pub as 'dirty hulkin brutes', or uncivilised and unwashed, by Maggie. (1) From at least one other part of the text: as above for up to 6 marks. Possible references include: ▸ John's less-than-convincing efforts to support his family ▸ John's refusal to visit Bertie, inability to come to terms with Bertie's illness

Question number	Question text	Marks available	Commentary, hints and tips
25 *(continued)*			▸ John's inability to cope with Jenny in any of their major confrontations ▸ John's passivity in general and especially at the end where he is physically drained and unable to respond ▸ Alec's laziness, slovenly habits, and occasional resorting to violence when unable to express his feelings ▸ Alec's rather pathetic reliance on his mother ▸ Alec's submissiveness to Isa ▸ Alec's inability to cope with Isa's infidelity and desertion.

Example 2

Question number	Question text	Marks available	Commentary, hints and tips
26	Look at lines 1–8. Analyse how language and stage directions are used to reveal the characters' emotions about the Bertie situation. For full marks, both characters' emotions should be included. 2 marks may be awarded for detailed/insightful comment plus quotation/reference; 1 mark for more basic comment plus quotation/reference; 0 marks for quotation/reference alone. (Marks may be awarded 2+2, 2+1+1 or 1+1+1+1.)	4	Possible answers include: ▸ Maggie is in denial, pretending that everything is well with Bertie (repetition of 'getting on fine'). ▸ When Maggie gets caught out, she is 'guilty and bewildered.' She feels ashamed that she has lied to Jenny and the family, but also confused over what she should do. ▸ Maggie finds it difficult to cope in the hospital: 'I get that excited'; 'ma heid gets intae a kind o a buzz'; 'I canna rightly think back on what they said tae dae' but she keeps going back as she loves her son. ▸ Jenny is more practical than her mother and wants to sort it out. She's 'been up' and 'seen the sister and doctor' which tells us she has been to the hospital and found out the truth. ▸ Jenny is frustrated: 'you … tae *dae* something!' and 'why d'you no listen tae them at the hospital?' ▸ Jenny's frustration is emphasised by the use of exclamation and question marks.
27	Look at lines 9–14. Analyse how language is used to create a sense that argument is building between Jenny and Maggie. 2 marks may be awarded for detailed/insightful comment plus quotation/reference; 1 mark for more basic comment plus quotation/reference; 0 marks for quotation/reference alone. (Marks may be awarded 1+1+1+1, 2+1+1 or 2+2.)	4	Possible answers include: ▸ contrast between Jenny trying to persuade Maggie to get a council house and Maggie explaining they have been trying. Emphasised by: ▸ back-and-forth argument ▸ the suggestion that Maggie is shouting via the exclamation marks ▸ the gentle response by Jenny 'But if they … Bertie' ▸ Jenny's complaints about Maggie's house 'No here. No tae this' ▸ Jenny's demanding tone 'You've to see the Corporation for a council hoose' ▸ Maggie's retort and repetition of frustration and irritation: 'A cooncil hoose! A cooncil hoose' ▸ Maggie's helplessness: 'Yer daddy's … scunnert'. ▸ Maggie desperately explaining it's not her fault 'you've tae wait yer turn in the queue'.

Question number	Question text	Marks available	Commentary, hints and tips
28	Look at lines 15–20. Analyse how language is used to reveal the more complex aspects of Jenny's character. 2 marks may be awarded for detailed/insightful comment plus quotation/reference; 1 mark for more basic comment plus quotation/reference; 0 marks for quotation/reference alone. (Marks may be awarded 1+1 or 2.)	2	Possible answers include: ▸ Jenny comes across as thoughtful. ▸ 'it was ma daddy's face in the water' – the fact she saw her father reminded her of their love. ▸ stage directions: 'More to herself than others' suggests that she is being reflective and contemplative. ▸ the poetic language suggests deep thought 'shimmerin on the blackness'; 'slinks alang slow' (emphasised by the sibilance). ▸ she's been quite depressed and considered suicide 'I was meaning to let it tak me alang wi it'.
29	By referring to this extract and to elsewhere in the play, discuss how Lamont Stewart explores the theme of poverty. You can answer in bullet points in this final question, or write a number of linked statements.	10	You can gain up to 2 marks for identifying elements of commonality as identified in the question, i.e. how Lamont Stewart explores the theme of poverty. A further 2 marks can be achieved for reference to the extract given. 6 additional marks can be gained for discussion of similar references to at least one other part of the text. In practice this means: Identification of commonality (1+1), e.g. Poverty is a major theme in the book, examining how once in poverty it is almost impossible to get out. (1) This is exemplified by the setting of 1930s depression in Glasgow. (1) From the extract: 2 marks for detailed/insightful comment plus quotation/reference; 1 mark for more basic comment plus quotation/reference; 0 marks for quotation alone. For example, even though the family has a bit more money, conditions in the house are still too bad for the hospital to allow Bertie to return. The solution to this is to get a council house: the extent of poverty in this society is demonstrated by the fact that there is a long wait to get one. From at least one other part of the text: as above for up to 6 marks. Possible references include: ▸ The setting oozes poverty: the house is said to be a 'midden' by Jenny, there are lots of them in a very small space and there is barely any space for them to all sleep. ▸ Food is very limited: Lily brings them 'beans' and no one is to touch them as Maggie wants to use them for the next day's dinner. Maggie hangs about at the grocer's at closing time to get fruit and veg no one else wants. Ernest complains about being hungry. Maggie has 'nae biscuits' to go with Mrs Harris's tea. ▸ Their clothes are very limited: Edie has no pants. Maggie is overjoyed with her new hat. ▸ Poverty has a direct impact on John and his lack of work – blaming the 'dirty rotten buggers in parliament'. He feels ashamed because he cannot provide for his family.

Question number	Question text	Marks available	Commentary, hints and tips
29 (continued)			▸ Jenny can't stand living in poverty any more so moves out. She calls the house a 'pig-sty'. ▸ Bertie's illness is a direct result of living in poverty. ▸ Alec turns to theft to get money.

Prose – *The Cone-Gatherers* by Robin Jenkins

Example 1

Question number	Question text	Marks available	Commentary, hints and tips
30	Look at lines 1–6. Analyse how the language in these lines conveys Duror's loathing for Calum. 2 marks may be awarded for detailed/insightful comment plus quotation/reference; 1 mark for more basic comment plus quotation/reference; 0 marks for quotation/reference alone. (Marks may be awarded 2 or 1+1.)	2	Possible answers include: ▸ 'feebleminded' suggests he sees him as stupid, subnormal ▸ 'hunchback' – a very belittling, offensive word, suggests he focuses on the deformity ▸ 'grovelling' distorts Calum's attempts at mercy into something demeaning, as if he's begging, bowing and scraping ▸ 'obscene' suggests that any sound from Calum would be seen as something disgusting, lascivious.
31	Look at lines 7–14. By referring to at least two examples, analyse how the writer makes the reader aware of Duror's disturbed state of mind. 2 marks may be awarded for detailed/insightful comment plus quotation/reference; 1 mark for more basic comment plus quotation/reference; 0 marks for quotation/reference alone. (Marks may be awarded 2+2, 2+1+1 or 1+1+1+1.)	4	Possible answers include: ▸ that he had 'waited over an hour' just to see them suggests it is an obsession ▸ 'purgatory of humiliation' is an exaggerated way to describe his feelings, it suggests how deeply affected he is ▸ 'as if … forced to wait upon them as upon his masters' – a reversal of the norm, suggests how distorted his view is ▸ his apparent desire to see the cone-gatherers come to harm, a sense of relish in 'come crashing down' and 'lie dead on the ground' ▸ the extended metaphor in which he imagines himself standing on the floor of the sea and sees features around him as if they were underwater – bizarre, dreamlike, surreal ▸ 'standing on the floor of a fantastic sea' – acknowledges that it's dreamlike, fanciful ▸ 'with an owl and a herd of roe-deer flitting by quiet as fish' – terrestrial creatures are transformed in his mind into aquatic ones ▸ 'ferns and bronzen brackens … gleamed like seaweed' – terrestrial flora are transformed into aquatic ones, ironically described in terms of great beauty ▸ 'spruce trees … like submarine monsters' – distorted view of trees as dangerous/threatening underwater beasts.

Question number	Question text	Marks available	Commentary, hints and tips
32	Look at lines 15–23. By referring to at least two examples, analyse how the imagery in these lines gives insight into Duror's feelings. 2 marks may be awarded for detailed/insightful comment plus quotation/reference; 1 mark for more basic comment plus quotation/ reference; 0 marks for quotation/reference alone. (Marks may be awarded 2+2, 2+1+1 or 1+1+1+1.)	4	Possible answers include: ▸ 'the overspreading tree of revulsion in him' – recognises the hatred within him as organic, taking him over totally ▸ 'his stronghold and sanctuary' gives the idea of him being at war, needing to defend himself, being isolated ▸ 'fortify his sanity and hope' shows awareness that he is mentally unstable and wishes to fight against this ▸ 'invaded and defiled' depicts the cone-gatherers as an enemy, a threat, corrupting, dirty ▸ 'its cleansing and reviving virtues' depicts the wood as a place of healing, suggests he views nature as perhaps more powerful than human agency ▸ 'like the whining prostrations of a heathen in front of an idol' – he sees Calum as something alien, primitive, submissive, lacking dignity, entirely different ▸ 'diabolical joke' – as if dreamed up by the devil, intended to cause him (Duror) suffering; 'joke' because of the incongruity of the ugly features and the beautiful face.
33	By referring to this extract and to elsewhere in the novel, discuss the conflict between Duror and the cone-gatherers. You can answer in bullet points in this final question, or write a number of linked statements.	10	You can gain up to 2 marks for identifying elements of commonality as identified in the question, i.e. how Jenkins explores the conflict between Duror and the cone-gatherers. A further 2 marks can be achieved for reference to the extract given. 6 additional marks can be gained for discussion of similar references to at least one other part of the text. In practice this means: Identification of commonality (1+1), e.g. Duror conflicts with the cone-gatherers for several reasons, but one in particular is his hatred of anything deformed (i.e. Calum). (1) In this sense, the conflict is symbolic of good and evil. (1) From the extract: 2 marks for detailed/insightful comment plus quotation/reference; 1 mark for more basic comment plus quotation/reference; 0 marks for quotation alone. For example, in this extract, Duror is hiding in the bushes thinking about what it would be like to kill Calum, in particular. He hates Calum because he sees him as 'deformed' and 'humpbacked'. It annoys him that the cone-gatherers have come to infect the purity of the nature of the wood. From at least one other part of the text: as above for up to 6 marks. Possible references include: ▸ the general idea of the eternal struggle of good and evil, innocence and worldliness ▸ Duror's irrational dislike of the cone-gatherers from the moment of their arrival ▸ the different attitudes to wildlife (the injured rabbit) ▸ Duror's support for the Nazis' treatment of disabled people

Question number	Question text	Marks available	Commentary, hints and tips
33 (continued)			▶ Duror's manipulation of Lady Runcie-Campbell to enlist the cone-gatherers in the deer drive ▶ Duror's lying about Calum exposing himself ▶ the deaths at the end – Calum as Christ, Duror as Judas/devil.

Example 2

Question number	Question text	Marks available	Commentary, hints and tips
34	Look at lines 1–7. Analyse how the language in these lines conveys Neil's determination that he will not save Roderick. 2 marks may be awarded for detailed/insightful comment plus quotation/reference; 1 mark for more basic comment plus quotation/reference; 0 marks for quotation/reference alone. (Marks may be awarded 2 or 1+1.)	**2**	Possible answers include: ▶ the assertive tone of 'we will not go' and 'we are not her servants' ▶ 'shook his head' emphasises that under no circumstances will he help Lady Runcie-Campbell ▶ 'I can hear you – I am not deaf' explains that he is ignoring Graham rather than stupid ▶ 'in agitation' suggests he does not find it easy and is wound up over it, but feels it is necessary.
35	Look at lines 8–17. By referring to at least two examples, analyse how the theme of inequality is explored in these lines. 2 marks may be awarded for detailed/insightful comment plus quotation/reference; 1 mark for more basic comment plus quotation/reference; 0 marks for quotation/reference alone. (Marks may be awarded 2+2, 2+1+1 or 1+1+1+1.)	**4**	Possible answers include: ▶ irritation 'if men we are in her eyes' explains that Neil thinks Lady Runcie-Campbell sees them as less than animals ▶ 'with passion, crushing a cone' suggests he is so annoyed about it he physically feels stress ▶ the contrast of 'lower than dogs' and 'order us to do her bidding' emphasises how immoral he thinks the landed classes are ▶ pride – 'we will starve first' suggests he is so annoyed at the unjust treatment they have been subjected to that he would rather not eat than do as she orders him ▶ 'let her come and ask for it' suggests he is past caring how he is seen by Lady Runcie-Campbell ▶ 'I expect nothing of her. Let her expect nothing of us'. Parallel sentences/repetition emphasise that he does not care any more about how they are seen. He wants Lady Runcie-Campbell to see the consequences of her actions.
36	Look at lines 18–24. By referring to at least two examples, analyse how these lines show Graham's desperation.	**4**	Possible answers include: ▶ 'jump of rage' he is pulled back in anger at Neil not doing his bidding ▶ 'listen to me' – ordering Neil to listen shows he urgently needs him to understand the situation ▶ the begging nature of 'Save the boy and you can name your price' suggests Neil will be able to get anything he wants if he saves Roderick

Question number	Question text	Marks available	Commentary, hints and tips
36 *(continued)*	2 marks may be awarded for detailed/insightful comment plus quotation/reference; 1 mark for more basic comment plus quotation/reference; 0 marks for quotation/reference alone. (Marks may be awarded 2+2, 2+1+1 or 1+1+1+1.)		▸ 'boy's the heir and she loves him' is a fraught appeal to Neil that he will be rewarded because Lady Runcie-Campbell loves her son so much ▸ 'show you gratitude like a queen' continues the emphasis on the extent to which the brothers will be rewarded – Graham's continued persuasion ▸ 'both hands up to God … stupidity' suggests he is at the end of the line, wondering why Neil does not understand what he is asking ▸ 'went down on one knee' – now he realises what the issue is, he changes his plans to try and convince Neil by appealing to his 'reasonable' side.
37	By referring to this extract and to elsewhere in the novel, discuss how Neil's character is developed. You can answer in bullet points in this final question, or write a number of linked statements.	10	You can gain up to 2 marks for identifying elements of commonality as identified in the question, i.e. how Neil's character is developed in the novel. A further 2 marks can be achieved for reference to the extract given. 6 additional marks can be gained for discussion of similar references to at least one other part of the text. In practice this means: Identification of commonality (1+1), e.g. Neil is the protector of his brother and has had to give up his dreams because of it. (1) As his character develops, themes of inequality and injustice are brought to light. (1) From the extract: 2 marks for detailed/insightful comment plus quotation/reference; 1 mark for more basic comment plus quotation/reference; 0 marks for quotation alone. For example, this extract is very important to the development of Neil's character because it is here he stands up for what he believes in: the issue of inequality and how he and Calum are not seen as equals in Lady Runcie-Campbell's eyes. From at least one other part of the text: as above for up to 6 marks. Possible references include: ▸ Neil starts off as a despondent character, having been unable to fulfil his dreams as he has to look after Calum, his brother. ▸ He is concerned over class division: at the start of the novel he compares the manor house with their hut. ▸ He gets frustrated with his brother, but he loves him (i.e. the rabbit in Chapter 1). ▸ He does the 'deer drive' because he feels he has no other choice, due to Duror, even though he knows Calum will not cope. ▸ He gets even more outraged with their treatment by Lady Runcie-Campbell over the deer drive/beach hut/storm. ▸ By not rescuing Roderick, he inadvertently causes Duror to take revenge and kill his brother.

Poetry – *War Photographer* by Carol Ann Duffy

Question number	Question text	Marks available	Commentary, hints and tips
38	Look at lines 1–6. By referring to at least two examples, analyse how the poet contrasts the photographer's home with the war zones he photographs. For full marks both home and war zones should be covered but not necessarily in equal measure. 2 marks may be awarded for detailed/insightful comment plus quotation/reference; 1 mark for more basic comment plus quotation/reference; 0 marks for quotation/reference alone. (Marks may be awarded 2+2, 2+1+1 or 1+1+1+1.)	4	Possible answers include: ▶ 'which did not tremble then' points to the contrast in his ability to control his emotions now that he is reflecting on what he has seen ▶ 'Rural England' suggests an idealised view of England as countryside which is leafy, peaceful ▶ the minor sentence 'Rural England' sounds like a sigh (either of contentment reflecting its calmness or of despair reflecting its vacuousness) ▶ 'ordinary pain' suggests problems at home are insignificant, commonplace ▶ 'simple weather' suggests how easily problems at home can be dealt with ▶ 'dispel' suggests problems at home can be dismissed with little effort ▶ 'explode' suggests a sudden eruption of danger, unpredictable and injurious ▶ 'nightmare heat' suggests extreme climatic conditions, with additional suggestion of oppressive, recurring dreams ▶ 'running children' suggests both an idyllic, innocent image of Rural England and an image of terrified children trying to escape the horror of a war zone.
39	Look at lines 7–12. Analyse how the horror of the war zone is conveyed. 2 marks may be awarded for detailed/insightful comment plus quotation/reference; 1 mark for more basic comment plus quotation/reference; 0 marks for quotation/reference alone. (Marks may be awarded 2 or 1+1.)	2	Possible answers include: ▶ 'stranger' suggests the anonymity of the people he sees, they are not people he can feel any connection with ▶ 'twist' suggests the body is distorted by pain, writhing in agony ▶ 'half-formed ghost' suggests being haunted by memories of death ▶ 'cries' suggests the anguish and pain of the man's wife ▶ the enjambment in 'cries/of this man's wife' emphasises the long, drawn-out sound of her agony ▶ 'blood stained' suggests the indelible nature of the memory of the scale of the violence ▶ 'dust' has connotation of death.
40	Look at lines 13–18. By referring to at least two examples, analyse how the poet conveys the attitude of other people to his photographs. 2 marks may be awarded for detailed/insightful comment plus quotation/reference; 1 mark for more basic comment plus quotation/reference; 0 marks for quotation/reference alone.	4	Possible answers include: ▶ 'a hundred agonies' suggests the sheer weight of evidence he has of suffering, but only a handful will be given any attention ▶ 'black and white' suggests clear and truthful, yet they will be largely unpublished/ignored ▶ 'pick out' suggests the editor chooses to be selective, despite the fact they all show the suffering, because of the requirements of the newspaper ▶ 'supplement' suggests the images don't even merit inclusion in the main part of the paper, they are added on, as if a sort of bonus

Question number	Question text	Marks available	Commentary, hints and tips
40 *(continued)*	(Marks may be awarded 2+2, 2+1+1 or 1+1+1+1.)		► the contrast in numbers ('hundred … five or six') emphasises how little capacity the public have for such images ► 'prick with tears' suggests a very limited response, just a tiny stab of emotion ► 'between the bath and the pre-lunch beers' emphasises the public's lack of concern by focusing on self-indulgent, almost hedonistic activities; the alliteration adds a sense of the poet almost spitting out contempt ► the positioning (and final rhyming) of 'they do not care' reinforces the public's indifference to the suffering.
41	By referring to this poem and to at least one other poem by Duffy, discuss how she explores the emotions of the characters in her poems. You can answer in bullet points in this final question, or write a number of linked statements.	10	You can gain up to 2 marks for identifying elements of commonality as identified in the question, i.e. how emotions of characters are explored in the poems. A further 2 marks can be achieved for reference to the extract given. 6 additional marks can be gained for discussion of similar references to at least one other poem by the author. In practice this means: Identification of commonality (1+1), e.g. many characters in Duffy's poetry are dealing with a multitude of (often changing) emotions (1) and these are used to highlight everyday life themes, such as love, pain, bitterness and revenge. (1) From the extract: 2 marks for detailed/insightful comment plus quotation/reference; 1 mark for more basic comment plus quotation/reference; 0 marks for quotation alone. *War Photographer* – the photographer has to cope with the horrors of what he sees in the war zones, to treat the images professionally and not succumb to emotion; he has also to face up to the attitudes of his editor (driven by business decisions) and of the public (whose interest is transient). From at least one other poem as above for up to 6 marks. Possible references include: ► *Originally* – the speaker first wants to be 'home' and resents the move; then feels uncomfortable in new surroundings; then discovers she has fitted in without realising it; by the end she questions exactly what her origins are. ► *In Mrs Tilscher's Class* – the sheer joy of the speaker's early schooldays is vividly expressed; the innocence of being able to relegate Brady and Hindley to the sidelines; the growing sense that things are changing and the confusion that accompanies the move into adolescence. ► *The Way My Mother Speaks* – the speaker's fondness for her mother and the security provided by memories of her speech patterns; her feelings of isolation as she moves further away from home; her conflicting feelings: 'homesick, free'.

Question number	Question text	Marks available	Commentary, hints and tips
41 (continued)			▶ *Mrs Midas* – the wife's ambiguous feelings for her husband: she despises his stupidity, his greed, his selfishness and his lack of concern for her, but she retains some affection and still misses physical contact with him. ▶ *Valentine* – the powerful feelings of the speaker who mocks the conventional ideas of love as expressed through Valentine's cards and gifts; the feelings of pain and rejection in the way love is compared with an onion, something which causes tears; the association of love with violence.

The Way My Mother Speaks by Carol Ann Duffy

Question number	Question text	Marks available	Commentary, hints and tips
42	Look at lines 1–5. By referring to at least one example, analyse how language is used to create a soothing tone. 2 marks may be awarded for detailed/insightful comment plus quotation/reference; 1 mark for more basic comment plus quotation/reference; 0 marks for quotation/reference alone. (Marks may be awarded 2 or 1+1.)	2	Possible answers include: ▶ 'shallows' sounds gentle, like water ▶ 'restful' suggests peace and tranquillity (of the journey outside and inside her head) ▶ the repetition and rhythm of 'The day and ever' suggests the gentle, rhythmic movement of the train.
43	Look at lines 6–14. By referring to at least two examples, analyse how the poet uses contrast to emphasise change. For full marks there must be some recognition of the change from childhood to adulthood. 2 marks may be awarded for detailed/insightful comment plus quotation/reference; 1 mark for more basic comment plus quotation/reference; 0 marks for quotation/reference alone. (Marks may be awarded 1+1+1+1, 2+1+1 or 2+2.)	4	Possible answers include: ▶ 'goes down England' suggests moving from one country to another, a metaphor for change from childhood to adulthood ▶ 'browsing for the right sky' metaphor for searching for her place in life ▶ 'too blue … cold grey' contrast shows how idealistic childhood has changed to more complex and depressive adulthood ▶ using her mother's words to sooth herself suggests she is trying to change her state from anxiety to calm ▶ 'Nothing is silent … not silent' suggests that even though she is changing, she cannot leave the past behind and forget her mother's words.
44	Look at lines 15–23. By referring to at least two examples, analyse how the poet demonstrates she is 'happy and sad'.	4	Possible answers include: ▶ she is happy because she is moving on with her life, but sad because she is leaving her mother and childhood behind

Question number	Question text	Marks available	Commentary, hints and tips
44 *(continued)*	For full marks, there must be some recognition of why the character feels 'happy and sad'. 2 marks may be awarded for detailed/insightful comment plus quotation/reference; 1 mark for more basic comment plus quotation/reference; 0 marks for quotation/reference alone. (Marks may be awarded 2+2, 2+1+1 or 1+1+1+1.)		▸ 'the end of summer' sounds idyllic, which contrasts with the 'erotic pond' which sounds more dangerous ▸ the contrast of 'green' (naivety) and erotic (sexual connotations) suggests childhood was happy, but leaving is somewhat threatening ▸ 'dipped a net' suggests she is tentatively trying out her new 'adult' life (happy and sad at the same time) ▸ 'homesick' suggests she is upset at leaving her home, but 'free' suggests she is excited by the possibilities that present themselves ▸ 'in love with the way my mother speaks' suggests she is happy she has her mother's voice to sooth her, but sad because she is missing her.
45	By referring to this poem and to at least one other poem, discuss how journeys are a central concern in Duffy's poetry. You can answer in bullet points in this final question, or write a number of linked statements.	10	You can gain up to 2 marks for identifying elements of commonality as identified in the question, i.e. how journeys are a central concern in Duffy's poetry. A further 2 marks can be achieved for reference to the extract given. 6 additional marks can be gained for discussion of similar references to at least one other poem by the author. In practice this means: Identification of commonality (1+1), e.g. many characters in Duffy's poetry are going through both a metaphorical and physical journey (1) and these are used to highlight every day how life events mean change is inevitable. (1) From the extract: 2 marks for detailed/insightful comment plus quotation/reference; 1 mark for more basic comment plus quotation/reference; 0 marks for quotation alone. For example, in *The Way My Mother Speaks* the writer is reflecting on her movement from childhood to adulthood and this is mimicked by the train journey from Scotland to England. From at least one other poem as above for up to 6 marks. Possible references include: ▸ *War Photographer* – the photographer goes on journeys to foreign countries, but also a journey of realisation that our society has little concern for those in war, and his job is not as impactful as he hopes. ▸ *Originally* – the speaker moves from Scotland to England but also through childhood to adulthood. ▸ *In Mrs Tilscher's Class* – there are journeys in the classroom via learning, but the real journey is the speaker's movement from childhood to adolescence with her realisation of how she was born. ▸ *Mrs Midas* – Mrs Midas goes on a journey of realisation that her husband has ruined their lives with his selfish desires. There is also the section in the poem where she moves him out – metaphorically reflecting the end of their relationship. ▸ *Valentine* – Arguably, the speaker moves from a journey of romantic to dangerous love.

Reading for Understanding, Analysis and Evaluation

Duration: 90 minutes
Total marks: 30
Attempt ALL questions.
In the exam you must write your answers clearly in the answer booklet provided and clearly identify the question number you are attempting.
Use **blue** or **black** ink.

The following two passages consider zoos and the treatment of wild animals.

Passage 1

Read the passage below and then attempt questions 1–8.

From 'The sooner zoos become extinct the better' by Janice Turner

In the first passage, Janice Turner considers our attitudes to animal life in captivity.

How many rare gorillas are equal to a human life? To protect a three-year-old boy who fell into an enclosure at Cincinnati Zoo, keepers last week shot dead a 400lb silverback gorilla called Harambe. In a Chilean zoo last month, a suicidal man who clambered into the big cats' cage was saved at the expense of two lions.

That is how our scales of moral worth swing: a human is more precious than any number of animals. Who
5   wouldn't wipe out a whole ape family to save your child, an entire species even? But you don't need to be an internet troll sniping 'they killed the wrong mammal' to feel repulsed. We lock up these wild creatures all their lives, then when a human trespasses into their prisons and they dare manifest natural behaviour, we shoot them dead.

What a travesty is a zoo. How can it still exist in civilised societies, this legacy of gentlemen collectors and
10 capricious kings? We take our children to see animated taxidermy to reveal the glory of nature when it shows only our own stone hearts. I will never forget a bear I saw in Colchester Zoo: such a species is a solitary thing, who hides from view in the wild, but here he was exposed to gawping crowds, so in his boredom and anxiety he'd perform a series of repetitive moves. Stand up, bend down, turn around. Over and over, all day. He was — in human terms — quite mad.

15 Oh, but zoos have evolved, I will be told. They moved the elephants out of London Zoo where they'd stand chained all day: great mammals who traverse a continent, pinioned on a grey concrete slab. After decades in which their immobility gave them arthritis, their lifespan was half that of in the wild, they had less space than you'd allow a domestic cow and, in cooped-up despair, they killed a keeper.

Nowadays zoos have lavish landscaped enclosures, no heavy prison bars, to create the illusion of freedom.
20 London Zoo has its 'Land of the Lions'. It has a ranger's hut, a mocked-up Indian railway station, a little high street with a barber's shop. It is there to reassure visitors this is more natural and 'authentic', almost like the wild. But are lions really happier living in a cage that looks like a movie set?

Admittedly, the animal rights movement attracts a theocratic, purist cadre: the RSPCA activists who compare farming to the Holocaust; those more inclined to found donkey sanctuaries in Syria than care for suffering
25 children; those who argue that animals should have representation in parliament. For these people the moral scales balance: animal and human life have equal value. Yet beyond this often angry fringe are people like me, a happy meat-eater who isn't even particularly fond of dogs, but who can't in conscience see wild animals as exhibits, specimens, playthings.

30 A decade ago, I took my kids to SeaWorld in San Diego to watch the orcas perform. I booked tickets without thinking. It was the stuff of sunny childhood TV shows: happy whales, leaping and splashing, 'kissing' their keepers. Except that watching it live you'd have to turn off half your brain not to feel queasy, to wonder how these mighty and intelligent animals enjoyed living in tiny tanks not open oceans.

A recent documentary *Blackfish* followed the case of a male orca at SeaWorld called Tilikum: his capture as a baby, the dark solitary conditions in which whales are transported, how this perversion of their nature sends
35 them psychotic until eventually Tilikum ate his keeper. After this, SeaWorld attendance plummeted. The theme park has announced it will no longer breed orcas and the live shows will be phased out. Public tastes shifted.

The broad arc of human progress has a parallel animal ark. Bear-baiting, dog-fighting, circuses, chimps' tea parties were all once normal, innocent, fun. Yet each generation is a little kinder to other creatures. The furore about the killing of Cecil the Lion on a 'trophy hunt' in Zimbabwe was not media-led hysteria. Rather it was mass
40 shock that an ordinary guy, a dentist from Minnesota, would get pleasure from destroying such a creature. You could understand an impoverished African poacher. But didn't that impulse to 'bag' beasts, to measure your manhood against your obliteration of fur and ivory, to pose beside a tiger's corpse with a goofy grin, die out in the nineteenth century? Apparently not: lions and other big game are bred just for the thrill of humans killing them for trophy hunts in southern Africa, a lucrative business that purports to conserve as it trades in death.

45 Zoos too have their dark underside. As with the famous public dissection of Marius, a perfectly healthy giraffe at Copenhagen Zoo, they think nothing of slaughtering an inconvenient 'surplus' of lions or elephants. Their conservation work, the protection of very rare species may be valuable. But how can zoos still justify keeping polar bears, great apes and tigers, who fare badly in captivity but as 'charismatic megafauna' are good for profits?

50 It is time for these melancholy mammal museums to die out. Let kids watch wildlife documentaries on TV: in real life, they are just as excited to meet a snake or a giant spider. The species scale is tipping. Costa Rica has become the first country to disband all its zoos and sent its animals to conservation parks. Why shouldn't Britain be next?

Passage 2

Read the passage below and attempt question 9. While reading, you may wish to make notes on the main ideas and/or highlight key points in the passage.

From the website of PETA (People for the Ethical Treatment of Animals)

For the most up-to-date information about animals used in entertainment, visit peta.org.

Zoos evolved at a time when travel for most people was impractical. Nowadays, wildlife watchers can hop on a plane to Africa or Australia for photo safaris or even stay at home and catch nature documentaries on television or view live Internet video feeds, which capture animals' natural behaviour that is rarely, if ever, seen in zoos. Zoos once boasted attendance of over a hundred million each year. Now, however, attendance at some zoos
5 is dropping. This is likely because these zoos are of declining interest to a public that has become much more knowledgeable about the needs and behaviour of wild animals and is more aware of the toll that captivity takes on animals who are meant to roam free.

There is no excuse for keeping intelligent, social animals in cages for our fleeting distraction and amusement. Habitat loss and other perils of the wild are not prevented by confining animals in cramped conditions and
10 depriving them of everything that is natural and important to them.

Most zoo exhibits provide animals with little, if any, opportunity to express natural behaviour or make choices in their daily lives, and this can lead to boredom and neurosis. With nothing to do, animals in zoos may sleep too much, eat too much, and exhibit behaviour that is rarely, if ever, seen in the wild. Primates sometimes throw faeces and engage in 'regurgitation and reingestion' — vomiting and then consuming the vomit.

15 Wide-ranging animals such as bears and big cats often pace incessantly. Primates and birds may mutilate themselves, and chimpanzees and gorillas can become overly aggressive. Hooved animals sometimes lick and chew on fences and make strange lip, neck, and tongue movements. Giraffes may twist their necks, bending their heads back and forth repeatedly. Elephants frequently bob their heads and sway from side to side.

Marine mammals repeatedly swim in the same repetitive patterns in their tanks. Fish suffer too. A study
20 conducted by the Captive Animals' Protection Society concluded that 90 percent of public aquariums studied

had animals that showed stereotypic (neurotic) behaviour, such as interacting with transparent boundaries, repeatedly raising their heads above the surface of the water, spinning around an imaginary object, and frequently turning on one side and rubbing along the floor of the tank.

By their very nature, zoos leave animals vulnerable to a variety of dangers from which they have no defence
25 or opportunity to escape. Animals in zoos have been poisoned, left to starve, deprived of veterinary care, and burned alive in fires. Many have died after eating coins, plastic bags, and other items thrown into their cages. Animals have been beaten, bludgeoned, and stolen by people who were able to gain access to their exhibits. A bear starved to death at the Toledo Zoo after zoo officials locked her up to hibernate without food or water — not knowing that her species doesn't hibernate. At the Niabi Zoo in Illinois, a 3-month-old lion cub
30 was euthanized after his spinal cord was crushed by a falling exhibit door. Despite knowing that two Asiatic bears had fought dozens of times, the Denver Zoo continued to house them together until one finally killed the other.

Marine-mammal facilities are part of a billion-dollar industry built on the suffering of intelligent, social beings who are denied everything that is natural and important to them. In the wild, orcas and members of other
35 dolphin species live in large, intricate social groups and swim vast distances every day in the open ocean. In aquariums and marine parks, these animals can only swim endless circles in enclosures that to them are like bathtubs and are unable to engage in most natural behaviours. They are forced to perform silly tricks for food and are frequently torn away from family members as they're shuffled between parks. The chronic and debilitating stress of captivity can weaken their immune systems, causing them to die earlier than their wild
40 counterparts — even though they are safe from predators and receive regular meals and veterinary care.

		MARKS
1	Read lines 1–8. Using your own words as far as possible, explain the key points made in these lines about our attitudes to animal life.	2
2	Read lines 9–14. By referring to at least two examples, analyse how the writer's use of language makes clear her disapproval of zoos.	4
3 a)	Read lines 15–22. Using your own words as far as possible, explain what London Zoo has done to try to improve its treatment of animals.	2
b)	Analyse how the writer's use of language casts doubt on the validity of this change in approach.	2
4	Read lines 23–28. By referring to at least two examples, analyse how the writer's use of language creates a negative impression of the animal rights movement.	4
5	Read lines 29–36. Explain how the writer uses the example of the orcas at SeaWorld to develop her argument.	3
6	Read lines 37–44. Analyse how the writer uses sentence structure and word choice to emphasise her incredulous tone.	3
7	Read lines 45–49. Identify one positive and one negative of zoos today. Use your own words in your answer.	2
8	Evaluate the effectiveness of the last paragraph (lines 50–52) as a conclusion to the passage as a whole.	3
9	Look at both passages. Both writers express their views about zoos and the treatment of wild animals. Identify three key areas on which they agree. You should support the points by referring to important ideas in both passages. You may answer this question in continuous prose or in a series of developed bullet points.	5

[End of question paper]

Critical Reading

Duration: 90 minutes

Total marks: 40

Section 1 – Scottish Text – 20 marks

Read an extract from a Scottish text you have previously studied and attempt the questions.

Choose ONE text from

Part A – Drama

or

Part B – Prose

or

Part C – Poetry

Attempt ALL questions for your chosen text.

Section 2 – Critical Essay – 20 marks

Attempt ONE question from the following genres – Drama, Prose Fiction, Prose Non-Fiction, Poetry, Film and Television Drama, or Language.

Your answer must be on a different genre from that chosen in Section 1.

You should spend approximately 45 minutes on each Section.

In the exam you must write your answers clearly in the answer booklet provided and clearly identify the question number you are attempting.

Use **blue** or **black** ink.

Section 1 – Scottish Text – 20 marks

Choose ONE text from Drama, Prose or Poetry.

Read the text extract carefully and then attempt ALL the questions for your chosen text.

You should spend about 45 minutes on this section.

Part A – Scottish Text – Drama

Text 1 – Drama

If you choose this text you may not attempt a question on Drama in Section 2.

Read the extract below and then attempt the following questions.

From *The Slab Boys* by John Byrne

This extract is from near the beginning of Act One.

(*Enter* WILLIE CURRY)

	CURRY:	Ha … there you are, McCann. Where've you been this morning? Farrell there said you were unwell.
	PHIL:	Er … um … yes …
5	CURRY:	C'mon, what was up with you?
	PHIL:	Er … touch of the … er … drawhaw.
	CURRY:	The what?
	PHIL:	Dee-oh-raw-ho … the skitters … it was very bad.
	CURRY:	Why didn't you come to me earlier? I could've got Nurse to have a look at you …
10	PHIL:	No … it's not what ye'd cry a 'spectator sport', Mr Curly …

	CURRY:	In future you report all illnesses to me … first thing. How am I supposed to keep tabs on you lot if I don't know where the devil you are?
	PHIL:	Ah wis down the lavvies …
	CURRY:	You wouldn't get much done down there …
15	PHIL:	Oh, I wouldn't say that, Mr Corrie …
	CURRY:	Godstruth, I don't know … If I'd had you chaps out in Burma. Diarrhoea? There were men in my platoon fighting the Japanese with dysentery.
	SPANKY:	How did they fire it … from chip baskets?
20	CURRY:	Less of your damned cheek, Farrell. A couple of years in the Forces would smarten your ideas up a bit … they'd soon have those silly duck's arse haircuts off you. And what have I told you about bringing that bloody contraption in … eh?
	SPANKY:	What contraption?
	CURRY:	How do you expect to get any work done with that racket going on?
	SPANKY:	Pardon?
25	CURRY:	Whoever owns this gadget can ask Mr Barton for it back. (*Protests from boys*) I'll be calling back in five minutes and if you bunch are still lounging about you're for the high jump, understand? Now, get on with it … (*Exits*)

MARKS

1 Look at lines 1–8. Analyse how the dramatist presents Curry as an overbearing character in these lines. **4**

2 Look at lines 9–18. By referring to at least one example, analyse how the humour in these lines relies on deliberate misunderstanding of what Curry has said. **2**

3 Look at lines 19–27. By referring to at least two examples, analyse how the writer's use of language in these lines conveys Curry's dislike of the Slab Boys and their lifestyle. **4**

4 By referring to this extract and to elsewhere in the play, discuss the characterisation of Willie Curry. **10**

Text 2 – Drama

If you choose this text you may not attempt a question on Drama in Section 2.

Read the extract below and then attempt the following questions.

From *Men Should Weep* by Ena Lamont Stewart

In this extract from Act 2, Scene 1, Jenny leaves home.

	MAGGIE:	I dinna ken whit way we bring weans intae the world at a. Slavin an worryin for them a yer days, an naethin but heartbreak at the end o it.
	ALEC:	Aw, come on Ma, cheer up. (*He smooths her hair: she looks up at him gratefully, lovingly, and lays his hand to her cheek. ISA looks at them and laughs.*)
5	ISA:	Mammy's big tumphy! G'on, ye big lump o dough!

(ALEC *disengages himself from his mother and grins feebly.*)

	LILY:	My, you're a right bitch, Isa. Yin o they days you'll get whit's comin tae ye. Alec's no as saft as he looks.
	ISA:	Is he no, Auntie? I'm right gled tae hear it.

10 (JENNY *comes in with a suitcase.*)

	JENNY:	Well, I'm awa. Cheeribye, everybody.
	LILY:	Goodbye. And good riddance tae bad rubbish.

(JENNY *sticks out her tongue.*)

	MAGGIE:	Jenny, whit am I goin tae tell folks?
15	JENNY:	Folks? Ye mean the neighbours? If they've got the impidence tae ask, tell them it's nane o their bloomin business.
	MAGGIE:	Oh Jenny, Jenny! Whit's happened tae ye, Jenny?
	JENNY:	Whit's happened? I've wakened up, that's whit's happened. There's better places than this. Jist because I wis born here disnae mean I've got tae bide here.
20	LILY:	Gie yer Mammy a kiss.
	JENNY:	(*She wavers for a moment, then tosses her head*) I'm no in the mood for kissin. Cheerio, Isa. Mind whit I tellt ye.
	ALEC:	Aboot whit? (*He creeps forward, suspiciously to* ISA) Whit did she tell ye, eh?
	ISA:	(*Pushing his face away*) A bed-time story; but no for wee boys.

25 (MAGGIE *looks helplessly on, combing her hair with her fingers.*)

	LILY:	Clear aff then, if ye're gaun!
	ISA:	Ta ta, Jenny. See you roon the toon.
	JENNY:	Aye. Ta ta.

(*The door opens.* JOHN *comes in. He and* JENNY *look at each other.*)

30	JOHN:	(*Wretched*) I thought ye'd hev gone.
	JENNY:	Naw. Jist gaun.

(*He lowers his eyes from her face and stands aside to let her pass. He turns and watches her from the doorway until her footsteps die away and the outside door bangs.*)

			MARKS
5	**a)**	Look at lines 1–27. By referring to at least two examples in these lines, analyse how the playwright conveys Maggie's state of mind to the audience.	4
	b)	Analyse how the playwright makes the audience aware of Isa's character in these lines.	2
6		Look at lines 29–33. By referring to language and stage directions, explain how John's reaction to Jenny leaving is made clear.	4
7		By referring to this extract and to elsewhere in the play, discuss how Maggie changes in the course of the play.	10

Part B – Scottish Text – Prose

Text 1 – Prose

If you choose this text you may not attempt a question on Prose in Section 2.

Read the extract below and then attempt the following questions.

From *The Red Door* by Iain Crichton Smith

The extract is from near the end of The Red Door.

But really was he happy? That was the question. When he considered it carefully he knew that he wasn't. He didn't like eating alone, he didn't like sitting in the house alone, he didn't like having none who belonged to him, to whom he could tell his secret thoughts, for example that such and such was a mean devil and that that other one was an ungrateful rat.

5 He had to keep a perpetually smiling face to the world, that was his trouble. But the red door didn't do that. It was foreign and confident. It seemed to be saying what it was, not what it thought others expected it to say. On the other hand, he didn't like wellingtons and a fisherman's jersey. He hated them in fact: they had no elegance.

Now Mary had elegance. Though she was a bit odd, she had elegance. It was true that the villagers didn't understand her but that was because she read many books, her father having been a teacher. And on the other
0 hand she made no concessions to anybody. She seemed to be saying, 'You can take me or leave me.' She never gossiped. She was proud and distant. She had a world of her own. She paid for everything on the nail. She was quite well off. But her world was her own, depending on none.

She was very fond of children and used to make up masks for them at Hallowe'en. As well as this she would walk by herself at night, which argued that she was romantic. And it was said that she had sudden bursts of rage
5 which too might be the sign of a spirit without servility. One couldn't marry a clod.

Murdo stared at the door and as he looked at it he seemed to be drawn inside it into its deep caves with all sorts of veins and passages. It was like a magic door out of the village but at the same time it pulsed with a deep red light which made it appear alive. It was all very odd and very puzzling, to think that a red door could make such a difference to house and moors and streams.

0 Solid and heavy he stood in front of it in his wellingtons, scratching his head. But the red door was not a mirror and he couldn't see himself in it. Rather he was sucked into it as if it were a place of heat and colour and reality. But it was different and it was his.

It was true that the villagers when they woke would see it and perhaps make fun of it, and would advise him to repaint it. They might not even want him in the village if he insisted on having a red door. Still they could all
5 have red doors if they wanted to. Or they could hunt him out of the village.

MARKS

8 Look at lines 1–12. By referring to at least two examples, analyse how the sentence structure and word choice in these lines help to convey Murdo's feelings. **4**

9 By referring to lines 13–15, describe Murdo's attitude to Mary. **2**

10 Look at lines 16–22. By referring to at least two examples, analyse how the writer's use of language in these lines suggests the door has mystical qualities. **4**

11 By referring to this story and to at least one other by Crichton Smith, discuss to what extent you feel pity for characters he creates. **10**

Text 2 – Prose

If you choose this text you may not attempt a question on Prose in Section 2.

Read the extract below and then attempt the following questions.

From *A Time to Keep* by George Mackay Brown

I was baiting a line with mussels at the end of the house when I saw the black car coming between the hills and stopping where the road ended at the mouth of the valley. It was the first car ever seen in the island, a Ford.

A small, neat man with a beard and a watch-chain across his belly got out and came stepping briskly up our side of the valley.

5 'Ingi,' I shouted, 'your father's here.'

She was baking, going between the table, the cupboard, and the fire, a blue reek all about her.

But now all thought of bread was forgotten. She let out a cry of distress. She threw off her mealy apron, she filled a bowl of water and dipped face and hands in it and wiped herself dry with the towel. She put the text straight on the wall. She covered my six rationalist books with a cloth. She fell to combing her hair and twisting
10 it into a new bright knot at the back of her head. All the same, the house was full of the blue hot reek of baking. And the bed was unmade. And there was a litter of fish-guts and crab toes about the door. She tried hard, Ingi, but she was not the tidiest of the croft women.

Ingi came and stood at the door.

As for me, I went on with my lines. I was not beholden to him.

15 Mr Sinclair, merchant in Osmundwall – and forby kirk elder, Justice of the Peace, chairman of the district council – stood at the corner of the barn.

'Father,' said Ingi.

'My girl,' said Mr Sinclair. He touched her gently on the arm.

'Well, Bill,' he said to me.

20 'Well,' I said.

'Father, I'm glad to see you,' said Ingi.

'No happier than I am to see you,' said Mr Sinclair. 'Ingi,' said he, 'you're not looking well. Not at all well. What way is it that we haven't seen you for three whole months, eh? Ingi, I doubt you're working too hard, is that it?'

'On a croft,' I said, 'everybody must work.'

25 'Is that so, Bill?' said Mr Sinclair. 'Maybe so. At the present moment I'm speaking to Ingi, to my daughter. I'll be wanting to speak to you later, before I go.'

'Say what you have to say now,' I said, 'for I have work to do.'

'Bill,' said Ingi unhappily.

'Work to do, is that it, work to do,' said Mr Sinclair. 'Then if you have so much work to do, why don't you give
30 my daughter enough money for her to live on? Eh? Just answer me. Why don't you do that? Last month you cut down on her money. The van man told me. She couldn't buy jam or paraffin. Don't imagine I don't hear things.'

		MARKS
12	Look at lines 1–12. By referring to at least two examples, analyse how language is used to reveal aspects of Ingi's character.	4
13	Look at lines 17–23. Analyse how language is used to convey the concerns Ingi's father has for her.	2
14	Look at lines 25–31. By referring to at least two examples, analyse how the writer's use of language conveys Mr Sinclair's attitude to Bill.	4
15	By referring to *A Time to Keep* and to at least one other story by Mackay Brown, discuss the way he creates tension at key moments in his stories.	10

Text 3 – Prose

If you choose this text you may not attempt a question on Prose in Section 2.

Read the extract below and then attempt the following questions.

From *Dr Jekyll and Mr Hyde* by Robert Louis Stevenson

This extract is from the beginning of 'Henry Jekyll's Full Statement of the Case'.

I was born in the year 18—— to a large fortune, endowed besides with excellent parts, inclined by nature to industry, fond of the respect of the wise and good among my fellow-men, and thus, as might have been supposed, with every guarantee of an honourable and distinguished future. And indeed the worst of my faults was a certain impatient gaiety of disposition, such as has made the happiness of many, but such as I found it hard to reconcile with my
5 imperious desire to carry my head high, and wear a more than commonly grave countenance before the public.

Hence it came about that I concealed my pleasures; and that when I reached years of reflection, and began to look round me and take stock of my progress and position in the world, I stood already committed to a profound duplicity of life. Many a man would have even blazoned such irregularities as I was guilty of; but from the high views that I had set before me, I regarded and hid them with an almost morbid sense of shame. It was
10 thus rather the exacting nature of my aspirations than any particular degradation in my faults, that made me what I was and, with even a deeper trench than in the majority of men, severed in me those provinces of good and ill which divide and compound man's dual nature.

In this case, I was driven to reflect deeply and inveterately on that hard law of life, which lies at the root of religion and is one of the most plentiful springs of distress. Though so profound a double-dealer, I was in no
15 sense a hypocrite; both sides of me were in dead earnest; I was no more myself when I laid aside restraint and plunged in shame, than when I laboured, in the eye of day, at the furtherance of knowledge or the relief of sorrow and suffering. And it chanced that the direction of my scientific studies, which led wholly toward the mystic and the transcendental, reacted and shed a strong light on this consciousness of the perennial war among my members. With every day, and from both sides of my intelligence, the moral and the intellectual,
20 I thus drew steadily nearer to that truth, by whose partial discovery I have been doomed to such a dreadful shipwreck: that man is not truly one, but truly two.

		MARKS
16	Look at lines 1–5. Analyse how the language used in these lines creates a positive impression of Jekyll.	2
17	Look at lines 6–12. By referring to at least two examples, analyse how the language used in these lines reveals Jekyll's darker side.	4
18	Look at lines 13–21. By referring to at least two examples, analyse how imagery is used to enhance Jekyll's points.	4
19	By referring to this extract and to elsewhere in the novel, discuss the theme of duality in *Dr Jekyll and Mr Hyde*.	10

Text 4 – Prose

If you choose this text you may not attempt a question on Prose in Section 2.

Read the extract below and then attempt the following questions.

From *Sunset Song* by Lewis Grassic Gibbon

In this extract from Part IV (Harvest), Ewan has returned on leave from the army.

Drunk he had come from the station and more than two hours late. Standing at last in the kitchen in his kilts he'd looked round and sneered *Hell, Chris, what a bloody place!* as she ran to him. And he'd flung his pack one way and his hat the other and kissed her as though she were a tink, his hands on her as quickly as that, hot and questing and wise as his hands had never been. She saw the hot smoulder fire in his eyes then, but no blush on
5 his face, it was red with other things. But she smothered her horror and laughed, and kissed him and struggled from him, and cried *Ewan, who's this?*

Young Ewan held back, shy-like, staring, and just said *It's father.* At that the strange, swaying figure in the tartan kilts laughed, coarse-like, *Well, we'll hope so, eh Chris? Any supper left – unless you're too bloody stand-offish even to have that?*

10 She couldn't believe her own ears. *Stand-offish? Oh, Ewan!* and ran to him again, but he shook her away, *Och, all right, I'm wearied. For Christ's sake let a man sit down.* He staggered to the chair she'd made ready for him, a picture-book of young Ewan's lay there, he picked the thing up and flung it to the other side of the room, and slumped down into the chair. *Hell, what a blasted climb to a blasted place. Here, give us some tea.*

She sat beside him to serve him, she knew her face had gone white. But she poured the tea and spread the fine
15 supper she'd been proud to make, it might hardly have been there for the notice he paid it, drinking cup after cup of the tea like a beast at a trough. She saw him clearer then, the coarse hair that sprang like short bristles all over his head, the neck with its red and angry circle about the collar of the khaki jacket, a great half-healed scar across the back of his hand glinted putrescent blue. Suddenly his eyes came on her, *Well, damn't, is that all you've to say to me now I've come home? I'd have done better to spend the night with a tart in the town.*

20 She didn't say anything, she couldn't, the tears were choking in her throat and smarting and biting at her eyelids, pressing to come, the tears that she'd sworn she'd never shed all the time he was home on leave. And she didn't dare look at him lest he should see, but he saw and pushed back his chair and got up in a rage, *God Almighty, what are you snivelling about now? You always were snivelling, I mind.* And out he went, young Ewan ran to her side and flung his arms round her, *Mother, don't cry, I don't like him, he's a tink, that soldier!*

	MARKS
20 Look at lines 1–13. By referring to at least two examples, analyse how the writer's use of language in these lines shows the offensiveness of Ewan's behaviour.	4
21 Look at lines 14–19. By referring to at least two examples, analyse how the writer makes the reader aware of Chris's perception of Ewan.	4
22 By referring to the whole extract, describe the change in young Ewan's reaction to his father.	2
23 By referring to this extract and to elsewhere in the novel, discuss the development of the relationship between Chris and Ewan.	10

Text 5 – Prose

If you choose this text you may not attempt a question on Prose in Section 2.

Read the extract below and then attempt the following questions.

From *The Cone-Gatherers* by Robin Jenkins

This extract is from early in Chapter 1. The brothers are getting ready to climb down from the tree after a day gathering cones.

The time came when, thrilling as a pipe lament across the water, daylight announced it must go: there was a last blaze of light, an uncanny clarity, a splendour and puissance; and then the abdication began. Single stars appeared, glittering in a sky pale and austere. Dusk like a breathing drifted in among the trees and crept over the loch. Slowly the mottled yellow of the chestnuts, the bronze of beech, the saffron of birches, all the
5   magnificent sombre harmonies of decay, became indistinguishable. Owls hooted. A fox barked.

It was past time to climb down and go home. The path to the earth was unfamiliar; in the dark it might be dangerous. Once safely down, they would have to find their way like ghosts to their hut in the heart of the wood. Yet Neil did not give the word to go down. It was not zeal to fill the bags that made him linger, for he had given up gathering. He just sat, motionless and silent; and his brother, accustomed to these trances, waited in
10   sympathy: he was sure that even at midnight he could climb down any tree, and help Neil to climb down too. He did not know what Neil was thinking, and never asked; even if told he would not understand. It was enough that they were together.

For about half an hour they sat there, no longer working. The scent of the tree seemed to strengthen with the darkness, until Calum fancied he was resting in the heart of an enormous flower. As he breathed in the
15   fragrance, he stroked the branches, and to his gentle hands they were as soft as petals. More owls cried. Listening, as if he was an owl himself, he saw in imagination the birds huddled on branches far lower than this one on which he sat. He became an owl himself, he rose and fanned his wings, flew close to the ground, and then swooped, to rise again with vole or shrew squeaking in his talons. Part-bird then, part-man, he suffered in the ineluctable predicament of necessary pain and death. The owl could not be blamed; it lived according to
20   its nature; but its victim must be pitied. This was the terrifying mystery, why creatures he loved should kill one another. He had been told that all over the world in the war now being fought men, women, and children were being slaughtered in thousands; cities were being burnt down. He could not understand it, and so he tried, with success, to forget it.

'Well, we'd better make for down,' said Neil at last, with a heavy sigh.

25   'I could sit up here all night, Neil,' his brother assured him eagerly.

		MARKS
24	Look at lines 1–5. By referring to at least two examples, analyse how the writer's use of language in these lines creates a vivid atmosphere.	**4**
25	Look at lines 6–12. Explain the relationship between Calum and Neil which is revealed in these lines.	**2**
26	Look at lines 13–25. By referring to at least two examples, analyse how the writer reveals aspects of Calum's character in these lines.	**4**
27	By referring to the extract and to elsewhere in the novel, discuss how Jenkins portrays Calum's innocence.	**10**

Part C – Scottish Text – Poetry

Text 1 – Poetry

If you choose this text you may not attempt a question on Poetry in Section 2.

Read the extract below and then attempt the following questions.

From *A Poet's Welcome to His Love-Begotten Daughter* by Robert Burns

Thou's welcome, wean; mishanter fa' me,

If thoughts o' thee, or yet thy mamie,

Shall ever daunton me or awe me,

My bonie lady,

5   Or if I blush when thou shalt ca' me

Tyta or daddie.

Tho' now they ca' me fornicator,

An' tease my name in kintry clatter,

The mair they talk, I'm kent the better,

10   E'en let them clash;

An auld wife's tongue's a feckless matter

To gie ane fash.

Welcome! my bonie, sweet, wee dochter,

Tho' ye come here a wee unsought for,

15   And tho' your comin' I hae fought for,

Baith kirk and queir;

Yet, by my faith, ye're no unwrought for,

That I shall swear!

Wee image o' my bonnie Betty,

20   As fatherly I kiss and daut thee,

As dear, and near my heart I set thee

Wi' as gude will

As a' the priests had seen me get thee

That's out o' hell.

25   Sweet fruit o' monie a merry dint,

My funny toil is now a' tint,

Sin' thou came to the warl' asklent,

Which fools may scoff at;

In my last plack thy part's be in't

30   The better ha'f o't.

MARKS

28 Look at lines 1–12. By referring to at least two examples, analyse how the poet's language in these lines creates a contrast between his attitude to his daughter and his attitude to those who criticise him.

4

29 Look at lines 13–18. Analyse how the sentence structure in these lines creates a defiant tone.

2

30 Look at lines 19–30. By referring to at least two examples in these lines, analyse how the poet's language conveys the depth of his love for his daughter.

4

31 By referring to this poem and to at least one other by Burns, discuss his use of contrast to explore important ideas.

10

Text 2 – Poetry

If you choose this text you may not attempt a question on Poetry in Section 2.

Read the extract below and then attempt the following questions.

Mrs Midas by Carol Ann Duffy

It was late September. I'd just poured a glass of wine, begun
to unwind, while the vegetables cooked. The kitchen
filled with the smell of itself, relaxed, its steamy breath
gently blanching the windows. So I opened one,
5   then with my fingers wiped the other's glass like a brow.
He was standing under the pear tree snapping a twig.

Now the garden was long and the visibility poor, the way
the dark of the ground seems to drink the light of the sky,
but that twig in his hand was gold. And then he plucked
10   a pear from a branch – we grew Fondante d'Automne –
and it sat in his palm like a light bulb. On.
I thought to myself, Is he putting fairy lights in the tree?

He came into the house. The doorknobs gleamed.
He drew the blinds. You know the mind; I thought of
15   the Field of the Cloth of Gold and of Miss Macready.
He sat in that chair like a king on a burnished throne.
The look on his face was strange, wild, vain. I said,
What in the name of God is going on? He started to laugh.

I served up the meal. For starters, corn on the cob.
20   Within seconds he was spitting out the teeth of the rich.
He toyed with his spoon, then mine, then with the knives, the forks.
He asked where was the wine. I poured with a shaking hand,
a fragrant, bone-dry white from Italy, then watched
as he picked up the glass, goblet, golden chalice, drank.

MARKS

32 Look at lines 1–6. By referring to at least two examples, analyse how the poet's language creates an ordinary, everyday atmosphere in these lines.   **4**

33 Look at lines 7–12. Analyse how the poet's language conveys the confusion that is beginning to arise in the speaker's mind.   **2**

34 Look at lines 13–24. By referring to at least two examples, analyse how the poet's language conveys the strangeness of the husband's behaviour.   **4**

35 By referring to this poem and at least one other by Duffy, discuss how she introduces unusual or surprising ideas into her poems.   **10**

Text 3 – Poetry

If you choose this text you may not attempt a question on Poetry in Section 2.

Read the poem below and then attempt the following questions.

Revelation by Liz Lochhead

I can remember once being shown the black bull

when a child at the farm for eggs and milk.

They called him Bob – as though perhaps

you could reduce a monster

5 with the charm of a friendly name.

At the threshold of his outhouse, someone

held my hand and let me peer inside.

At first, only black

and the hot reek of him. Then he was immense,

10 his edges merging with the darkness, just

a big bulk and a roar to be really scared of,

a trampling, and a clanking tense with the chain's jerk.

His eyes swivelled in the great wedge of his tossed head.

He roared his rage. His nostrils gaped.

15 And in the yard outside,

oblivious hens picked their way about.

The faint and rather festive jingling

behind the mellow stone and hasp was all they knew

of that Black Mass, straining at his chains.

20 I had always half-known he existed –

this antidote and Anti-Christ, his anarchy

threatening the eggs, well rounded, self-contained –

and the placidity of milk.

I ran, my pigtails thumping on my back in fear,

25 past the big boys in the farm lane

who pulled the wings from butterflies and

blew up frogs with straws.

Past thorned hedge and harried nest,

scared of the eggs shattering –

30 only my small and shaking hand on the jug's rim

in case the milk should spill.

MARKS

36 Look at lines 1–14. By referring to at least two examples, analyse how the poet creates an intimidating atmosphere in these lines.

4

37 Look at lines 15–31. By referring to at least two examples, analyse how the poet presents masculinity as threatening.

4

38 By referring to the poem as a whole, explain the significance of the title of the poem.

2

39 By referring to this poem and to at least one other poem by Lochhead, discuss her use of contrast to explore important ideas.

10

Text 4 – Poetry

If you choose this text you may not attempt a question on Poetry in Section 2.

Read the poem below and then attempt the following questions.

Visiting hour by Norman MacCaig

The hospital smell

combs my nostrils

as they go bobbing along

green and yellow corridors.

5   What seems a corpse

is trundled into a lift and vanishes

heavenward.

I will not feel, I will not

feel, until

10   I have to.

Nurses walk lightly, swiftly,

here and up and down and there,

their slender waists miraculously

carrying their burden

15   of so much pain, so

many deaths, their eyes

still clear after

so many farewells.

Ward 7. She lies

20   in a white cave of forgetfulness.

A withered hand

trembles on its stalk. Eyes move

behind eyelids too heavy

to raise. Into an arm wasted

25   of colour a glass fang is fixed,

not guzzling but giving.

And between her and me

distance shrinks till there is none left

but the distance of pain that neither she nor I

30   can cross.

She smiles a little at this

black figure in her white cave

who clumsily rises

in the round swimming waves of a bell

35 and dizzily goes off, growing fainter,

not smaller, leaving behind only

books that will not be read

and fruitless fruits.

MARKS

40 Look at lines 1–10. By referring to at least two examples, analyse how the poet's use of language conveys the speaker's discomfort.   4

41 Look at lines 11–18. Analyse how the speaker's attitude to the nurses is conveyed.   2

42 Look at lines 19–38. By referring to at least two examples, analyse how the poet's use of language creates a bleak atmosphere.   4

43 By referring to this extract and to at least one other poem by MacCaig, discuss how he explores thought-provoking ideas in his poems.   10

Text 5 – Poetry

If you choose this text you may not attempt a question on Poetry in Section 2.

Read the extract below and then attempt the following questions.

Nil Nil by Don Paterson

Besides the one setback – the spell of giant-killing
in the Cup (Lochee Violet, then Aberdeen Bon Accord,
the deadlock with Lochee Harp finally broken
by Farquhar's own-goal in the replay)
5 nothing inhibits the fifty-year slide
into Sunday League, big tartan flasks,
open hatchbacks parked squint behind goal-nets,
the half-time satsuma, the dog on the pitch,
then the Boy's Club, sponsored by Skelly Assurance,
10 then Skelly Dry Cleaners, then nobody;
stud-harrowed pitches with one-in-five inclines,
grim fathers and perverts with Old English Sheepdogs
lining the touch, moaning softly.
Now the unrefereed thirty-a-sides,
15 terrified fat boys with callipers minding
four jackets on infinite, notional fields;
ten years of dwindling, half-hearted kickabouts
leaves two little boys – Alastair Watt,
who answers to 'Forty', and wee Horace Madden,
20 so smelly the air seems to quiver above him –
playing desperate two-touch with a bald tennis ball
in the hour before lighting-up time.
Alastair cheats, and goes off with the ball
leaving wee Horace to hack up a stone
25 and dribble it home in the rain;
past the stopped swings, the dead shanty-town
of allotments, the black shell of Skelly Dry Cleaners
and into his cul-de-sac, where, accidentally,
he neatly back-heels it straight into the gutter
30 then tries to swank off like he meant it.

		MARKS
44	Look at lines 1–13. By referring to at least two examples, analyse how the poet's use of language conveys the extent of the club's decline.	4
45	Look at lines 14–22. By referring to at least two examples, analyse how the poet's use of language creates a depressing mood in these lines.	4
46	Look at lines 23–30. Analyse how the poet's use of language creates sympathy for 'wee Horace'.	2
47	By referring to this poem and to at least one other by Paterson, discuss his use of symbolism to explore important themes.	10

[End of Section 1]

Section 2 – Critical Essay – 20 marks

Attempt **ONE** question from the following genres – Drama, Prose Fiction, Prose Non-Fiction, Poetry, Film and Television Drama, or Language.

Your answer must be on a different genre from that chosen in Section 1.

You should spend approximately 45 minutes on this Section.

Part A – Drama

Answers to questions on Drama should refer to the text and to such relevant features as characterisation, key scene(s), structure, climax, theme, plot, conflict, setting.

1   Choose a play which explores **one** of the following themes: revenge, betrayal, sacrifice.

   By referring to appropriate techniques, discuss how the dramatist explores your chosen theme and discuss how this contributes to your appreciation of the play as a whole.

2   Choose from a play an important scene which you find amusing **or** disturbing **or** moving.

   By referring to appropriate techniques, explain how the dramatist makes the scene amusing **or** disturbing **or** moving and discuss how this contributes to your appreciation of the play as a whole.

3   Choose a play in which a character makes a crucial error.

   By referring to appropriate techniques, explain what the error is and discuss to what extent it is important to your understanding of the character's situation in the play as a whole.

Part B – Prose Fiction

Answers to questions on Prose Fiction should refer to the text and to such relevant features as characterisation, setting, language, key incident(s), climax, turning point, plot, structure, narrative technique, theme, ideas, description.

4   Choose a novel **or** short story which explores the cruelty of human nature.

   By referring to appropriate techniques, explain how the writer explores this theme and discuss how the exploration of the theme adds to your appreciation of the text as a whole.

5   Choose a novel **or** short story in which a conflict between a central character and at least one other character is of central importance in the text.

   By referring to appropriate techniques, explain the circumstances of the conflict and discuss its importance to your appreciation of the text as a whole.

6   Choose a novel **or** short story which ends in a way you find particularly satisfying.

   By referring to appropriate techniques, briefly describe the ending and discuss why you find the ending satisfying in terms of your appreciation of the text as a whole.

Part C – Prose Non-Fiction

Answers to questions on Prose Non-Fiction should refer to the text and to such relevant features as ideas, use of evidence, stance, style, selection of material, narrative voice.

Non-fiction texts can include travel writing, journalism, autobiography, biography, essays.

7   Choose a non-fiction text in which the writer expresses outrage **or** shock about an issue which you feel is important.

   By referring to appropriate techniques, discuss how the writer conveys this emotion.

8   Choose a non-fiction text in which the writer brings one **or** more than one key incident vividly to life.

   By referring to appropriate techniques, discuss how the writer achieves this and how it adds to your understanding of the text as a whole.

9   Choose a non-fiction text which, in your opinion, deals with a fundamental truth about human nature.

   By referring to appropriate techniques, discuss how the writer explores this fundamental truth and to what extent your understanding of it is enhanced.

Part D – Poetry

Answers to questions on Poetry should refer to the text and to such relevant features as word choice, tone, imagery, structure, content, rhythm, rhyme, theme, sound, ideas.

10 Choose a poem which reveals a complex character.

With reference to appropriate techniques, explain how the poet reveals the complexity of the character and discuss how this adds to your appreciation of the poem as a whole.

11 Choose a poem in which there is a powerful evocation of place.

With reference to appropriate techniques, discuss how the poet presents the place and how this adds to your appreciation of the poem as a whole.

12 Choose a poem in which the poet presents an apparently ordinary situation **or** event in an extraordinary way.

With reference to appropriate techniques, discuss how the poet gives impact and meaning to the apparently ordinary situation **or** event and how this adds to your appreciation of the poem as a whole.

Part E – Film and Television Drama

Answers to questions on Film and Television Drama* should refer to the text and to such relevant features as use of camera, key sequence, characterisation, mise-en-scène, editing, music/sound, special effects, plot, dialogue.

13 Choose a film **or** television drama* in which a particular atmosphere is an important feature.

With reference to appropriate techniques, explain how the film **or** programme makers create this atmosphere and discuss how it contributes to your appreciation of the film **or** television drama as a whole.

14 Choose a film **or** television drama which explores a crisis in a relationship **or** the break-up of a family.

With reference to appropriate techniques, discuss how the film **or** programme makers' exploration of the crisis **or** break-up contributes to your appreciation of the film **or** television drama as a whole.

15 Choose from a film **or** television drama an important sequence in which a tense mood is created.

With reference to appropriate techniques, explain how the film **or** programme makers create the tension in the sequence and discuss the importance of the sequence to the film **or** television drama as a whole.

* 'Television drama' includes a single play, a series or a serial.

Part F – Language

Answers to questions on Language should refer to the text and to such relevant features as register, accent, dialect, slang, jargon, vocabulary, tone, abbreviation.

16 Choose the language of live broadcasting, such as news coverage, sports commentaries, award ceremonies.

Identify specific examples of this language and discuss to what extent it is effective in communicating the event to its target audience.

17 Choose some of the rhetorical devices which underpin success in speechmaking.

Identify specific examples of this language and discuss the effectiveness of your chosen rhetorical devices.

18 Choose aspects of language associated with a particular vocational group such as lawyers **or** doctors **or** engineers.

Identify specific examples of this language and discuss to what extent this shared language contributes to the effectiveness of the group's vocational activities.

[End of Practice Paper 1]

Reading for Understanding, Analysis and Evaluation

Duration: 90 minutes

Total marks: 30

Attempt ALL questions.

In the exam you must write your answers clearly in the answer booklet provided and clearly identify the question number you are attempting.

Use **blue** or **black** ink.

The following two passages consider the place of work in our lives.

Passage 1

Read the passage below and then attempt questions 1–7.

From 'The Culture of Overwork' by Johann Hari

In the first passage, Johann Hari describes two experiments which aimed to change the pattern of working lives.

The people of Utah, one of the most conservative states in the US, have stumbled across a simple policy that slashes greenhouse gas emissions by 13 percent, saves huge sums of money, improves public services, cuts traffic congestion, and makes 82 percent of workers happier. It all began in 2008, when the state was facing a budget crisis. One night, the Governor, Jon Huntsman, was staring at the red ink and rough sums when he had
5 an idea. Keeping the state's buildings lit and heated and manned cost a fortune. What if, instead of working 9 to 5, Monday to Friday, the state's employees only came in four days a week, but now from 8 to 6? The state would be getting the same forty hours a week out of its staff – but the costs of maintaining their offices would plummet. The employees would get a three-day weekend, and cut a whole day's worth of tiring, polluting commuting out of their week.

10 He took the step of requiring it by law for 80 percent of the state's employees (emergency services and prisons were exempted). At first, there was cautious support among the workforce but as the experiment has rolled on, it has gathered remarkable acclaim. Now, 82 percent of employees applaud the new hours, and hardly anyone wants to go back.

A whole series of unexpected benefits started to emerge. The number of sick days claimed by workers fell by 9
15 percent. Air pollution fell, since people were spending 20 percent less time in their cars. Some 17,000 tonnes of warming gases were kept out of the atmosphere. They have a new slogan in Utah – Thank God It's Thursday.

Work is the activity that we spend most of our waking lives engaged in – yet it is too often trapped in an outdated routine. Today, very few of us work in factories, yet we have clung to the habits of the factory with almost religious devotion. Clock in, sit at your terminal, be seen to work, clock out. Is this the best way to make
20 us as productive and creative and happy as we can be? Should we clamber into a steel box every morning to sit in a concrete box all day?

Some of the best creative works of recent years – think of Ricky Gervais' TV series The Office, for example – have distilled the strange anomie of living like this, constantly monitored, constantly sedentary, constantly staring at a screen. In a wired lap-topped world, far more people could work more effectively from home, in
25 hours of their own choosing, if only their bosses would have confidence in them. They would be better workers, better parents and better people – and we would take a huge number of cars off the road.

But the problem runs deeper than this. Britain now has the longest work hours in the developed world after the US – and in a recession, those of us with jobs scamper ever faster in our hamster-wheels. This is not how the 21st century was meant to turn out. If you look at the economists and thinkers of, say, the 1930s, they assumed that

30 once we had achieved abundance – once humans had all the food and clothes and heat and toys we could use – we would relax and work less. They thought that by now work would barely cover three days as we headed en masse for the beach and the concert-hall.

Instead, the treadmill is whirling ever-faster. This isn't our choice: virtually every study of this issue finds that huge majorities of people say they want to work less and spend more time with their friends, their families and

35 their thoughts. We know it's bad for us. You become 37 percent more likely to suffer a stroke or heart-attack if you work 60 hours a week – yet one in six of all Brits are doing just that.

We don't stop primarily because we are locked in an arms race with our colleagues. If we relax and become more human, we fall behind the person in the next booth down, who is chasing faster. Work can be one of the richest and most rewarding experiences, but not like this.

40 In the 1990s, the French government discovered an elegant way out of this, taking the Utah experiment deeper and further. They insisted that everyone work a maximum of 35 paid hours a week. It was a way of saying: in a rich country, life is about more than serving corporations and slogging. Wealth generation and consumerism should be our slaves, not our masters: where they make us happy, we should embrace them; where they make us miserable, we should cast them aside. Enjoy yourself. True wealth lies not only in having enough, but in

45 having the time to enjoy everything and everyone around you.

It was the equivalent of an arms treaty: we all stop, together, now, at the 35 hour mark. The French population became fitter, their relationships were less likely to break down, their children became considerably happier, and voluntary organisations came back to life. But under pressure from corporations enraged that their staff couldn't be made to slog all the time, France has abandoned this extraordinary national experiment. The

50 French people were dismayed: the polls show a majority still support the cap.

From the unlikely pairing of Utah and Paris, a voice is calling. It is telling us that if we leave our offices empty a little more, we can find a happier, healthier alternative lying in the great free spaces beyond.

Passage 2

Read the passage below and attempt question 8. While reading, you may wish to make notes on the main ideas and/or highlight key points in the passage.

From 'Free Us from the Drudgery of Work' by Owen Jones

In the second passage, Owen Jones argues that work threatens to take up even more of our lives in the future.

Work already consumes too much of our lives: for the next generation, it could consume even more. The state pension age will be bumped up to 66 by 2020; and those lucky young things now joining the world of employment could be waiting into their 70s for a state pension. An inevitable by-product of rising life expectancy perhaps; but surely a gift of progress should be the granting of more healthy years of leisure, not fewer.

5 We should be aspiring to a more balanced life: a period of contributing to the nation before decades of global sightseeing, babysitting for grandchildren, back-to-back boxsets and quality time with partners. Think of septuagenarians chained to desks, performing brain surgery or stacking shelves, and tell me you don't shudder. Will employers even be willing to take on workers of that vintage?

In any case, we already work too much. Research released by the TUC last week showed that British workers

10 put in unpaid overtime worth £31.5bn last year. Five million toiled an average of 7.7 hours a week for zilch. Ever more employees are working excessive hours, defined as more than 48 a week; 3.4 million workers (excluding the self-employed) now work excessive hours, a jump of 15% since 2010.

This simply cannot be good for us. It's hardly a surprise that 9.9 million days were lost to work-related stress, depression or anxiety in 2014/15, though I suspect many suffer in silence. But it is surely time that can be better

15 spent: hours robbed from watching children grow up, taking up new hobbies, widening cultural horizons, or just catching up with sleep.

Should we resign ourselves to a bleak future of work devouring even our old age? Surely we should start planning for a world where we work less, rather than more. At the centre of my vision is a society where our lives no longer revolve around work. Work represents the loss of our autonomy, where we are under the control of

20 bosses and employers, a full one-third of our adult lives is spent in submission to them. The alternative is not laziness: reading a book or playing sport all require effort, but these are things we freely do. As we work less, our lives become our own.

It was once taken for granted that progress and working less would go hand in hand. At the outset of the Great Depression, economists suggested we would be working only 15 hours a week by now; but the average full-time

25 British worker today puts in nearly 28 hours more than that. It was presumed that advances in technology would reduce the need for human labour: actually, it can fuel demand for new types of work: the arrival of the personal computer has led to the creation of more than 1,500 new types of job.

The postwar western world enjoyed near-full employment, but that era has long since passed. Not only are unemployment and inactivity rates higher than they once were, but work has become more precarious, with

30 zero-hours contracts, insecure self-employment and reluctant part-time workers. The trend will surely be towards even more precarious work.

This isn't alarmism. Research suggests that technology could, in the next 20 years, mean the automation of 60% of retail jobs. Because technology is destroying more jobs than it is creating, 11m jobs could go.

But threats can be opportunities too. Rather than regarding the march of the robots as an existential threat,

35 why not aim for the automation of the entire economy? Wealth would still be created – albeit by an army of machines – but we would be freed from the drudgery of work.

We have a choice: a society where work becomes ever more dominant even as it becomes ever more precarious, where some work until they drop and others are demonised for being unable to work; or a society where we can realise our full potential in every sense, with more time for leisure, for love, for each other. I

40 choose the latter.

		MARKS
1	Read lines 1–9. Identify two benefits to Jon Huntsman's introduction of a four-day working week. Use your own words as far as possible.	2
2	Read lines 17–21. By referring to **at least two** examples, analyse how the writer's use of language creates a negative impression of work.	4
3	Read lines 22–26. By referring to at least two examples, analyse how language is used to clarify what the writer is saying.	4
4 a)	Read lines 27–39. Using your own words as far as possible, explain the difference between what 'economists and thinkers' predicted in the 1930s and what has actually happened.	4
b)	By referring to **at least two** examples of imagery in these lines, analyse how the writer conveys his attitude to modern working practices.	4
5	Read lines 40–45. Using your own words as far as possible, explain the thinking behind what the French government did in the 1990s.	3
6	Read lines 46–50. By referring to at least one example, analyse how sentence structure is used to clarify what the writer is saying.	2
7	Read lines 51–52. Analyse how the writer's use of language creates a positive tone on which to conclude the passage.	2
8	Look at both passages. Both writers express their views about work. Identify **three** key areas on which they agree. You should support the points by referring to important ideas in both passages. You may answer this question in continuous prose or in a series of developed bullet points.	5

[End of question paper]

Critical Reading

Duration: 90 minutes
Total marks: 40
Section 1 – Scottish Text – 20 marks
Read an extract from a Scottish text you have previously studied and attempt the questions.
Choose ONE text from
Part A – Drama
or
Part B – Prose
or
Part C – Poetry
Attempt ALL questions for your chosen text.
Section 2 – Critical Essay – 20 marks
Attempt ONE question from the following genres – Drama, Prose Fiction, Prose Non-Fiction, Poetry, Film and Television Drama, or Language.
Your answer must be on a different genre from that chosen in Section 1.
You should spend approximately 45 minutes on each Section.
In the exam you must write your answers clearly in the answer booklet provided and clearly identify the question number you are attempting.
Use **blue** or **black** ink.

Section 1 – Scottish Text – 20 marks

Choose ONE text from Drama, Prose or Poetry.

Read the text extract carefully and then attempt ALL the questions for your chosen text.

You should spend about 45 minutes on this section.

Part A – Scottish Text – Drama

Text 1 – Drama

If you choose this text you may not attempt a question on Drama in Section 2.

Read the extract below and then attempt the following questions.

From *The Slab Boys* by John Byrne

In this extract, from Act Two of the play, Alan intervenes on Hector's behalf.

	HECTOR:	D'you like it, Alan?
	ALAN:	It's … er … (PHIL *threatens to snap pen*) … really gadgey, Heck.
	HECTOR:	Will I go now and ask her? Will I? (*Heads for door*)
	SPANKY:	(*Cutting him off*) Not just yet, Hector … Remember you've still got to go and see Willie.
5	HECTOR:	Yeh, but I can do that after I've asked Lucille …
	PHIL:	No, Spanky's right, kiddo … better go and see Willie first. It's important. Lucille'll not go off the boil. Here, I'll give you my coat to put on … (*Takes off coat*)
	HECTOR:	What do I want that for? I don't mind doing a bit of swanking now that my clothes are up to date.
10	PHIL:	Yeh, but you don't want anybody else to get a preview, do you? Lessen the impact … know what I mean? Get the coat on. (*Forces HECTOR's arms into sleeves*)

	SPANKY:	(*Pulling balaclava helmet from cupboard*) You better put this on and all … it's draughty in Willie's room. (*Pulls helmet over* HECTOR's *head*) Cosy, eh?
	HECTOR:	(*Slightly bamboozled*) Yeh, but will he not think I'm a bit happed up?
15	PHIL:	That's just it. You've been down at Nurse. Influenza verging on pleurisy. She ordered you home but you decided to soldier on. He'll like that. Maybe not give you your … (*Stops*)
	SPANKY:	(*Quickly*) Wireless back.
	HECTOR:	I'm not expecting my wireless back. You know what he's like.
	SPANKY:	Well, you can't just expect it back cos you've got the flu, Heck …
20	PHIL:	Triple pneumonia, Spanks.
	HECTOR:	I'm all mixed up … what've I got again?
	SPANKY:	Triple pneumonia …
	PHIL:	Double rupture …
	HECTOR:	I'll away along then.
25	SPANKY:	Good man. All the best.
	PHIL:	Good luck, son … (*They shove* HECTOR *out the door*) You'll need it.

(*They hold onto each other laughing*)

	ALAN:	Well, I hope you're proud of yourselves … that was a pretty lousy trick to play!
	SPANKY:	Oh, was it, by jove?
30	PHIL:	A trick, you cad! Take that! (*Bops* ALAN's *head a smack*)
	ALAN:	Hey, watch it! That was sore … Chuckit! Okay, so I'm speaking out of turn but that poor little bastard's gone off to Willie Curry's office thinking that underneath that dustcoat and helmet he really does cut a dash … and he'll probably stop off on the way back to have a word with Lucille … doff the coat and hat and you know what'll happen then … she'll wet herself. Which
35		will probably give you and your crummy friend a big laugh, won't it?
	PHIL:	Gosh and All Serene … the Fifth Form at St Dominic's. Listen, Steerforth Minor, if it wasn't for me and Spanks there that 'poor little bastard' wouldn't have any pals. Yeh, that's right. So, we do take the piss … set him up a bit …
	ALAN:	More than a bit.

MARKS

1 Look at lines 1–27. By referring to at least two examples, analyse how dialogue and stage directions make the audience feel sympathy for Hector.

4

2 Look at lines 28–30. Analyse how the playwright's use of language in these lines allows Phil and Spanky to make fun of Alan.

2

3 Look at lines 31–39. By referring to at least two examples, analyse how the playwright emphasises the animosity between Alan and Phil.

4

4 By referring to this extract and to elsewhere in the play, discuss the importance of the conflict between Phil and Alan in exploring at least one theme in the play.

10

Text 2 – Drama

If you choose this text you may not attempt a question on Drama in Section 2.

Read the extract below and then attempt the following questions.

From *Men Should Weep* by Ena Lamont Stewart

In this extract from near the end of Act 1, scene 2, Jenny arrives home late.

(JOHN *comes in holding* JENNY *by the arm. She is about eighteen, made up boldly for the nineteen-thirties: her lipstick is spread over her mouth, her coat and blouse undone, her hair tousled.*)

JENNY: (*furious*) Leave me go!

(*She shakes herself free and she and* JOHN *stand glaring at each other.* MAGGIE *is watching fearfully.*)

5   Makin a bloomin fool o me in front o ma friend!

JOHN: Where hae you been till this time o night?

JENNY: That's nane o your business. I'm grown up noo.

JOHN: Don't you speak tae me like that. I asked ye where ye'd been.

JENNY: An I tellt ye! Nane o your damned interferin business!

10 MAGGIE: Jenny! John!

(JOHN *takes* JENNY *by the shoulders and shakes her.*)

JOHN: Where wis ye? Answer me!

JENNY: At the pickshers.

JOHN: The pickchers comes oot at hauf ten. Where wis ye efter?

15 JENNY: (*sullen*) Wi Nessie Tate an a coupla friends.

(*He lets her go and she flops into a chair, glaring sullenly at him and rubbing her shoulder.*)

JOHN: I don't approve o yon Nessie Tait.

JENNY: That's a peety. I dae.

JOHN: Ye impident little bitch! What I ought tae dae is tak ma belt

20   tae ye.

JENNY: Jist you try it!

JOHN: The next time you come in here at this time o night wi yer paint smeared a ower yer face, I wull! Look at yersel!

(*He drags her over to a mirror, then propels her, resisting, to the sink, where, holding her head under his arm, he*
25 *scrubs off her make-up.*)

                      There! And in the future, you'll let yer hair grow tae the colour God meant it tae be an leave it that wey.

	MARKS
5 Look at lines 1–9. By referring to at least **two** aspects of character, explain what impressions are created of Jenny in these lines.	3
6 Look at lines 11–21. By referring to at least **two** features, analyse how a dramatic conflict between John and Jenny is created.	4
7 Look at lines 22–27. By referring to at least **two** examples, analyse how dialogue and/or stage directions are used to convey John's anger.	3
8 By referring to this extract and to elsewhere in the play, discuss the role of Jenny in *Men Should Weep*.	10

Part B – Scottish Text – Prose

Text 1 – Prose

If you choose this text you may not attempt a question on Prose in Section 2.

Read the extract below and then attempt the following questions.

From *Mother and Son by* Iain Crichton Smith

His clothes were dripping as he came in. The water was streaming down his cheeks, a little reddened by the wind and the rain. He shook back his long hair and threw his jacket on the bed post, then abruptly remembering, he looked through the pockets for a box of matches. The house was in partial darkness, for, though the evening was not dark, the daylight was hooded by thick yellow curtains which were drawn across
5 the width of the window. He shivered slightly as he lit the match: it had been a cold, dismal afternoon in the fields. The weather was extraordinarily bad for the time of year and gathering the sheaves into stacks was both monotonous and uncomfortable.

He held the match cupped within his hands to warm them and to light his way to the box where he kept the peats. The flickering light showed a handsome face. The forehead was smooth and tanned, the nose thin
10 though not incisive, the mouth curved and petulant, and the chin small and round. It was a good-looking face, though it was a face which had something childish about it. The childishness could be seen by a closer look, a look into the wide blue eyes which were rather stolid and netted by little red lines which divided them up like a graph. These eyes were deep and unquestioning as a child's, but they gave an unaccountable impression that they could be as dangerous and irresponsible as a child's. As the match flickered and went out with an
15 apologetic cough, he cursed weakly and searched his pockets. Then he remembered he had left the box on the table, reached out for it impatiently, and lit another match. This he carried over to the lamp which lay on the table. The light clung to the wick, and he put the clean globe gently inside the brackets.

When the lamp was lit, it showed a moderately sized kitchen, the walls of which were painted a dull yellow. The dresser was surmounted by numerous shelves which held numerous dishes, some whole, some broken. A little
20 china dog looked over the edge as if searching for crumbs: but the floor was clean and spotless, though the green linoleum looked a bit worn. Along one wall of the room was a four-poster bed with soiled pillows and a coverlet of some dark, rough material. In the bed was a woman.

		MARKS
9	Look at lines 1–7. By referring to at least two examples, analyse how the writer creates a hostile atmosphere.	4
10	Look at lines 8–17. Analyse how the writer's use of language shows two sides to the son's personality.	4
11	Look at lines 18–22. Analyse how the writer creates a vivid impression of the room.	2
12	By referring to this extract and to at least one other story by Iain Crichton Smith, discuss how he creates complex central characters in his stories.	10

Text 2 – Prose

If you choose this text you may not attempt a question on Prose in Section 2.

Read the extract below and then attempt the following questions.

From *The Eye of the Hurricane* by George Mackay Brown

In this extract Captain Stevens tries to convince the narrator to buy him alcohol.

'Now, Barclay, about this cold of mine.'

'Miriam says you haven't got a cold at all,' I said.

'The little bitch,' he said. 'Did she go into your room? She had no right to be disturbing you. I'll speak to her about that. I expect she told you also that I have drinking bouts.'

5   'She did,' I said.

'Well,' he said, 'everybody knows. Can't do a thing about it, Barclay. It's a natural thing, like a storm, you just have to let it blow itself out, keep the ship headed into it. Do you understand that, Barclay?'

'I know nothing about it,' I said.

'I thought writers are supposed to understand things,' he said, 'the quirks of human nature. That's what they're
10   for. Don't take hard what I say, Barclay. I like you. I'm very glad you're living in this house. I'm just explaining the situation to you, setting the course through the storm, so that you can take your turn at navigating if the need arises. The best way you can help the voyage, Barclay, is just do what I say. I'm the skipper of this ship. And the first thing I want you to do is open that drawer and you'll see a wallet.'

'No,' I said, and got to my feet.

15   'There should be four five-pound notes in it. Take one of them out.'

'No,' I said.

'Two bottles of navy rum from Wilson's, as quick as you can.'

Charity is no hard-minted currency to be distributed according to whim, a shilling here and a sovereign there – it is the oil and wine that drop uncertainly through the fingers upon the wounds of the world, wherever the roads
20   of pity and suffering cross. It might help this old man, as he said, if I stood close beside him on the bridge till this particular hurricane blew itself out. But I trusted the older wisdom of women. I had made a promise to Miriam.

'No,' I said.

'Very well, Mr Barclay,' he said after a pause. 'Let me see. At the moment you are paying me a rent of two pounds a week, I think. As from Monday next you will pay me four pounds a week. In fact, I think you should make
25   arrangements to leave this house before the end of the month. I find you an unsatisfactory tenant. Now get out.'

All night, till I fell into a drowse around three o'clock in the morning, I heard him pacing back and fore, back and fore in his room, an ancient mariner in a ship of dark enchantment.

MARKS

13 By referring to the whole extract, analyse how the Captain tries to convince the narrator to buy him alcohol.   **4**

14 Look at lines 18–21. By referring to at least two examples, analyse how the narrator uses imagery in these lines to explain his views on charity.   **4**

15 Explain what the last paragraph (lines 26–27) suggests about the narrator's feelings for the Captain.   **2**

16 By referring to this extract and to at least one other story by Mackay Brown, discuss how he creates confrontations between characters.   **10**

Text 3 – Prose

If you choose this text you may not attempt a question on Prose in Section 2.

Read the extract below and then attempt the following questions.

From *Dr Jekyll and Mr Hyde* by Robert Louis Stevenson

In this extract Utterson has been attending a dinner party hosted by Jekyll.

Hosts loved to detain the dry lawyer, when the light-hearted and the loose-tongued had already their foot on the threshold; they liked to sit a while in his unobtrusive company, practising for solitude, sobering their minds in the man's rich silence after the expense and strain of gaiety. To this rule, Dr. Jekyll was no exception; and as he now sat on the opposite side of the fire – a large, well-made, smooth-faced man of fifty, with something of a
5   slyish cast perhaps, but every mark of capacity and kindness – you could see by his looks that he cherished for Mr. Utterson a sincere and warm affection.

"I have been wanting to speak to you, Jekyll," began the latter. "You know that will of yours?"

A close observer might have gathered that the topic was distasteful; but the doctor carried it off gaily. "My poor Utterson," said he, "you are unfortunate in such a client. I never saw a man so distressed as you were by my
10 will; unless it were that hide-bound pedant, Lanyon, at what he called my scientific heresies. Oh, I know he's a good fellow – you needn't frown – an excellent fellow, and I always mean to see more of him; but a hide-bound pedant for all that; an ignorant, blatant pedant. I was never more disappointed in any man than Lanyon."

"You know I never approved of it," pursued Utterson, ruthlessly disregarding the fresh topic.

"My will? Yes, certainly, I know that," said the doctor, a trifle sharply. "You have told me so."

15 "Well, I tell you so again," continued the lawyer. "I have been learning something of young Hyde."

The large handsome face of Dr. Jekyll grew pale to the very lips, and there came a blackness about his eyes. "I do not care to hear more," said he. "This is a matter I thought we had agreed to drop."

"What I heard was abominable," said Utterson.

"It can make no change. You do not understand my position," returned the doctor, with a certain incoherency of
20 manner. "I am painfully situated, Utterson; my position is a very strange – a very strange one. It is one of those affairs that cannot be mended by talking."

"Jekyll," said Utterson, "you know me: I am a man to be trusted. Make a clean breast of this in confidence; and I make no doubt I can get you out of it."

"My good Utterson," said the doctor, "this is very good of you, this is downright good of you, and I cannot find
25 words to thank you in. I believe you fully; I would trust you before any man alive, ay, before myself, if I could make the choice; but indeed it isn't what you fancy; it is not so bad as that; and just to put your good heart at rest, I will tell you one thing: the moment I choose, I can be rid of Mr. Hyde. I give you my hand upon that; and I thank you again and again; and I will just add one little word, Utterson, that I'm sure you'll take in good part: this is a private matter, and I beg of you to let it sleep."

MARKS

17   Look at lines 1–6. Analyse how the writer's language presents a positive impression of Jekyll.   2

18   Look at lines 7–17. By referring to at least two examples, analyse how the tension between Utterson and Jekyll is conveyed.   4

19   Look at lines 18–29. By referring to at least two examples, analyse how the writer reveals aspects of the relationship between Jekyll and Utterson.   4

20   By referring to this extract and to elsewhere in the novel, discuss how Stevenson presents the character of Henry Jekyll.   10

Text 4 – Prose

If you choose this text you may not attempt a question on Prose in Section 2.

Read the extract below and then attempt the following questions.

From *Sunset Song* by Lewis Grassic Gibbon

In this extract from Part III (Seed-time), a disagreement arises at the wedding celebration.

Up at Rob's table an argument rose, Chris hoped that it wasn't religion, she saw Mr Gordon's wee face pecked up to counter Rob. But Rob was just saying what a shame it was that folk should be shamed nowadays to speak Scotch – or they called it Scots if they did, the split-tongued sourocks! Every damned little narrow dowped rat that you met put on the English if he thought he'd impress you – as though Scotch wasn't good enough now, it
5   had words in it that the thin bit scraichs of the English could never come at. And Rob said *You can tell me, man, what's the English for sotter, or greip, or smore, or pleiter, gloaming or glunching or well-kenspeckled? And if you said gloaming was sunset you'd fair be a liar; and you're hardly that, Mr Gordon.*

But Gordon was real decent and reasonable, *You can't help it, Rob. If folk are to get on in the world nowadays, away from the ploughshafts and out of the pleiter, they must use the English, orra though it be.* And Chae cried
10   out that was right enough, and God! who could you blame? And a fair bit breeze got up about it all, every soul in the parlour seemed speaking at once; and as aye when they spoke of the thing they agreed that the land was a coarse, coarse life, you'd do better at almost anything else, folks that could send their lads to learn a trade were right wise, no doubt of that, there was nothing on the land but work, work, work, and chave, chave, chave, from the blink of day till the fall of night, no thanks from the soss and sotter, and hardly a living to be made.

15   Syne Cuddiestoun said that he'd heard of a childe up Laurencekirk way, a banker's son from the town he was, and he'd come to do farming in a scientific way. So he'd said at first, had the childe, but God! by now you could hardly get into the place for the clutter of machines that lay in the yard; and *he* wouldn't store the kiln long. But Chae wouldn't have that, he swore *Damn't, no, the machine's the best friend of man, or it would be so in a socialist state. It's coming and the chaving'll end, you'll see, the machine'll do all the dirty work.* And Long Rob
20   called out that he'd like right well to see the damned machine that would muck you a pigsty even though they all turned socialist to-morrow.

		MARKS
21	Look at lines 1–7. By referring to at least two examples, analyse how the writer conveys the strength of Rob's feelings about language.	4
22	Look at lines 8–14. Explain how the writer conveys in these lines the harshness of life working the land.	2
23	Look at lines 15–21. By referring to at least two examples, analyse how the writer's use of language conveys the conflicting views about 'scientific' farming methods.	4
24	By referring to this extract and to elsewhere in the novel, discuss how *Sunset Song* celebrates the traditional way of life.	10

Text 5 – Prose

If you choose this text you may not attempt a question on Prose in Section 2.

Read the extract below and then attempt the following questions.

From *The Cone-Gatherers* by Robin Jenkins

In this extract from Chapter 6, Calum witnesses the killing of a deer.

Calum no longer was one of the beaters; he too was a deer hunted by remorseless men. Moaning and gasping, he fled after them, with no hope of saving them from slaughter but with the impulse to share it with them. He could not, however, be so swift or sure of foot. He fell and rose again; he avoided one tree only to collide with another close to it; and all the time he felt, as the deer must have, the indifference of all
5 nature; of the trees, of tall withered stalks of willowherb, of the patches of blue sky, of bushes, of piles of cut scrubwood, of birds lurking in branches, and of the sunlight: presences which might have been expected to help or at least sympathise.

The dogs barked fiercely. Duror fired his gun in warning to those waiting in the ride. Neil, seeing his brother rush into the danger, roared to him to come back. All the beaters, except Charlie in the rear, joined in the
10 commotion; the wood resounded with their exultant shouts. Realising this must be the finish or kill, Graham, recuperating on the road, hopped back over the fence into the wood and bellowed loudest of all.

As Duror bawled to his dogs to stop lest they interfere with the shooting, and as the deer hesitated before making the dash across the ride, Calum was quite close to them as, silent, desperate, and heroic, they sprang forward to die or escape. When the guns banged he did not, as Neil had vehemently warned him to do, fall
15 flat on the ground and put his fingers in his ears. Instead, with wails of lament, he dashed on at demented speed and shot out onto the broad green ride to hear a deer screaming and see it, wounded in the breast and forelegs, scrabbling about on its hindquarters. Captain Forgan was feverishly reloading his gun to fire again. Calum saw no one else, not even the lady or Mr. Tulloch, who was standing by himself about twenty yards away.

Screaming in sympathy, heedless of the danger of being shot, Calum flung himself upon the deer, clasped it
20 round the neck, and tried to comfort it. Terrified more than ever, it dragged him about with it in its mortal agony. Its blood came off onto his face and hands.

While Captain Forgan, young Roderick, and Lady Runcie-Campbell stood petrified by this sight, Duror followed by his dogs came leaping out of the wood. He seemed to be laughing in some kind of berserk joy. There was a knife in his hand. His mistress shouted to him: what it was she did not know herself, and he never heard. Rushing
25 upon the stricken deer and the frantic hunchback, he threw the latter off with furious force, and then, seizing the former's head with one hand cut its throat savagely with the other. Blood spouted. Lady Runcie-Campbell closed her eyes. Captain Forgan shook his head slightly in some kind of denial. Roderick screamed at Duror. Tulloch had gone running over to Calum.

The deer was dead, but Duror did not rise triumphant; he crouched beside it, on his knees, as if he was
30 mourning over it. His hands were red with blood; in one of them he still held the knife.

		MARKS
25	Look at lines 1–7. Analyse how the sentence structure in these lines helps to convey how Calum is feeling.	2
26	Look at lines 8–21. By referring to at least two examples, analyse how the writer's use of language in these lines creates a sense of 'commotion' (line 10).	4
27	Look at lines 22–30. By referring to at least two examples, analyse how the writer makes the reader aware in these lines of Duror's state of mind.	4
28	By referring to this extract and to elsewhere in the novel, discuss how the writer presents the character of Calum.	10

Part C – Scottish Text – Poetry

Text 1 – Poetry

If you choose this text you may not attempt a question on Poetry in Section 2.

Read the extract below and then attempt the following questions.

From *Tam o' Shanter* by Robert Burns

In this extract Tam manages to outrun the witches.

As bees bizz out wi' angry fyke,

When plundering herds assail their byke;

As open pussie's mortal foes,

When, pop! she starts before their nose;

5   As eager runs the market-crowd,

When 'Catch the thief!' resounds aloud;

So Maggie runs, the witches follow,

Wi' mony an eldritch skriech and hollo.

Ah, Tam! ah, Tam! thou'll get thy fairin!

10   In hell they'll roast thee like a herrin!

In vain thy Kate awaits thy comin!

Kate soon will be a woefu' woman!

Now, do thy speedy utmost, Meg,

And win the key-stane o' the brig;

15   There at them thou thy tail may toss,

A running stream they dare na cross.

But ere the key-stane she could make,

The fient a tail she had to shake!

For Nannie far before the rest,

20   Hard upon noble Maggie prest,

And flew at Tam wi' furious ettle;

But little wist she Maggie's mettle –

Ae spring brought aff her master hale,

But left behind her ain grey tail:

25   The carlin claught her by the rump,

And left poor Maggie scarce a stump.

Now, wha this tale o' truth shall read,

Ilk man and mother's son, take heed;

Whene'er to drink you are inclin'd,

30   Or cutty-sarks run in your mind,

Think! ye may buy the joys o'er dear –

Remember Tam o' Shanter's mare.

MARKS

29 Look at lines 1–8. By referring to at least **two** examples, analyse how the extended simile in these lines creates a vivid picture of what is happening.

4

30 Look at lines 9–26. By referring to at least **two** examples, analyse how Burns makes this part of the poem dramatic.

4

31 Look at lines 27–32. Analyse how far these lines can be read as a warning to the reader.

2

32 Referring to this poem and at least one other poem by Burns, discuss the way his poetry passes judgement on people and/or institutions.

10

Text 2 – Poetry

If you choose this text you may not attempt a question on Poetry in Section 2.

Read the poem below and then attempt the following questions.

Valentine by Carol Ann Duffy

Not a red rose or a satin heart.

I give you an onion.
It is a moon wrapped in brown paper.
It promises light
5   like the careful undressing of love.

Here.
It will blind you with tears
like a lover.
It will make your reflection
10   a wobbling photo of grief.

I am trying to be truthful.

Not a cute card or a kissogram.

I give you an onion.
Its fierce kiss will stay on your lips,
15   possessive and faithful
as we are,
for as long as we are.

Take it.
Its platinum loops shrink to a wedding-ring,
20   if you like.
Lethal.
Its scent will cling to your fingers,
cling to your knife.

	MARKS

33 Look at lines 1–5. By referring to at least **two** examples, analyse how the poet's language in these lines creates a dramatic opening to the poem. — **4**

34 Look at lines 6–17. By referring to at least **two** examples, analyse how the poet's language in these lines describes love in an unusual way. — **4**

35 Look at lines 18–23. Analyse how the poet's language in these lines creates an unsettling mood. — **2**

36 By referring to this poem and to at least one other poem by Duffy, discuss her use of striking imagery. — **10**

Text 3 – Poetry

If you choose this text you may not attempt a question on Poetry in Section 2.

Read the extract below and then attempt the following questions.

From *The Bargain* by Liz Lochhead

The extract is from the end of the poem.

We queue in a blue haze of hot fat

for Danny's Do-Nuts that grit

our teeth with granules of sugar

I keep

5   losing you and finding you –

two stalls away you thumb

through a complete set of manuals for

primary teachers in the thirties

I rub my sleeve

10   on a dusty Chinese saucer

till the gilt shows through.

Oh come on we promised

we'd not let our affection for the slightly cracked

trap us into such expenditure again.

15   Oh even if it is a bargain

we won't buy.

The stallholder says we'll be the death of her

she says see January

it's been the doldrums the day.

20   And it's packing up time

with the dark coming early

and as cold as the river.

By the bus stop I show you

the beady bag and the maybe rosewood box

25   with the inlaid butterfly and the broken catch.

You've bought a record by the Shangri-las

a pin-stripe waistcoat that needs a stitch

it just won't get and a book called *Enquire*

Within – Upon Everything.

30   The raw cold gets colder.

There doesn't seem to be a lot to say.

I wish we could either mend things

or learn to throw them away.

MARKS

37 Look at lines 1–19. By referring to at least **two** examples, analyse how the poet's language in these lines conveys the uneasy atmosphere between the couple.

4

38 Look at lines 20–29. By referring to at least **two** examples, analyse how the poet's language in these lines conveys the bleak mood of the speaker.

4

39 Look at lines 30–33. Analyse how the poet's language in these lines creates a conclusion you find either optimistic or pessimistic.

2

40 By referring to this poem and to at least one other poem by Lochhead, discuss how she explores the tension that can arise in relationships.

10

Text 4 – Poetry

If you choose this text you may not attempt a question on Poetry in Section 2.

Read the poem below and then attempt the following questions.

Assisi by Norman MacCaig

The dwarf with his hands on backwards
sat, slumped like a half-filled sack
on tiny twisted legs from which
sawdust might run,
5   outside the three tiers of churches built
in honour of St Francis, brother
of the poor, talker with birds, over whom
he had the advantage
of not being dead yet.

10   A priest explained
how clever it was of Giotto
to make his frescoes tell stories
that would reveal to the illiterate the goodness
of God and the suffering
15   of His Son. I understood
the explanation and
the cleverness.

A rush of tourists, clucking contentedly,
fluttered after him as he scattered
20   the grain of the Word. It was they who had passed
the ruined temple outside, whose eyes
wept pus, whose back was higher
than his head, whose lopsided mouth
said *Grazie* in a voice as sweet
25   as a child's when she speaks to her mother
or a bird's when it spoke
to St Francis.

		MARKS
41	Look at lines 1–4. Analyse how the poet's use of sound in these lines enhances the description of the beggar.	2
42	Look at lines 5–17. By referring to at least **two** examples, analyse how the poet creates an ironic tone in these lines.	4
43	Look at lines 20–27. ('It was they … St Francis.') By referring to at least **two** examples, analyse how the poet's language develops the idea of the beggar as a 'ruined temple'.	4
44	By referring to this poem and to at least one other by MacCaig, discuss his use of wry humour in his poetry.	10

Text 5 – Poetry

If you choose this text you may not attempt a question on Poetry in Section 2.

Read the extract below and then attempt the following questions.

From *The Ferryman's Arms* by Don Paterson

When I set down the cue-ball inside the parched D
it clacked on the slate; the nap was so threadbare
I could screw back the globe, given somewhere to stand –
as physics itself becomes something negotiable
5   a rash of small miracles covers the shortfall:
I went on to make an immaculate clearance.
A low punch with a wee dab of side, and the black
did the vanishing trick while the white stopped
before gently rolling back as if nothing had happened,
10   shouldering its way through the unpotted colours.

The boat chugged up to the little stone jetty
without breaking the skin of the water, stretching,
as black as my stout, from somewhere unspeakable
to here, where the foaming lip mussitates endlessly,
15   trying, with a nutter's persistence, to read
and re-read the shoreline. I got aboard early,
remembering the ferry would leave on the hour
even for only my losing opponent;
but I left him there, stuck in his tent of light, sullenly
20   knocking the balls in, for practice, for next time.

MARKS

45 Look at lines 1–10. By referring to at least two examples, analyse how the poet combines ordinary detail with suggestions of the unworldly in his description of the pool game.   **4**

46 Look at lines 11 ('The boat chugged …') to 16 ('… the shoreline.'). By referring to at least two examples, analyse how the poet creates a sinister atmosphere in these lines.   **4**

47 Look at lines 16 ('I got aboard …') to 20 ('… for next time.'). Explain the significance of the term 'losing opponent' to the extract as a whole.   **2**

48 By referring to this extract and to at least one other poem by Paterson, discuss the effectiveness of the way he ends his poems.   **10**

[End of Section 1]

Section 2 – Critical Essay – 20 marks

Attempt **ONE** question from the following genres – Drama, Prose Fiction, Prose Non-Fiction, Poetry, Film and Television Drama, or Language.

Your answer must be on a different genre from that chosen in Section 1.

You should spend approximately 45 minutes on this Section.

Part A – Drama

Answers to questions on Drama should refer to the text and to such relevant features as characterisation, key scene(s), structure, climax, theme, plot, conflict, setting.

1   Choose a play in which a central character experiences rejection **or** isolation **or** loneliness.

    By referring to appropriate techniques, discuss how the dramatist makes you aware of the character's rejection **or** isolation **or** loneliness and how this contributes to your appreciation of the play as a whole.

2   Choose a play in which the opening scene establishes important elements of theme and/or character.

    By referring to appropriate techniques, explain how these elements are established in the opening scene and discuss how this contributes to your appreciation of the play as a whole.

3   Choose a play in which the setting in time and/or place is an important feature.

    By referring to appropriate techniques, explain how the dramatist presents the setting and discuss why this is important to your appreciation of the play as a whole.

Part B – Prose Fiction

Answers to questions on Prose Fiction should refer to the text and to such relevant features as characterisation, setting, language, key incident(s), climax, turning point, plot, structure, narrative technique, theme, ideas, description.

4   Choose a novel **or** short story in which a key incident leads to a change in the text.

    By referring to appropriate techniques, explain why the incident leads to a change and discuss how this change contributes to your appreciation of the text as a whole.

5   Choose a novel **or** short story which explores one of the following ideas: loss **or** futility **or** celebration.

    By referring to appropriate techniques, explain how the writer explores this idea and discuss how its exploration adds to your appreciation of the text as a whole.

6   Choose a novel **or** short story in which a central character has to overcome obstacles to reach his or her central goal.

    By referring to appropriate techniques, explain how the character overcomes these obstacles and discuss how this adds to your appreciation of the text as a whole.

Part C – Prose Non-Fiction

Answers to questions on Prose Non-Fiction should refer to the text and to such relevant features as ideas, use of evidence, stance, style, selection of material, narrative voice.

Non-fiction texts can include travel writing, journalism, autobiography, biography, essays.

7   Choose a non-fiction text in which you feel the style of writing is a key factor in developing a persuasive argument.

    With reference to appropriate techniques, discuss how the writer's presentation of the argument is made persuasive.

8   Choose a non-fiction text in which the writer presents the life of an individual in a negative **or** positive light.

    With reference to appropriate techniques, discuss how the writer creates this impression of the individual.

9   Choose a non-fiction text in which the writer describes an experience which is frightening **or** amusing **or** educational.

    With reference to appropriate techniques, discuss how the writer conveys that aspect of the experience and how it enhances your appreciation of the text as a whole.

Part D – Poetry

Answers to questions on Poetry should refer to the text and to such relevant features as word choice, tone, imagery, structure, content, rhythm, rhyme, theme, sound, ideas.

10 Choose a poem in which the use of contrast is important in developing the central concern(s).

With reference to appropriate techniques, discuss how the poet's use of contrast contributes to the development of the central concerns and to your appreciation of the poem as a whole.

11 Choose a poem which explores aspects of human relationships.

With reference to appropriate techniques, discuss how the poet explores the aspects of human relationships and how this contributes to your appreciation of the poem as a whole.

12 Choose a poem whose closing lines you find particularly effective as a conclusion.

With reference to appropriate techniques, discuss why you find the closing lines an effective conclusion to the poem as a whole.

Part E – Film and Television Drama

Answers to questions on Film and Television Drama* should refer to the text and to such relevant features as use of camera, key sequence, characterisation, mise-en-scène, editing, music/sound, special effects, plot, dialogue.

13 Choose a film **or** television drama which focuses on a rivalry **or** a friendship between two characters.

With reference to appropriate techniques, explain how the film **or** programme makers present the characters and discuss how the rivalry **or** friendship contributes to your appreciation of the film **or** television drama as a whole.

14 Choose a film **or** television drama which deals with violence but does not glorify it.

With reference to appropriate techniques, discuss how the film **or** programme makers explore violence in this way and how this helps you appreciate the film **or** television drama as a whole.

15 Choose a film **or** television drama in which the opening sequence successfully establishes key features of the text such as setting, mood, genre, character, theme.

With reference to appropriate techniques, explain how the film **or** programme makers achieve this success and discuss the importance of the sequence to your appreciation of the film **or** television drama as a whole.

* 'Television drama' includes a single play, a series or a serial.

Part F – Language

Answers to questions on Language should refer to the text and to such relevant features as register, accent, dialect, slang, jargon, vocabulary, tone, abbreviation.

16 Choose some of the ways language differs across generations.

Identify specific examples of this difference in language and discuss to what extent this is advantageous to those involved.

17 Choose the technical language associated with a sport, a craft, a profession or one of the arts.

Identify specific examples of this language and discuss to what extent you feel such language leads to clearer communication among its users.

18 Choose the language of advertising aimed at promoting goods **or** entertainment **or** campaigns **or** causes.

Identify specific examples of this language and discuss how successful the advertising is.

[End of Practice Paper 2]

Practice Paper 1
Reading for Understanding, Analysis and Evaluation
Passage 1

Question number	Question text	Marks available	Commentary, hints and tips
1	Read lines 1–8. Using your own words as far as possible, explain the key points made in these lines about our attitudes to animal life. No marks for straight lifts from the passage. 2 marks may be awarded for detailed/insightful comment; 1 mark for more basic comment. (Marks may be awarded 2 or 1+1.)	2	Possible answers include: ▶ human life is always given priority over animal life ▶ we will go to any lengths to preserve human life regardless of the impact on the animal world ▶ we treat animals in captivity with contempt ▶ we respond violently when a captive animal poses a threat, despite the fact that it is only obeying instinct.
2	Read lines 9–14. By referring to at least two examples, analyse how the writer's use of language makes clear her disapproval of zoos. For full marks there should be comments on at least two examples. 2 marks may be awarded for detailed/insightful comment plus quotation/reference; 1 mark for more basic comment plus quotation/reference; 0 marks for quotation/reference alone. (Marks may be awarded 2+2, 2+1+1 or 1+1+1+1.)	4	Possible answers include: ▶ exclamatory tone of 'What a travesty is a zoo' suggests contempt ▶ 'travesty' suggests perversion, corruption ▶ question 'How can it still exist …?' suggests disbelief that it does still exist ▶ 'legacy' suggests a relic, something left over ▶ 'gentlemen collectors and capricious kings' suggests zoos belong in a bygone age of upper-class dilettantes, detached from ordinary life ▶ 'animated taxidermy' – dark humour in the idea that the animals are as good as dead and merely brought to life artificially for our entertainment ▶ 'exposed' suggests thrown open against his will, at the mercy of the onlookers ▶ 'gawping crowds' suggests stupid, mindless, prepared to stare at anything ▶ structure of 'Stand up, bend down, turn around' replicates the simple, limited, repetitive movement of the captive bear ▶ 'quite mad' shows deep sympathy for the result of the bear's treatment in the zoo.

Question number		Question text	Marks available	Commentary, hints and tips
3	a)	Read lines 15–22. Using your own words as far as possible, explain what London Zoo has done to try to improve its treatment of animals. No marks for straight lifts from the passage. 2 marks may be awarded for detailed/ insightful comment; 1 mark for more basic comment. (Marks may be awarded 2 or 1+1.)	2	Possible answers include: ▶ elephants, which were once housed in very restricted space and denied the ability to move in a natural way, are no longer kept in the zoo ▶ lions are no longer confined in cages but are now kept in an area which makes an attempt to replicate their natural environment.
	b)	Analyse how the writer's use of language casts doubt on the validity of this change in approach. 2 marks may be awarded for detailed/ insightful comment plus quotation/ reference; 1 mark for more basic comment plus quotation/reference; 0 marks for quotation/reference alone. (Marks may be awarded 2 or 1+1.)	2	Possible answers include: ▶ 'Oh, but …' at the start of defenders' claim sounds a little bit insincere ▶ 'lavish' suggests it is a little bit overdone, extravagant ▶ 'illusion' suggests it is a deception, a piece of trickery ▶ use of inverted commas at 'Land of the Lions' suggests disapproval of the term, implying 'so-called', that it's a bit pompous ▶ 'mocked-up' suggests artificial, rather cheap ▶ 'little (high street)' is rather dismissive, reductive ▶ use of inverted commas at 'authentic' casts doubt on the zoo's claim ▶ 'movie set' suggests contrived, designed to appear as something it is not ▶ the use of 'really' in the concluding question suggests strongly that the writer thinks it is not the case.
4		Read lines 23–28. By referring to at least two examples, analyse how the writer's use of language creates a negative impression of the animal rights movement. For full marks there should be comments on at least two examples. 2 marks may be awarded for detailed/ insightful comment plus quotation/ reference; 1 mark for more basic comment plus quotation/reference; 0 marks for quotation/reference alone. (Marks may be awarded 2+2, 2+1+1 or 1+1+1+1.)	4	Possible answers include: ▶ 'theocratic' suggests religious zeal, a blinkered outlook ▶ 'purist' suggests intolerance if any deviation from one point of view ▶ 'cadre' suggests a closed, almost secretive group, well organised, dedicated to a single cause ▶ 'activists' has a hint of militancy ▶ list of 'who compare … more inclined … who argue' suggests a substantial number of extreme points of view ▶ exaggeration of 'compare farming to the Holocaust' suggests how ridiculous some of their beliefs can be ▶ extreme comparison ('donkey sanctuaries in Syria … suffering children') suggests how outrageous some of their beliefs can be ▶ simplicity of the sentence 'For these people …' – statement; colon; statement – imitates their dogmatic way of thinking ▶ 'fringe' suggests they are not part of mainstream belief, are out on the edge.

Question number	Question text	Marks available	Commentary, hints and tips
5	Read lines 29–36. Explain how the writer uses the example of the orcas at SeaWorld to develop her argument. 2 marks may be awarded for detailed/insightful comment; 1 mark for more basic comment. (Marks may be awarded 1+2 or 2+1 or 1+1+1.)	3	Possible answers include: ▶ she uses her own experience of going to SeaWorld as an example: she admits she was wrong to expect an innocent, enjoyable experience – it was in fact very disturbing to see the way the orcas were treated ▶ she references the documentary *Blackfish* as a telling example of how exposure of the way orcas are treated at SeaWorld had a major influence on public attitudes ▶ she argues that falling attendance at SeaWorld in response to the film is evidence that public opinion is changing (for the better) ▶ she uses emotional language such as 'turn off half your brain', 'perversion of their nature', 'psychotic' in her descriptions of the orcas at SeaWorld to influence the reader to disapprove of their treatment.
6	Read lines 37–44. Analyse how the writer uses sentence structure and word choice to emphasise her incredulous tone. 2 marks may be awarded for detailed/insightful comment; 1 mark for more basic comment. (Marks may be awarded 2+1 or 1+2 or 1+1+1.)	3	Possible answers include: **Sentence structure:** ▶ parenthesis of 'a dentist from Minnesota' emphasises how shocking it is that an everyday person can do such an evil thing ▶ question emphasises the outrage that this killing is still being done ▶ colon explains the answer to the question, that the horror of killing animals for fun still continues. **Word choice:** ▶ 'mass shock' indicates the horror of the population (and the writer) that this could take place ▶ 'bag beasts' suggests counting up the number of animals destroyed ▶ 'measure your manhood' the shock that it takes the act of killing something to prove how male you are ▶ 'obliteration' suggests complete destruction ▶ 'destroying' suggests not just killed, but maliciously so ▶ 'thrill' explains that people are doing this evil for excitement ▶ 'trophy hunts' suggests people are doing it for pride (i.e. keeping a 'trophy' (horns etc.)) ▶ 'trades in death' emphasises horror that money is being made by such cruelty.

Question number	Question text	Marks available	Commentary, hints and tips
7	Read lines 45–49. Identify one positive and one negative of zoos today. Use your own words in your answer. For full marks, one positive and one negative should be identified. No marks for straight lifts from the passage. 1 mark for each point from the 'Commentary, hints and tips' column.	2	**Negative:** ▸ They will kill any animals they have too many of. ▸ They keep many animals who do not belong in small spaces just to make money. **Positive:** ▸ Making sure species in danger do not die out.
8	Evaluate the effectiveness of the last paragraph (lines 50–52) as a conclusion to the passage as a whole. 2 marks may be awarded for detailed/insightful comment (plus quotation/reference if appropriate); 1 mark for more basic comment (plus quotation/reference if appropriate); 0 marks for quotation/reference alone. (Marks may be awarded 2+1 or 1+1+1.)	3	Possible answers include: ▸ scathing tone of 'melancholy mammal museums' sums up her strong disapproval of zoos ▸ she offers a simple solution (documentaries on TV) as if there is nothing very difficult about it – and the use of colloquial 'kids' emphasises the simplicity of it ▸ short blunt sentence 'The species scale is tipping' provides assertive, unambiguous statement that change is coming ▸ the imagery of 'scales' links back to 'scales of moral worth' in the second paragraph, rounding off the passage ▸ reference to Costa Rica is perhaps surprising since it is a relatively poor country, not often used as an example of enlightened thinking ▸ question at the end is a direct challenge to the reader, almost defying anyone to contradict her.

Passage 2

Question number	Question text	Marks available	Commentary, hints and tips
9	Look at both passages. Both writers express their views about zoos and the treatment of wild animals. Identify three key areas on which they agree. You should support the points by referring to important ideas in both passages. You may use bullet points in this final question, or write a number of linked statements. Evidence from the passage may include quotations, but these should be supported by explanations. The approach to marking is shown in the 'Commentary, hints and tips' column. Key areas of agreement are shown in the table below. Other answers are possible.	5	The following guidelines should be used: ▶ 5 marks – identification of three key areas of agreement with detailed/insightful use of supporting evidence ▶ 4 marks – identification of three key areas of agreement with appropriate use of supporting evidence ▶ 3 marks – identification of three key areas of agreement ▶ 2 marks – identification of two key areas of agreement ▶ 1 mark – identification of one key area of agreement ▶ 0 marks – failure to identify one key area of agreement and/or misunderstanding of task. **NB** If you identify only two key areas of agreement, you may be awarded up to a maximum of 4 marks, as follows: ▶ 2 marks for identification of two key areas of agreement plus either ▶ a further 1 mark for appropriate use of supporting evidence to a total of 3 marks or ▶ a further 2 marks for detailed/insightful use of supporting evidence to a total of 4 marks. If you identify only one key area of agreement, you may be awarded up to a maximum of 2 marks, as follows: ▶ 1 mark for identification of one key area of agreement ▶ a further 1 mark for use of supporting evidence to a total of 2 marks.

	Area of agreement	Passage 1	Passage 2
1	moral objection to zoos	an affront to civilised society to treat animals as exhibits for our entertainment	no excuse for confining animals for 'our fleeting distraction and amusement'
2	natural behaviour is inhibited by zoos	freedom of movement is limited	animals are denied the ability to behave the way they would in the wild
3	physical harm caused by zoos	animals killed to protect humans; the arthritic elephants at London Zoo	over-eating; injury from fire, or from ingestion of foreign bodies
4	psychological harm caused by zoos	effect of repetitive actions, the bear in Colchester Zoo, the orcas in SeaWorld	incessant pacing, boredom, neurosis, stress
5	changing public attitudes	some progress over the years in our acceptance of mistreatment of animals	public is now more aware of animals' needs
6	interest in zoos waning	attendance at SeaWorld has declined; orca shows have been discontinued	attendances, once in the millions, now going down
7	the financial imperative	the safari business in Africa, the exploitation of 'charismatic megafauna' for income	marine parks part of a billion-dollar industry

Critical Reading
Section 1 – Scottish Text – 20 marks
Part A – Scottish Text – Drama

Text 1 – Drama – *The Slab Boys* by John Byrne

Question number	Question text	Marks available	Commentary, hints and tips
1	Look at lines 1–8. Analyse how the dramatist presents Curry as an overbearing character in these lines. 2 marks may be awarded for detailed/insightful comment plus quotation/reference, 1 mark for more basic comment plus quotation/reference; 0 marks for quotation/reference alone. (Marks may be awarded 1+1+1+1, 2+1+1 or 2+2.)	4	Possible answers include: ▸ nearly everything he says is a question, suggesting he has a right to know everything, can probe into every aspect of their lives ▸ the 'Ha' at the start suggests a kind of triumphant 'got you at last' tone ▸ use of surnames only ('McCann … Farrell') suggests he is treating them as inferiors ▸ 'C'mon …' suggests demanding more information, not prepared to settle for vagueness ▸ 'The what?' – insisting that Phil reveal in detail what was (allegedly) wrong with him.
2	Look at lines 9–18. By referring to at least one example, analyse how the humour in these lines relies on deliberate misunderstanding of what Curry has said. 2 marks may be awarded for detailed/insightful comment plus quotation/reference; 1 mark for more basic comment plus quotation/reference; 0 marks for quotation/reference alone. (Marks may be awarded 1+1 or 2.)	2	Possible answers include: ▸ 'Nurse to have a look at you' is a reasonably caring suggestion that he could have consulted the nurse, but Phil pretends to take it literally, as if the nurse would be 'looking at' him during a bout of diarrhoea ▸ 'You wouldn't get much done down there' refers to not getting much company business done, but Phil turns it into a lavatorial joke, suggesting that he did in fact get 'a lot done' ▸ 'fighting the Japanese with dysentery' means they were suffering from dysentery while they were fighting, but Spanky pretends to take it as using dysentery as a weapon, and asks with assumed naivety how they fired it.

Question number	Question text	Marks available	Commentary, hints and tips
3	Look at lines 19–27. By referring to at least two examples, analyse how the writer's use of language in these lines conveys Curry's dislike of the Slab Boys and their lifestyle. 2 marks may be awarded for detailed/ insightful comment plus quotation/ reference; 1 mark for more basic comment plus quotation/reference; 0 marks for quotation/reference alone. (Marks may be awarded 2+2, 2+1+1 or 1+1+1+1.)	4	Possible answers include: ▶ 'damned cheek' suggests he sees them as insubordinate, insolent ▶ 'silly duck's arse haircuts' suggests he finds their hairstyles stupid, probably uses the slang term with some distaste ▶ 'that bloody contraption' suggests he disapproves of the radio, sees no value in it ▶ 'that racket' suggests he has a low opinion of the music, sees it only as noise ▶ 'this gadget' suggests he sees the radio as trivial, a mere contraption ▶ 'you bunch' suggests he has no respect for them, just a group like a little gang, not committed to the company ethic ▶ 'lounging about' suggests he sees them as lazy, not dedicated to their work.
4	By referring to this extract and to elsewhere in the play, discuss the characterisation of Willie Curry. You can answer in bullet points in this final question, or write a number of linked statements.	10	Up to 2 marks can be achieved for identifying elements of commonality as identified in the question, i.e. how Willy is characterised. A further 2 marks can be achieved for reference to the extract given. 6 additional marks can be gained for discussion of similar references to at least one other part of the text by the author. In practice this means: Identification of commonality (1+1), e.g. Willy is authoritarian and finds it difficult to understand the Slab Boys. (1) He has a 'typical' ex-Army, disciplinarian, follow-orders-without-question approach, but is not all bad as seen at the end. (1) From the extract: 2 marks for detailed/ insightful comment plus quotation/reference; 1 mark for more basic comment plus quotation/reference; 0 marks for quotation/ reference alone. 2 marks only for discussion of extract. For example, he treats Phil as if he is overreacting to his diarrhoea ('men in my platoon … dysentery) (1) and doesn't respond well to jokes ('less of your dammed cheek'). (1) From at least one other part of the text as above for up to 6 marks. Possible answers include: ▶ puffed up, self-important, has created a self-mythology around his exploits in Burma ▶ despairs of and criticises younger generation, their attitude, their music, their clothes

Question number		Question text	Marks available	Commentary, hints and tips
4 (continued)				▸ sycophantic towards Alan ▸ fondness for clichés ('pull your socks up', 'toe the line') and for his own linguistic creations ('faster than you can say Axminster broadloom') ▸ dull, straight-laced: Phil and Spanky's patter usually goes over his head, he misses the double entendres, knows Phil and Spanky are making fun of him but doesn't know how ▸ but not all bad: surprises audience at end by supporting Phil against Barton (and for having kept the secret about Jimmy Robertson).

Text 2 – Drama – *Men Should Weep* by Ena Lamont Stewart

Question number		Question text	Marks available	Commentary, hints and tips
5	a)	Look at lines 1–27. By referring to at least two examples in these lines, analyse how the playwright conveys Maggie's state of mind to the audience. 2 marks may be awarded for detailed/ insightful comment plus quotation/ reference; 1 mark for more basic comment plus quotation/reference; 0 marks for quotation/reference alone. (Marks may be awarded 2+2, 2+1+1 or 1+1+1+1.)	4	Possible answers include: ▸ 'I dinna ken … at a' expresses her bewilderment, anguish, sadness ▸ 'Slavin an worryin … an naethin but heartbreak' conveys the lack of fulfilment she feels despite all the effort ▸ 'a yer days' emphasises the lifelong commitment ▸ her response to Alec's comforting gesture ('*she looks up at him gratefully, lovingly, and lays his hand to her cheek*') is a measure of how upset she is – that she is touched by such a simple gesture (from Alec of all people) emphasises her need for comfort ▸ 'whit am I goin tae tell folks?' suggests despair, that she is lost, out of her depth ▸ the pleading, despairing 'Oh Jenny, Jenny! Whit's happened tae ye, Jenny?' is emphasised by an exclamation followed by a question and by the almost lamenting tone from the repetition of her name ▸ the stage direction '*Maggie looks helplessly on*' makes clear her vulnerability ▸ '*combing her hair with her fingers*' is a visual indication of her misery.

Question number		Question text	Marks available	Commentary, hints and tips
5	b)	Analyse how the playwright makes the audience aware of Isa's character in these lines. 2 marks may be awarded for detailed/insightful comment plus quotation/reference; 1 mark for more basic comment plus quotation/reference; 0 marks for quotation/reference alone. (Marks may be awarded 2 or 1+1.)	2	Possible answers include: ▸ she is openly contemptuous of Alec: sneering language of 'tumphy' and 'big lump o dough' ▸ she has a forceful personality: her dominance over Alec is seen when her sneering at his affection for his mother causes him to move away from her ▸ her response when Lily says Alec is 'no as saft as he looks' is mock polite ('I'm right gled'), but really shows her contempt for Alec ▸ her physical rejection of Alec '(*Pushing his face away*)' shows her attitude ▸ 'but no for wee boys' is openly demeaning ▸ her friendly comment when Jenny leaves ('Ta ta, Jenny. See you roon the toon') is rather provocative in face of others' disapproval.
6		Look at lines 29–33. By referring to language and stage directions, explain how John's reaction to Jenny leaving is made clear. 2 marks may be awarded for detailed/insightful comment plus quotation/reference; 1 mark for more basic comment plus quotation/reference; 0 marks for quotation/reference alone. (Marks may be awarded 2+2, 2+1+1 or 1+1+1+1.)	4	Possible answers include: ▸ the silent moments when they look at each other will be filled with tension emphasising neither are comfortable with this departure ▸ John's anguish is described in the stage direction 'Wretched', which emphasises his distress for the audience ▸ The pathetic nature of his 'I thought ye'd hev gone' is melancholic as the audience are led to believe John has been waiting to avoid seeing her departure ▸ John lowers his eyes and stands aside, which suggests he has to inevitably accept what is happening ▸ his wordless watching her could be defeat, longing, guilt ▸ the dying sound of footsteps emphasises her leaving and his despair ▸ the banging of the door concludes that Jenny has gone and there is nothing he can do about it.

Question number	Question text	Marks available	Commentary, hints and tips
7	By referring to this extract and to elsewhere in the play, discuss how Maggie changes in the course of the play. You can answer in bullet points in this final question, or write a number of linked statements.	10	Up to 2 marks can be achieved for identifying elements of commonality as identified in the question, i.e. how Maggie changes throughout the play. A further 2 marks can be achieved for reference to the extract given. 6 additional marks can be awarded for discussion of similar references to at least one other part of the text by the author. In practice this means: Identification of commonality (1+1), e.g. to begin with, she is hopelessly overburdened but is resigned to her role; by the end she is, to an extent, emancipated when she goes against John's wishes (1) showing that women are not always downtrodden in this time and place. (1) From the extract: 2 marks for detailed/insightful comment plus quotation/reference; 1 mark for more basic comment plus quotation/reference; 0 marks for quotation/reference alone. 2 marks only for discussion of extract. At this point in the play, Maggie is contemplating women's role in 1930s Glasgow. (1) We see this when she wonders why women have children when they have to look after them, often without male support, and then they (the children) disappoint them. (1) From at least one other part of the text as above for up to 6 marks. Possible answers include: ▶ at the start of the play she is very supportive of John; gives him his place and makes sure others do the same (e.g. her defence of him to Lily) ▶ by the end she no longer subordinates herself to the needs (and weaknesses) of others ▶ she makes a personal journey and becomes a stronger woman through the play, in many ways under the influence of the younger women in the play, e.g. she doesn't reject Jenny because of her lifestyle; even Isa teaches her that men can be weak ▶ her journey reaches fruition at the end, when she stands up to John, humiliates him, accepts Jenny's money to enable the family to move to a healthier environment for Bertie, thus taking control of her own life and her family's future.

Part B – Scottish Text – Prose

Text 1 – Prose – *The Red Door* by Iain Crichton Smith

Question number	Question text	Marks available	Commentary, hints and tips
8	Look at lines 1–12. By referring to at least two examples, analyse how the sentence structure and word choice in these lines helps to convey Murdo's feelings. 2 marks may be awarded for detailed/insightful comment plus quotation/reference; 1 mark for more basic comment plus quotation/reference; 0 marks for quotation/reference alone. (Marks may be awarded 2+2, 2+1+1 or 1+1+1+1.)	4	Possible answers include: **Sentence structure:** ▶ question 'But really was he happy?' shows uncertainty, doubt in his mind ▶ repetition of 'He didn't like …' emphasises his dissatisfaction with current lifestyle ▶ listing of the things he 'didn't like' shows how many things displeased him ▶ 'that such and such … that that other one' hints at willingness to snipe at anyone ▶ 'But the red door didn't do that': short affirmative sentence of how the red door represents the antithesis ▶ colon introduces the key thing he feels is missing from his life – 'elegance' ▶ 'Now Mary had elegance': short opening to new paragraph introduces the explanation of her 'elegance' ▶ repetition of 'elegance' suggests its importance to him ▶ use of concessionary words/expressions ('Though … It was true … And on the other hand') show him as being thoughtful, undogmatic ▶ sequence of short sentences ('She seemed … She never … She was … She had …. She paid … She was') suggests he is enumerating her many qualities ▶ 'But' at start of last sentence introduces her key quality. **Word choice:** ▶ 'perpetually smiling face' explains that he was miserable yet had to keep up a façade for the world to see ▶ 'eating alone/being alone/having none' all suggest his want for human company ▶ 'foreign and confident' suggests that he wants to be accepted for his difference, like the door ▶ 'had elegance' suggests he admires Mary's grace ▶ 'no concessions' suggests he admires Mary's honesty.
9	By referring to lines 13–15, describe Murdo's attitude to Mary. 2 marks may be awarded for detailed/insightful comment plus quotation/reference; 1 mark for more basic comment plus quotation/reference; 0 marks for quotation/reference alone. (Marks may be awarded 2 or 1+1.)	2	Possible answers include: ▶ admires her generosity, altruism (care for children) ▶ sees her as a free spirit ('walk by herself'), a little quixotic ('romantic') ▶ prepared to see a usually negative quality ('sudden bursts of rage') in a positive way as a sign of her refusal to bend to anybody.

Question number	Question text	Marks available	Commentary, hints and tips
10	Look at lines 16–22. By referring to at least two examples, analyse how the writer's use of language in these lines suggests the door has mystical qualities. 2 marks may be awarded for detailed/insightful comment plus quotation/reference; 1 mark for more basic comment plus quotation/reference; 0 marks for quotation/reference alone. (Marks may be awarded 2+2, 2+1+1 or 1+1+1+1.)	4	Possible answers include: ▶ 'seemed to be drawn inside it' suggests hypnotic powers ▶ 'deep caves' suggests profound, unfathomable ▶ 'all sorts of' suggests it is undefinable, mysterious ▶ 'veins and passages' suggests almost human ▶ 'like a magic door …' suggests something out of a fairy tale, enchanted ▶ 'pulsed with a deep red light' suggests deliberately mesmerising, sci-fi overtones ▶ 'make such a difference to house and moors and streams' suggests supernatural powers ▶ 'sucked into it' suggests the door has physical power over him ▶ 'a place of heat and colour and reality' suggests an inanimate object is vividly alive.
11	By referring to this story and to at least one other by Crichton Smith, discuss to what extent you feel pity for characters he creates. You can answer in bullet points in this final question, or write a number of linked statements.	10	Up to 2 marks can be achieved for identifying elements of commonality as identified in the question, i.e. how Crichton Smith makes us feel pity for his characters. A further 2 marks can be achieved for reference to the extract given. 6 additional marks can be gained for discussion of similar references to at least one other short story by the author. In practice this means: identification of commonality. (1+1) We are driven to feel pity for Crichton Smith's characters because they are often dealing with difficult situations where they feel trapped (1) helping us appreciate the themes of frustration and isolation. (1) From the extract: 2 marks for detailed/insightful comment plus quotation/reference; 1 mark for more basic comment plus quotation/reference; 0 marks for quotation/reference alone. 2 marks only for discussion of extract. In this extract, we feel sorry for Murdo because of his sense of isolation in the village (1), and that making the door red worries him in terms of the reaction from others, but also gives him a sense of rebellion. (1) From at least one other short story as above for up to 6 marks.

Question number	Question text	Marks available	Commentary, hints and tips
11 *(continued)*			Possible answers include: ▶ *The Telegram* – pity for both women because of the danger their sons are in, because of dread that the telegram is for her; pity for the elder ▶ *Mother and Son* – pity for son's having to endure nagging, having no life of his own, his unrewarding life of grinding routine ▶ *Home* – pity for the man seeing how his hometown has changed, facing his wife's lack of enthusiasm for the visit, his treatment at the hands of the factor, his sense of feeling out of place; for both husband and wife at the way they have adopted the racial prejudices of southern Africa.

Text 2 – Prose – *A Time to Keep* by George Mackay Brown

Question number	Question text	Marks available	Commentary, hints and tips
12	Look at lines 1–12. By referring to at least two examples, analyse how language is used to reveal aspects of Ingi's character. 2 marks may be awarded for detailed/insightful comment plus quotation/reference; 1 mark for more basic comment plus quotation/reference; 0 marks for quotation/reference alone. (Marks may be awarded 2+2, 2+1+1 or 1+1+1+1.)	4	Possible answers include: ▶ 'a blue reek all about her' suggests she is a messy baker. ▶ 'all thought of bread was forgotten' suggests she is a panicker when it comes to her father ▶ 'let out a cry of distress' suggests she is afraid of her father ▶ flurry of tidying up, emphasised by sentence structure/repeated pattern indicating frantic activity suggests she is desperate to impress/not to be thought ill of ▶ straightening of the text/covering of the anti-religious books again suggests she is afraid of her father's reaction. ▶ 'combing her hair' suggests she wants to hide the reality of the mess of herself ▶ 'bed was unmade' and 'litter of fish-guts' suggests she is messy/too busy to be a good housekeeper ▶ 'tried hard' suggests she wants to be good at her work but finds it difficult.

Question number	Question text	Marks available	Commentary, hints and tips
13	Look at lines 17–23. Analyse how language is used to convey the concerns Ingi's father has for her. 2 marks may be awarded for detailed/insightful comment plus quotation/reference; 1 mark for more basic comment plus quotation/reference; 0 marks for quotation/reference alone. (Marks may be awarded 2 or 1+1.)	2	Possible answers include: ▶ 'gently' suggests her father may be worried about her. ▶ 'you're not looking well' suggests he is concerned for her welfare ▶ Repetition of 'not … well' emphasises he is concerned she is sick ▶ 'haven't seen you for three whole months' suggests he is concerned there is a worrying reason for her disappearance ▶ 'working too hard' suggests he is concerned Ingi is not being treated properly ▶ use of questions suggests he wants answers to his worries.
14	Look at lines 25–31. By referring to at least two examples, analyse how the writer's use of language conveys Mr Sinclair's attitude to Bill. 2 marks may be awarded for detailed/insightful comment plus quotation/reference; 1 mark for more basic comment plus quotation/reference; 0 marks for quotation/reference alone. (Marks may be awarded 2+2, 2+1+1 or 1+1+1+1.)	4	Possible answers include: ▶ Sinclair's reply 'Is that so, Bill?' is fairly disrespectful, as if saying 'You must think I'm stupid if I don't know that …' ▶ dismissive tone of 'Maybe so. At the present moment I'm speaking to Ingi …' suggests he feels he is superior to Bill ▶ 'I'll be wanting to speak to you later' – peremptory tone, assuming he calls the shots and that Bill needs to be taken in hand ▶ Sinclair's sarcastic repetition of 'work' is designed to mock Bill, suggesting he suspects he is a lazy, good-for-nothing ▶ 'enough money to live on' suggests that he knows Bill spends his money irresponsibly ▶ 'Just answer me.' suggests he finds Bill frustrating ▶ 'Don't imagine I don't hear things' – asserting his superiority, perhaps threatening further revelations.
15	By referring to A Time to Keep and to at least one other story by Mackay Brown, discuss the way he creates tension at key moments in his stories. You can answer in bullet points in this final question, or write a number of linked statements.	10	Up to 2 marks can be achieved for identifying elements of commonality as identified in the question, i.e. how Mackay Brown creates tension at key moments in his stories. A further 2 marks can be achieved for reference to the extract given. 6 additional marks can be gained for discussion of similar references to at least one other short story by the author. In practice this means: Identification of commonality. (1+1) Tension is built by using the unknown and the uncertain between characters and situations in Mackay Brown's stories. (1) This keeps the reader 'hooked' as they want to discover the outcome of the tension. (1)

Question number	Question text	Marks available	Commentary, hints and tips
15 *(continued)*			From the extract: 2 marks for detailed/insightful comment plus quotation/reference; 1 mark for more basic comment plus quotation/reference; 0 marks for quotation/reference alone.
			2 marks only for discussion of extract.
			In this extract, tension is built because of the characters' dislike for each other: as Mr Sinclair arrives to check on his daughter it becomes obvious he is concerned about her ('why don't you give her enough money to live on?') and that the reader suspects he has come to confront Bill. (2)
			From at least one other short story as above for up to 6 marks.
			Possible answers include:
			▸ *Andrina* – tension as Bill waits for Andrina to return; when the postman calls and Bill is unable to call for help; when Bill rejects Sigrid; when he reads the contents of the letter; pervading tension over whether or not Andrina is 'real'
			▸ *The Wireless Set* – tension in the reactions to Lord Haw Haw; in the uncertainty about the accuracy of news; at the arrival of the telegram
			▸ *The Eye of the Hurricane* – tension between Barclay and Stevens; between Barclay and Miriam; during the presence of Stevens' old shipmates.

Text 3 – Prose – *Dr Jekyll and Mr Hyde* by Robert Louis Stevenson

Question number	Question text	Marks available	Commentary, hints and tips
16	Look at lines 1–5. Analyse how the language used in these lines creates a positive impression of Jekyll. 2 marks may be awarded for detailed/insightful comment plus quotation/reference; 1 mark for more basic comment plus quotation/reference; 0 marks for quotation/reference alone. (Marks may be awarded 2 or 1+1.)	2	Possible answers include: ▸ 'large fortune' suggests he is well off, free of financial worries ▸ 'excellent parts' suggests all features of his personality are of the best ▸ 'inclined … to industry' suggests he is hard-working ▸ 'respect of the wise …' suggests he is held in high esteem by people of standing ▸ 'honourable' suggests upright, moral ▸ 'distinguished' suggests eminent, illustrious ▸ admission of 'faults' is followed by 'but' to deny that he derives any 'happiness' from them ▸ 'carry my head high' suggests he wishes to maintain dignity ▸ 'grave countenance' suggests he aspires to seriousness, a lack of frivolity.
17	Look at lines 6–12. By referring to at least two examples, analyse how the language used in these lines reveals Jekyll's darker side. 2 marks may be awarded for detailed/insightful comment plus quotation/reference; 1 mark for more basic comment plus quotation/reference; 0 marks for quotation/reference alone. (Marks may be awarded 2+2, 2+1+1 or 1+1+1+1.)	4	Possible answers include: ▸ 'concealed' suggests deception, secretiveness ▸ 'committed' suggests he has given himself over to the secret side of his nature ▸ 'duplicity' suggests dishonesty, malicious deception ▸ 'irregularities … I was guilty of' suggests he is aware of a number of faults ▸ 'morbid sense of shame' suggests a deep, dark self-knowledge ▸ 'degradation' suggests serious moral shortcomings ▸ 'trench' suggests something deep and dark.
18	Look at lines 13–21. By referring to at least two examples, analyse how imagery is used to enhance Jekyll's points. 2 marks may be awarded for detailed/insightful comment plus quotation/reference; 1 mark for more basic comment plus quotation/reference; 0 marks for quotation/reference alone. (Marks may be awarded 2+2, 2+1+1 or 1+1+1+1.)	4	Possible answers include: ▸ 'root' – suggests that the 'law of life' is the basis of all religion, from which all religious belief grows ▸ 'springs' – suggests that much distress originates and flows from the 'law of life' ▸ 'double-dealer' – suggests he is presenting different faces to different people, to the detriment of both ▸ 'the eye of day' – suggests that day was watching him, could see him easily, unlike during his darker exploits ▸ 'shed a strong light' – suggests that his studies allowed him to see clearly ▸ 'perennial war' – suggests a constant struggle between the different aspects of his personality ▸ 'dreadful shipwreck' – suggests total destruction and devastation brought about by forces beyond his control.

Question number	Question text	Marks available	Commentary, hints and tips
19	By referring to this extract and to elsewhere in the novel, discuss the theme of duality in *Dr Jekyll and Mr Hyde*. You can answer in bullet points in this final question, or write a number of linked statements.	10	Up to 2 marks can be achieved for identifying elements of commonality as identified in the question, i.e. how the theme of duality is portrayed in *Dr Jekyll and Mr Hyde*. A further 2 marks can be achieved for reference to the extract given. 6 additional marks can be gained for discussion of similar references to at least one other part of the text by the author. In practice this means: Identification of commonality. (1+1) Much of the text is concerned with the duality of man, and how man has both good and bad within him. (1) This theme is demonstrated through the character of Jekyll who 'splits' himself into two different characters – the good Dr Jekyll and the evil Mr Hyde. (1) From the extract: 2 marks for detailed/insightful comment plus quotation/reference; 1 mark for more basic comment plus quotation/reference; 0 marks for quotation/reference alone. 2 marks only for discussion of extract. Jekyll's explanation of the theory in the *Statement*: 'man's dual nature', 'man is not truly one, but truly two', 'the thorough and primitive duality of man' explains how there are two sides to man – the respectable and the 'concealed … pleasures'. Jekyll explains how he wrestled with the more risky side of his personality. (2) From at least one other part of the text as above for up to 6 marks. Possible answers include: ▶ his early life: outwardly respectable but at times depraved ▶ his 'beloved day-dream' for the 'separation of these elements' resulting in his experiments ▶ his realisation that he can unleash the 'lower elements of my soul' ▶ the reality of his creation: the malevolence and violence of Edward Hyde, witnessed throughout the novel ▶ Jekyll's original belief that good can control evil ▶ the idea that evil, although it is in a sense a natural part of him, is a more powerful force and takes over.

Text 4 – Prose – *Sunset Song* by Lewis Grassic Gibbon

Question number	Question text	Marks available	Commentary, hints and tips
20	Look at lines 1–13. By referring to at least two examples, analyse how the writer's use of language in these lines shows the offensiveness of Ewan's behaviour. 2 marks may be awarded for detailed/insightful comment plus quotation/reference; 1 mark for more basic comment plus quotation/reference; 0 marks for quotation/reference alone. (Marks may be awarded 2+2, 2+1+1 or 1+1+1+1.)	4	Possible answers include: ▶ 'sneered' suggests contempt in his voice ▶ *'Hell, Chris, what a bloody place!'* – the coarse language suggests a lack of respect ▶ 'flung his pack one way and his hat the other' suggests a lack of care, self-respect ▶ 'as though she were a tink' compares Chris to someone to be looked down on, of no value ▶ 'hot and questing and wise' suggests he is being sexually aggressive, selfish, that he is more experienced now than he was and isn't afraid to make Chris aware of it ▶ 'the hot smoulder fire in his eyes' suggests he is almost demonic, malevolent ▶ 'red with other things' suggests he is sexually aroused in a frightening way ▶ *'Well, we'll hope so, eh Chris*?' – crude, sexual innuendo ▶ *'unless you're too bloody stand-offish'* – open insult to his wife coarsened by use of offensive language ▶ 'picked the thing up and flung it …' – such lack of respect for his own child's picture book (emphasised by 'thing' and 'flung') is an especially upsetting detail ▶ the commanding tone of *'Here, give us some tea'* as if Chris were a servant to be bossed about.
21	Look at lines 14–19. By referring to at least two examples, analyse how the writer makes the reader aware of Chris's perception of Ewan. 2 marks may be awarded for detailed/insightful comment plus quotation/reference; 1 mark for more basic comment plus quotation/reference; 0 marks for quotation/reference alone. (Marks may be awarded 2+2, 2+1+1 or 1+1+1+1.)	4	Possible answers include: ▶ 'like a beast at a trough' suggests she sees him as non-human, merely satisfying basic needs, no self-respect; the harsh, plosive consonants at 'beast' and 'trough' add a hint of disgust ▶ 'coarse hair that sprang like short bristles' suggests she sees him as rough, unrefined, compares him with an inanimate object ▶ 'red and angry circle about the collar' shows that she can sense his aggressiveness in the chafing left by his uniform ▶ 'a great half-healed scar … glinted putrescent blue' – a revolting description of something deeply unhealthy, unnatural, almost alive.

Question number	Question text	Marks available	Commentary, hints and tips
22	By referring to the whole extract, describe the change in young Ewan's reaction to his father. 2 marks may be awarded for detailed/insightful comment plus quotation/reference; 1 mark for more basic comment plus quotation/reference; 0 marks for quotation/reference alone. (Marks may be awarded 2 or 1+1.)	2	Possible answers include: ▸ at first, he is cautious, but acknowledges Ewan as his father, albeit with little or no emotion: 'just said *It's father.*' ▸ at the end he is scared/seeks Chris's protection, calling him 'that soldier', i.e. denying any relationship.
23	By referring to this extract and to elsewhere in the novel, discuss the development of the relationship between Chris and Ewan. You can answer in bullet points in this final question, or write a number of linked statements.	10	Up to 2 marks can be achieved for identifying elements of commonality as identified in the question, i.e. how Chris and Ewan's relationship develops. A further 2 marks can be achieved for reference to the extract given. 6 additional marks can be gained for discussion of similar references to at least one other part of the text by the author. In practice this means: Identification of commonality. (1+1) When Chris and Ewan meet they are very much in love and Ewan is a hard-working and kind husband. (1) However, the war changes him, but although he is violent on his return home, his final words to Chae let us know he still loves Chris. (1) From the extract: 2 marks for detailed/insightful comment plus quotation/reference; 1 mark for more basic comment plus quotation/reference; 0 marks for quotation/reference alone. 2 marks only for discussion of extract.

Question number	Question text	Marks available	Commentary, hints and tips
23 (continued)			This extract shows the effect war can have on relationships through the reaction of Ewan coming home (getting drunk and being obnoxious) and Chris ('her face had gone white'). Their relationship is no longer what it once was. (2) From at least one other part of the text as above for up to 6 marks. Possible answers include: ▶ the initial wooing – nervous, occasionally comic ▶ early passion, happy domestic life with Chris and young Ewan ▶ problems emerge (e.g. his temper when asked about Sarah Sinclair) ▶ Chris's growing sense that Ewan doesn't understand her (e.g. over the 'realm of the dead') ▶ the disparity in intellect (e.g. his attitude to history at Dunnottar Castle) ▶ the disagreements about going to war; his treatment of her on his leave; the report from Chae about his love for her at the end; her vision of him after his death.

Text 5 – Prose – The Cone-Gatherers by Robin Jenkins

Question number	Question text	Marks available	Commentary, hints and tips
24	Look at lines 1–5. By referring to at least two examples, analyse how the writer's use of language in these lines creates a vivid atmosphere. 2 marks may be awarded for detailed/insightful comment plus quotation/reference; 1 mark for more basic comment plus quotation/reference; 0 marks for quotation/reference alone. (Marks may be awarded 2+2, 2+1+1 or 1+1+1+1.)	4	Possible answers include: ▶ 'thrilling as a pipe lament' suggests uplifting, musical, emotional ▶ 'daylight announced' – personification suggests power of nature ▶ 'a last blaze of light' suggests sudden burst of powerful sunlight ▶ 'an uncanny clarity' suggests almost mystical sense of brightness ▶ 'splendour and puissance' suggests magnificence and power ▶ 'abdication' suggests a grand, important change as in a monarch stepping down ▶ alliteration in 'Single stars' adds poetic weight to the description ▶ 'glittering' suggests brightness, attractiveness ▶ unusual, old-fashioned word order in 'a sky pale and austere' adds a sense of gravity, importance

Question number	Question text	Marks available	Commentary, hints and tips
24 *(continued)*			▸ 'Dusk like a breathing' – synaesthesia makes the moment seem dreamlike, unworldly ▸ 'drifted … crept' suggests stealthy, gentle, peaceful ▸ periodic structure of the sentence 'Slowly … became indistinguishable' lists all the different colours and climaxes in the idea of their merging into one ▸ 'mottled yellow … bronze … saffron' creates a palette of soft colours ▸ 'sombre harmonies of decay' – a highly poetic image of the beauty of nature ▸ 'Owls hooted. A fox barked' – the two short sentences focus on sound and create a haunting mood.
25	Look at lines 6–12. Explain the relationship between Calum and Neil which is revealed in these lines. 2 marks may be awarded for detailed/insightful comment plus quotation/reference; 1 mark for more basic comment plus quotation/reference; 0 marks for quotation/reference alone. (Marks may be awarded 2 or 1+1.)	2	Possible answers include: ▸ an almost telepathic understanding: nothing is said, but they seem to know what each other is doing ▸ clearly, if unspoken, defined roles: Calum will lead the way down the tree, and help Neil ▸ implicit understanding, trust in each other: Calum doesn't ask what Neil is thinking, but their being together is all he asks.
26	Look at lines 13–25. By referring to at least two examples, analyse how the writer reveals aspects of Calum's character in these lines. 2 marks may be awarded for detailed/insightful comment plus quotation/reference; 1 mark for more basic comment plus quotation/reference; 0 marks for quotation/reference alone. (Marks may be awarded 2+2, 2+1+1 or 1+1+1+1.)	4	Possible answers include: ▸ patience: waits for 'about half an hour' without complaint ▸ one-ness with nature: 'fancied he was resting in the heart of an enormous flower' ▸ love of nature: 'as he breathed in the fragrance' ▸ tenderness: 'he stroked the branches, and to his gentle hands they were as soft as petals' ▸ child-like imagination: 'as if he was an owl himself' ▸ complete absorption in the fantasy: 'He became an owl himself …' ▸ awareness of suffering in nature: 'he suffered in the ineluctable predicament of necessary pain and death' ▸ inability to understand suffering in nature: 'This was the terrifying mystery' ▸ detachment from world events: 'he tried, with success, to forget it' ▸ contentment with what he has: '"I could sit up here all night …" … assured him eagerly'.

Question number	Question text	Marks available	Commentary, hints and tips
27	By referring to the extract and to elsewhere in the novel, discuss how Jenkins portrays Calum's innocence. You can answer in bullet points in this final question, or write a number of linked statements.	10	Up to 2 marks can be achieved for identifying elements of commonality as identified in the question, i.e. how Calum's innocence is portrayed. A further 2 marks can be achieved for reference to the extract given. 6 additional marks can be gained for discussion of similar references to at least one other part of the text by the author. In practice this means: Identification of commonality. (1+1) Calum represents all that is good in the world (1): he is kind to nature (he loves birds and being in the trees) and can't understand evil (like Duror). (1) From the extract: 2 marks for detailed/insightful comment plus quotation/reference; 1 mark for more basic comment plus quotation/reference; 0 marks for quotation/reference alone. 2 marks only for discussion of extract. Calum's innocence comes across in this extract through the writer telling us he doesn't understand war or why nature can be cruel (the natural food chain). (2) From at least one other part of the text as above for up to 6 marks. Possible references include: ▶ constant comparisons with nature (especially birds) ▶ inability to understand Duror's hatred ▶ desire to help the injured rabbit; confusion/inner conflict about death in nature ▶ doesn't share/understand Neil's resentment of the aristocracy ▶ doesn't mind being stared at by Roderick and Sheila 'as if you were a monkey' ▶ not upset by the child on the bus ▶ his concern for the cones when the storm breaks ▶ doesn't take part in the exclusion of the conscientious objectors in Lendrick ▶ child-like attraction to the broken doll ▶ defence of Neil in beach hut ▶ the 'innocence' of his death; comparisons with crucifixion.

Part C – Scottish Text – Poetry

Text 1 – Poetry – *A Poet's Welcome to His Love-Begotten Daughter* by Robert Burns

Question number	Question text	Marks available	Commentary, hints and tips
28	Look at lines 1–12. By referring to at least two examples, analyse how the poet's language in these lines creates a contrast between his attitude to his daughter and his attitude to those who criticise him. For full marks both the daughter and the critics should be covered but not necessarily in equal measure. 2 marks may be awarded for detailed/insightful comment plus quotation/reference; 1 mark for more basic comment plus quotation/reference; 0 marks for quotation/reference alone. (Marks may be awarded 2+2, 2+1+1 or 1+1+1+1.)	4	Possible answers include: **Attitude to daughter – love, affection, pride:** ▶ informal 'Thou's' ▶ 'welcome' – she is openly and warmly received ▶ wishes ill on himself ('mishanter') if he thinks of her badly ▶ 'My bonie lady' – playfully grants her title of 'lady' ▶ happy, not ashamed to be called by childish names 'Tyta or daddie'. **Attitude to critics – defiant, defensive, contemptuous:** ▶ 'Tho' now …' implies he is not concerned at what they call him ▶ use of 'they' suggests a contempt in not defining them ▶ 'fornicator' is a particularly strong word, suggesting the strength of their criticism ▶ 'kintry clatter' – alliteration mimics the harsh sound of their chatter ▶ 'clatter' – onomatopoeia mimics noisy gossip ▶ 'let them clash' – dismissive tone ▶ 'clash' – suggests pointless, aimless chatter ▶ 'auld wife's' – dismisses his critics as old women ▶ 'feckless' suggests puny, silly ▶ 'gie ane fash' – not even worth a single worry.
29	Look at lines 13–18. Analyse how the sentence structure in these lines creates a defiant tone. 2 marks may be awarded for detailed/insightful comment plus quotation/reference; 1 mark for more basic comment plus quotation/reference; 0 marks for quotation/reference alone. (Marks may be awarded 2 or 1+1.)	2	Possible answers include: ▶ the exclamatory interjection 'Welcome!' reinforces his defiance of the criticism in the previous stanza ▶ 'bonie, sweet, wee dochter,' piles up a list of the many reasons to love her ▶ 'Tho' ye … tho' your' concedes possible reasons for criticism; they will almost inevitably be followed by 'Yet …' ▶ parenthetical 'by my faith' asserts his strength of feeling ▶ 'That I shall swear!' – short robust declaration of intent.

Question number	Question text	Marks available	Commentary, hints and tips
30	Look at lines 19–30. By referring to at least two examples in these lines, analyse how the poet's language conveys the depth of his love for his daughter. 2 marks may be awarded for detailed/insightful comment plus quotation/reference; 1 mark for more basic comment plus quotation/reference; 0 marks for quotation/reference alone. (Marks may be awarded 2+2, 2+1+1 or 1+1+1+1.)	4	Possible answers include: ▸ compares her with her mother whom he calls 'bonie' ▸ 'fatherly' implies he feels a loving bond ▸ 'daut' suggests handling gently and lovingly ▸ the rhyme 'dear … near' adds a gentle, musical touch ▸ prepared to defend her against criticism from the whole church ▸ 'Sweet fruit' suggests something natural, attractive, wholesome ▸ 'mony a merry dint' recalls with pleasure (heightened by the alliteration) the activities which led to her conception ▸ those who would 'scoff' at her birth are dismissed as 'fools' ▸ asserts that he will support her to the 'last plack', i.e. the tiniest remaining coin.
31	By referring to this poem and to at least one other by Burns, discuss his use of contrast to explore important ideas. You can answer in bullet points in this final question, or write a number of linked statements.	10	Up to 2 marks can be achieved for identifying elements of commonality as identified in the question, i.e. how Burns uses contrast to explore important ideas. A further 2 marks can be achieved for reference to the extract given. 6 additional marks can be gained for discussion of similar references to at least one other poem by the author. In practice this means: Identification of commonality. (1+1) Burns uses contrast to explore ideas such as social class, pretensions and hypocrisy. (1) He often does this through human and animal characters. (1) From the extract: 2 marks for detailed/insightful comment plus quotation/reference; 1 mark for more basic comment plus quotation/reference; 0 marks for quotation/reference alone. 2 marks only for discussion of extract. ▸ *A Poet's Welcome* – contrasts his love with others' condemnation; contrasts his free spirit with the narrow-mindedness of others. (2) From at least one other poem as above for up to 6 marks.

Question number	Question text	Marks available	Commentary, hints and tips
31 (continued)			Possible references include: ▸ *To a Louse* – contrasts the vulgarity of the louse with the social pretensions of the lady on whose bonnet it is creeping; contrasts the way we see ourselves with the way 'others see us' ▸ *To a Mouse* – contrasts 'Man's dominion' with 'nature's social union'; contrasts hopes with reality ▸ *A Red, Red Rose* – contrasts the enduring nature of his love with imagined changes in nature ('the seas gang dry', 'the rocks melt wi' the sun') ▸ *Tam o' Shanter* – contrasts the bonhomie in the tavern with the terrors outside; contrasts men's stupidity with women's common sense; contrast in use of Scots and English ▸ *Holy Willie's Prayer* – contrasts impression Holy Willie is trying to create with the reality; contrasts genuine prayer with the travesty that is Holy Willie's spiteful, self-promoting effort.

Text 2 – Poetry – *Mrs Midas* by Carol Ann Duffy

Question number	Question text	Marks available	Commentary, hints and tips
32	Look at lines 1–6. By referring to at least two examples, analyse how the poet's language creates an ordinary, everyday atmosphere in these lines. 2 marks may be awarded for detailed/ insightful comment plus quotation/ reference; 1 mark for more basic comment plus quotation/reference; 0 marks for quotation/reference alone. (Marks may be awarded 2+2, 2+1+1 or 1+1+1+1.)	4	Possible answers include: ▸ the use of simple statement 'It was late September', as if recounting a simple recollection ▸ the use of informal contraction 'I'd just poured' suggests relaxed tone ▸ the absence of 'and' between 'wine' and 'begun' is informal, sounds comfortable ▸ everyday detail ('a glass of wine') suggests relaxation, contentment ▸ word choice of 'unwind' suggests calmness, composure ▸ imagery/personification of 'The kitchen/ filled with the smell of itself' suggests warmth, pleasant smells, promise of good food ▸ 'steamy breath/gently blanching the windows' – personification of kitchen as something alive, warm, tender ▸ conversational tone of 'So I opened one' as if continuing a simple story ▸ 'wiped the other's glass like a brow' – affectionate, caring, unthreatening gesture ▸ simple description of what husband is doing 'standing under the pear tree …' ▸ 'snapping a twig' suggests a small, unthreatening action.

Question number	Question text	Marks available	Commentary, hints and tips
33	Look at lines 7–12. Analyse how the poet's language conveys the confusion that is beginning to arise in the speaker's mind. 2 marks may be awarded for detailed/insightful comment plus quotation/reference; 1 mark for more basic comment plus quotation/reference; 0 marks for quotation/reference alone. (Marks may be awarded 2 or 1+1.)	2	Possible answers include: ▸ tone of 'Now the garden was long and the visibility poor' – as if offering an excuse for possibly not seeing correctly ▸ the imagery of 'the dark of the ground seems to drink the light of the sky' suggests something mysterious, dark, deprived of light, uncertain ▸ the delayed assertion 'but that twig in his hand was gold' as if unwilling to state what she is seeing ▸ the parenthetical '– we grew Fondante d'Automne –' seems an unnecessary detail as if trying to hold onto reality by including it ▸ the minor sentence 'On' conveys a sense of stupefaction, unable to say anything more than a single syllable ▸ question 'Is he putting fairy lights in the tree?' suggests doubt, almost an attempt to rationalise.
34	Look at lines 13–24. By referring to at least two examples, analyse how the poet's language conveys the strangeness of the husband's behaviour. 2 marks may be awarded for detailed/insightful comment plus quotation/reference; 1 mark for more basic comment plus quotation/reference; 0 marks for quotation/reference alone. (Marks may be awarded 2+2, 2+1+1 or 1+1+1+1.)	4	Possible answers include: ▸ the juxtaposition of the ordinary ('He came into the house') with the extraordinary ('The doorknobs gleamed') ▸ the way his behaviour causes her mind to jump to a schoolroom memory ▸ the simile 'like a king on a burnished throne' presents him as a regal figure amid great splendour ▸ 'strange, wild, vain' – use of three monosyllables to convey a wide range of emotions ▸ 'He started to laugh' suggests an almost irrational response to the situation ▸ 'spitting out the teeth of the rich' – a grotesque image combining pain/discomfort with association of wealth ▸ structure of 'toyed with his spoon, then mine, then with the knives, the forks' suggests random actions, as if he is confused ▸ 'glass, goblet, golden chalice' shows the progression from simple drinking vessel to exotic 'chalice'; emphasised by the alliteration ▸ structure of 'picked up the glass, goblet, golden chalice, drank' – suggests staccato movement, unusual behaviour.

Question number	Question text	Marks available	Commentary, hints and tips
35	By referring to this poem and at least one other by Duffy, discuss how she introduces unusual or surprising ideas into her poems. You can answer in bullet points in this final question, or write a number of linked statements.	10	Up to 2 marks can be achieved for identifying elements of commonality as identified in the question, i.e. how Duffy introduces unusual or surprising ideas into her poems. A further 2 marks can be achieved for reference to the extract given. 6 additional marks can be gained for discussion of similar references to at least one other poem by the author. In practice this means: Identification of commonality. (1+1) Surprising and unusual ideas are introduced through strange images and obscure occurrences to show that things are not as simple as we may think. (1) Duffy does this by challenging what we would normally expect, i.e. a 'romantic gift' as an onion in *Valentine*. (1) From the extract: 2 marks for detailed/insightful comment plus quotation/reference; 1 mark for more basic comment plus quotation/reference; 0 marks for quotation/reference alone. 2 marks only for discussion of extract. In the extract, we see a surprisingly updated version of the Midas legend; the husband is 'spitting out the teeth of the rich' and everything is turning to gold. The husband is delighted with this sinister occurrence which builds suspense for the reader. (2) From at least one other poem as above for up to 6 marks. Possible references include: ▶ *The Way My Mother Speaks* – the disorientation suggested by 'Nothing is silent. Nothing is not silent'; the image of the child and the net; the power of the repeated phrase 'The day and ever' ▶ *Valentine* – the rejection of the conventional love message; the surprise of 'I give you an onion'; the association of love and violence ▶ *In Mrs Tilscher's Class* – the imagery of 'the chalky Pyramids rubbed in to dust'; Brady and Hindley as the 'uneasy smudge of a mistake'; the tadpoles and frogs comparison; the onset of puberty as 'the air tasted of electricity', 'fractious under the heavy, sexy sky' ▶ *Originally* – the surreal imagery of the 'room/which fell through fields'; the notion of childhood as an 'emigration'; the idea of culture etc. being lost/replaced ▶ *War Photographer* – the photographer as priest.

Text 3 – Poetry – *Revelation* by Liz Lochhead

Question number	Question text	Marks available	Commentary, hints and tips
36	Look at lines 1–14. By referring to at least two examples, analyse how the poet creates an intimidating atmosphere in these lines. 2 marks may be awarded for detailed/insightful comment plus quotation/reference; 1 mark for more basic comment plus quotation/reference; 0 marks for quotation/reference alone. (Marks may be awarded 2+2, 2+1+1 or 1+1+1+1.)	4	Possible answers include: ▸ contrast of 'black bull' and 'child' suggests innocence threatened by bulk ▸ 'monster' suggests an aggressive beast, supernatural qualities ▸ 'threshold' suggests being on the brink of a dangerous discovery ▸ 'held my hand' suggests the need for protection ▸ 'only black' suggests total darkness, unable to distinguish any features ▸ 'hot reek' suggests overwhelming, repulsive smell ▸ 'immense' suggests awe-inspiring size ▸ 'edges merging with the darkness' suggests the bull's features cannot be made out, are consumed by the blackness ▸ 'big bulk' – alliteration suggests heaviness ▸ 'roar … scared of' suggests a terrifyingly loud noise ▸ onomatopoeia of 'trampling … clanking' suggests heavy, dangerous sound ▸ 'chain's jerk' suggests the bull is straining to break free ▸ 'great wedge' suggests the enormous bulk of his head is seen like a destructive tool ▸ alliteration and onomatopoeia in 'roared his rage' suggest fearsome aggression ▸ 'nostrils gaped' suggests pent-up violence, naked aggression.
37	Look at lines 15–31. By referring to at least two examples, analyse how the poet presents masculinity as threatening. 2 marks may be awarded for detailed/insightful comment plus quotation/reference; 1 mark for more basic comment plus quotation/reference; 0 marks for quotation/reference alone. (Marks may be awarded 2+2, 2+1+1 or 1+1+1+1.)	4	Possible answers include: ▸ the hens' behaviour depicts them as innocent of the bull's violence ▸ 'Black Mass' suggests not just size and colour, but attributes satanic qualities to the bull ▸ 'straining at his chains' suggests the bull is fighting to escape and poses a threat ▸ 'always half-known' suggests the speaker already has a subconscious understanding of the evil represented by the bull ▸ 'Anti-Christ' suggests the bull is the complete opposite of the Christian values of love and compassion ▸ 'anarchy' suggests his desire to disturb the natural order ▸ 'threatening … eggs … milk' depicts him as the enemy of these symbols of femininity

Question number	Question text	Marks available	Commentary, hints and tips
37 *(continued)*			▶ the goodness of the eggs ('well rounded, self-contained') and the milk ('placidity') is in direct contrast with the evil of the bull ▶ the activities of the 'big boys' depict them as sadists, torturing innocent creatures; and the specific examples are of animals who have changed their life form, in the same way as the speaker has moved from innocence to an awareness of the evil around her ▶ 'thronged hedge and harried nest' suggests she now sees danger and menace all around her ▶ 'eggs shattering … milk should spill' suggests she is fearful of the damage male aggression can cause, her vulnerability as a woman.
38	By referring to the poem as a whole, explain the significance of the title of the poem. 2 marks may be awarded for detailed/insightful comment plus quotation/reference; 1 mark for more basic comment plus quotation/reference; 0 marks for quotation/reference alone. (Marks may be awarded 2 or 1+1.)	**2**	Possible answers include: ▶ the incident at the farm has revealed to the speaker an important truth ▶ a previously half-understood idea that evil and aggression exist just below the surface in the world is now fully formed ▶ the feminine virtues represented by the eggs and the milk are under threat from male violence, as represented by the dark, mysterious bulk of the bull and by the casual sadism of the 'big boys' ▶ the word 'Revelation' has apocalyptic associations, emphasising how deeply she is affected; this is linked to the reference to 'Anti-Christ'.
39	By referring to this poem and to at least one other poem by Lochhead, discuss her use of contrast to explore important ideas. You can answer in bullet points in this final question, or write a number of linked statements.	**10**	Up to 2 marks can be achieved for identifying elements of commonality as identified in the question, i.e. how Lochhead uses contrast to explore important ideas. A further 2 marks can be achieved for reference to the extract given. 6 additional marks can be gained for discussion of similar references to at least one other poem by the author. In practice this means: Identification of commonality. (1+1) Lochhead often contrasts characters and situations (1) to explore ideas such as masculinity and femininity, love and growing up. (1)

Question number	Question text	Marks available	Commentary, hints and tips
39 (continued)			From the extract: 2 marks for detailed/insightful comment plus quotation/reference; 1 mark for more basic comment plus quotation/reference; 0 marks for quotation/reference alone.
			2 marks only for discussion of extract.
			Revelation – the hens' perception of the bull and the speaker's; the bull's name and the reality of his appearance links to female vulnerability and male aggression; innocence and experience. (2)
			From at least one other poem as above for up to 6 marks.
			Possible references include:
			▸ *Last Supper* – the actual meal with the man and the imagined follow-up with the Girls; traditional feminine gentleness and the hostility of the imagined conversation; the predatory attitude at the end contrasts with conventional views of female behaviour
			▸ *View of Scotland/Love Poem* – Hogmanay past and present; past and present in general; childhood innocence and adult scepticism; mother's devotion to tradition and speaker's rather amused attitude; 'new view' in the calendar and the mother's adherence to tradition
			▸ *My Rival's House* – the speaker and the woman; the woman's outward politeness and her inner hostility; surface versus reality in general
			▸ *The Bargain* – 'looking back, looking forward'; past love in relationship and current discontent; the items at the market: once of use/value, now broken, worthless
			▸ *Box Room* – the mother's outward politeness and obvious inner dislike; hope of permanence and the reality of the 'weekend case'; 'Invited guest among abandoned objects'; boyfriend's past and present.

Text 4 – Poetry – *Visiting hour* by Norman MacCaig

Question number	Question text	Marks available	Commentary, hints and tips
40	Look at lines 1–10. By referring to at least two examples, analyse how the poet's use of language conveys the speaker's discomfort. 2 marks may be awarded for detailed/ insightful comment plus quotation/ reference; 1 mark for more basic comment plus quotation/reference; 0 marks for quotation/reference alone. (Marks may be awarded 2+2, 2+1+1 or 1+1+1+1.)	4	Possible answers include: ▸ 'smell/combs' suggests the smell is invasive and pervasive ▸ 'they go bobbing' suggests surreal dislocation of nose from the rest of the body ▸ 'green and yellow' suggests a colour combination reminiscent of sickness and illness ▸ 'seems a corpse' suggests inability to discern the true nature of something ▸ 'corpse' suggests presence of death ▸ 'is trundled' – passive voice creates absence of human agency in the action ▸ 'vanishes' suggests mysterious disappearance ▸ the enjambment in 'vanishes/heavenward' suggests a gaping void into which the corpse disappears ▸ the fragmented structure of 'I will not feel …' suggests struggling to control emotions.
41	Look at lines 11–18. Analyse how the speaker's attitude to the nurses is conveyed. 2 marks may be awarded for detailed/ insightful comment plus quotation/ reference; 1 mark for more basic comment plus quotation/reference; 0 marks for quotation/reference alone. (Marks may be awarded 2 or 1+1.)	2	Possible answers include: ▸ admiration for their efficiency ('lightly, swiftly') ▸ recognition of the demanding nature of their job ('here and up and down and there') ▸ appreciation of their ability to cope with suffering 'carrying their burden …' ▸ acknowledgement of the dark side of their job ('so much pain …') ▸ awe/wonder at their ability to carry on ('still clear …').
42	Look at lines 19–38. By referring to at least two examples, analyse how the poet's use of language creates a bleak atmosphere. 2 marks may be awarded for detailed/ insightful comment plus quotation/ reference; 1 mark for more basic comment plus quotation/reference; 0 marks for quotation/reference alone. (Marks may be awarded 2+2, 2+1+1 or 1+1+1+1.)	4	Possible answers include: ▸ minor sentence 'Ward 7' – suggests sudden pause for thought, as if having to face up to something unpleasant ▸ 'white cave of forgetfulness' suggests the patient is cut off from the rest of the world, deep in a world of her own ▸ 'withered hand' suggests wasted, emaciated ▸ 'trembles' suggests shivering, weakness ▸ 'stalk' suggests her arm is thin, fragile, insubstantial ▸ 'eyelids too heavy' suggests an almost permanent drowsiness ▸ 'wasted of colour' suggests life has faded, vitality has drained ▸ the vampire imagery in 'fang … guzzling' is dark and suggests unnatural behaviour

Question number	Question text	Marks available	Commentary, hints and tips
42 (continued)			▶ 'distance shrinks' suggests a fading away ▶ 'distance of pain' suggests that all that lies between them is suffering ▶ the 'black figure' in the 'white cave' suggests he feels out of place, a negative presence ▶ 'swimming waves … dizzily' suggests he is confused by the sound, is disorientated ▶ 'books that will not be read and fruitless fruits' suggests loss of purpose, futility.
43	By referring to this extract and to at least one other poem by MacCaig, discuss how he explores thought-provoking ideas in his poems. You can answer in bullet points in this final question, or write a number of linked statements.	10	Up to 2 marks can be achieved for identifying elements of commonality as identified in the question, i.e. how MacCaig explores thought-provoking ideas in his poems. A further 2 marks can be achieved for reference to the extract given. 6 additional marks can be gained for discussion of similar references to at least one other poem by the author. In practice this means: Identification of commonality. (1+1) MacCaig uses characters and situations to reveal thought-provoking ideas (1) surrounding life and death, humanity's cruel nature and moral values. (1) From the extract: 2 marks for detailed/insightful comment plus quotation/reference; 1 mark for more basic comment plus quotation/reference; 0 marks for quotation/reference alone. 2 marks only for discussion of extract. *Visiting hour* – explores the idea that it is impossible to switch off emotions no matter how hard one tries, that visiting a sick person reminds the poet of his own mortality. (2) From at least one other poem as above for up to 6 marks. Possible references include: ▶ *Hotel room 12th floor* – explores the idea that a city renowned for advanced technology is still subject to violence and fear, that we are not as civilised as we might think we are, that the 'frontier' between the civilised and the uncivilised is still with us

Question number	Question text	Marks available	Commentary, hints and tips
43 (continued)			▶ *Brooklyn cop* – explores the idea that underneath the intimidating appearance of the cop is an ordinary husband with a wife who fears for his safety, that as a policeman he patrols the 'thin tissue over violence', which could 'tear' at any moment, that his 'victims' are perhaps to be pitied as much as he is ▶ *Assisi* – explores the idea that the Church is failing in its duty to care for the poor and disabled, that the Church in Assisi is too elaborate, that the beggar's outward deformities detract from his inner worth ▶ *Basking shark* – explores the idea that the difference between apparently civilised humans and the notoriously single-minded and destructive shark is simply an accident of evolution, questions exactly who the 'monster' is ▶ *Aunt Julia* – explores the disappearance of a traditional, elemental way of life and its language, which is no longer understood or valued by modern ways of living.

Text 5 – Poetry – *Nil Nil* by Don Paterson

Question number	Question text	Marks available	Commentary, hints and tips
44	Look at lines 1–13. By referring to at least two examples, analyse how the poet's use of language conveys the extent of the club's decline. 2 marks may be awarded for detailed/insightful comment plus quotation/reference; 1 mark for more basic comment plus quotation/reference; 0 marks for quotation/reference alone. (Marks may be awarded 2+2, 2+1+1 or 1+1+1+1.)	4	Possible answers include: ▶ the sentence structure (long, rambling list, dominated by 'then') suggests an almost endless, unstoppable process ▶ the ironic reference to their one success as a 'setback' suggests just how inexorable the decline actually was ▶ 'fifty-year slide' suggests the decline lasted for a long time, and was relentless ▶ 'Sunday League' suggests second-rate, not comparable with serious Saturday games ▶ 'big tartan flasks' suggests refreshments brought from home, not provided by the club ▶ 'open hatchbacks' suggests players have driven themselves right up to the pitch, no team transport ▶ 'half-time satsuma' suggests very limited, frugal nourishment provided ▶ 'the dog on the pitch' is slightly humorous, suggests a ground where no one pays much attention

Question number	Question text	Marks available	Commentary, hints and tips
44 (continued)			▶ 'Boy's Club' implies it has lost senior status ▶ 'then nobody' is a bleak description of the end of sponsorship ▶ spectators are reduced to 'grim fathers' (no enjoyment) and 'perverts' (disturbing image of people there for the wrong reason).
45	Look at lines 14–22. By referring to at least two examples, analyse how the poet's use of language creates a depressing mood in these lines. 2 marks may be awarded for detailed/insightful comment plus quotation/reference; 1 mark for more basic comment plus quotation/reference; 0 marks for quotation/reference alone. (Marks may be awarded 2+2, 2+1+1 or 1+1+1+1.)	4	Possible answers include: ▶ 'unrefereed thirty-a-sides' suggests chaotic, anarchic ▶ 'terrified' suggests the lame boys have been bullied into their roles ▶ 'fat boys with callipers' suggests the insensitive language used by others ▶ 'infinite, notional fields' suggests the lack of order, control ▶ 'dwindling' suggests steady decline, loss of status ▶ 'half-hearted' suggests lack of enthusiasm ▶ 'kickabouts' suggests informal, unstructured, without any passion ▶ 'so smelly the air seems to quiver above him' – the description of Horace is vivid and direct ▶ 'desperate' suggests frantic, uncontrolled ▶ 'bald tennis ball' suggests over-used, well past its usefulness ▶ 'the hour before lighting-up time' symbolises approaching dark.
46	Look at lines 23–30. Analyse how the poet's use of language creates sympathy for 'wee Horace'. 2 marks may be awarded for detailed/insightful comment plus quotation/reference; 1 mark for more basic comment plus quotation/reference; 0 marks for quotation/reference alone. (Marks may be awarded 2 or 1+1.)	2	Possible answers include: ▶ his being left alone by someone who 'cheats' ▶ 'hack up' suggests the process is clumsy, crude, inelegant ▶ 'in the rain' – pathetic fallacy to suggest misery ▶ 'stopped swings' suggests the park is deserted, implying loneliness, isolation ▶ 'dead shanty-town' suggests the area he lives in is run-down, almost primitive ▶ 'black shell' suggests environment is dark, dirty, empty ▶ 'cul-de-sac' symbolises a dead-end existence ▶ the pathetic attempt to 'swank off' after a mere fluke.
47	By referring to this poem and to at least one other by Paterson, discuss his use of symbolism to explore important themes. You can answer in bullet points in this final question, or write a number of linked statements.	10	Up to 2 marks can be achieved for identifying elements of commonality as identified in the question, i.e. how Paterson uses symbolism to explore important themes. A further 2 marks can be achieved for reference to the extract given.

Question number	Question text	Marks available	Commentary, hints and tips
47 (continued)			6 additional marks can be gained for discussion of similar references to at least one other poem by the author.
			In practice this means: Identification of commonality. (1+1)
			Paterson uses symbols of situation and character (1) to explore themes such as growing up, what it means to be human, life, birth and death. (1)
			From the extract: 2 marks for detailed/insightful comment plus quotation/reference; 1 mark for more basic comment plus quotation/reference; 0 marks for quotation/reference alone.
			2 marks only for discussion of extract.
			Nil Nil – symbolism in the rise and fall of the football team's fortunes; in 'a game of two halves'; in the 'dog on the pitch'; the 'bald tennis ball'; the pilot's crash; the gallstone. (2)
			From at least one other poem as above for up to 6 marks.
			Possible references include:
			▸ *Rain* – symbolism in each of the scenarios: e.g. 'braiding a windowpane', 'a hung-out dress'; 'the woman sits alone', 'the dress lies ruined on the grass'; in rain as a 'fatal watercourse'; in 'ink … milk … blood'; in the power of rain and water to give birth ('we rose up from …'), refresh ('all was washed clean')
			▸ *11.00: Baldovan* – symbolism in the journey itself; in the bus stop as 'Steel flag'; in the details of the coins; in the 'wrong streets that suddenly forget their names'; in 'all the houses have gone'
			▸ *Waking With Russell* – symbolism in the 'true path' and 'mezzo del cammin' ideas; the smile as 'river'; the 'true gift' that 'never leave the giver'
			▸ *The Circle* – symbolism in the references to 'outer space … comets, planets, moon and sun'; in the idea of 'circuitry'; in 'he's all the earth/and sky'; in 'the dream is taxed'; in the 'target' references: 'between the bowstring and the mark', 'keep our arrows …', 'draws our aim'; in the 'spoiled work'; in the religious references ('Krishna', 'avatar'); in 'the perfect ring'
			▸ *The Ferryman's Arms* – symbolism in the ferry/ferryman; in the mysterious table; in the 'rash of small miracles'; in the leaving behind of 'my losing opponent'.

Practice Paper 2
Reading for Understanding, Analysis and Evaluation
Passage 1

Question number	Question text	Marks available	Commentary, hints and tips
1	Read lines 1–9. Identify two benefits to Jon Huntsman's introduction of a four-day working week. Use your own words as far as possible. No marks for straight lifts from the passage. 1 mark for each point from the 'Commentary, hints and tips' column. (Marks may be awarded 2 or 1+1.)	2	Possible answers include: ▶ the state saved money ▶ workers would have more time off at the weekend ▶ less commuting, therefore healthier, happier employees and less contribution to global warming.
2	Read lines 17–21. By referring to at least two examples, analyse how the writer's use of language creates a negative impression of work. For full marks there should be comments on at least two examples. 2 marks may be awarded for detailed/insightful comment plus quotation/reference; 1 mark for more basic comment plus quotation/reference; 0 marks for quotation/reference alone. (Marks may be awarded 2+2, 2+1+1 or 1+1+1+1.)	4	Possible answers include: ▶ 'trapped' suggests imprisoned, confined ▶ 'outdated' suggests old-fashioned, invalid ▶ 'routine' suggests done without thinking, dull, boring ▶ 'clung' suggests holding on desperately, reluctant to think of alternatives ▶ 'religious devotion' suggests a possibly irrational belief in something with no foundation ▶ 'Clock in, sit at your terminal, be seen to work, clock out' – listing of activities suggests a fixed, unshakeable pattern; minor sentence suggests that overall it is a dull, lifeless activity ▶ rhetorical questions ('Is this …', 'Should we …') suggest the writer's contempt for the ideas in the questions ▶ 'clamber' suggests unpleasant, ungainly movement involving discomfort ▶ 'steel box … concrete box' suggests car and office are both restrictive, inhuman.

Question number		Question text	Marks available	Commentary, hints and tips
3		Read lines 22–26. By referring to at least two examples, analyse how language is used to clarify what the writer is saying. 2 marks may be awarded for detailed/insightful comment plus quotation/reference; 1 mark for more basic comment plus quotation/reference; 0 marks for quotation/reference alone. (Marks may be awarded 2+2 or 2+1+1 or 1+1+1+1.)	4	Possible answers include: **Sentence structure:** ▶ parenthetical reference to *The Office* provides a specific example of the type of work the writer is referring to ▶ repetition of 'constantly' reinforces the idea of an oppressive routine ▶ list ('constantly … screen') suggests the large number of routine activities to be endured ▶ repetition of 'better' emphasises the improvement in lifestyle that could be achieved ▶ additional comment after the dash shows almost as an afterthought that there are even more benefits to be gained. **Word choice:** ▶ 'anomie' – the alienation of our way of life has led to us trying to make meaning out of nothing ▶ 'monitored' – we are always being watched; possible pun on screen monitor ▶ 'sedentary' – sit still/don't move ▶ 'wired lap-topped world' – the whole world is glued to their screens.
4	a)	Read lines 27–39. Using your own words as far as possible, explain the difference between what 'economists and thinkers' predicted in the 1930s and what has actually happened. No marks for straight lifts from the passage. For full marks, there must be reference to both the prediction and to the reality, but these do not have to be evenly divided. 2 marks may be awarded for detailed/insightful comment; 1 mark for more basic comment; 0 marks for quotation/reference alone. (Marks may be awarded 2+2, 2+1+1 or 1+1+1+1.)	4	Possible answers include: **Prediction:** ▶ once we reached the point when we had all we needed as basics, work would feature less in our lives ▶ the working week could be reduced to three days ▶ we would be able to devote more time to leisure and culture. **Reality:** ▶ rather than improving, the situation has become worse ▶ despite people's wishes, we find ourselves working even longer hours ▶ there is a culture of competitiveness and long hours which impacts on our health.

Question number		Question text	Marks available	Commentary, hints and tips
4	b)	By referring to at least two examples of imagery in these lines, analyse how the writer conveys his attitude to modern working practices. For full marks there should be comments on at least two examples. 2 marks may be awarded for detailed/insightful comment plus quotation/reference; 1 mark for more basic comment plus quotation/reference; 0 marks for quotation/reference alone. (Marks may be awarded 2+2, 2+1+1 or 1+1+1+1.)	4	Possible answers include: ▸ 'scamper ever faster in our hamster-wheels' compares workers to caged animals engaged in repetitive, ultimately futile activity; suggests that we have no control, are simply doing as our bosses demand, have been drained of our humanity ▸ 'treadmill is whirling ever-faster' compares working life to a gruelling, boring task of generating motion carried out by animals (or prisoners); suggests workers are mere functionaries, engaged in monotonous drudgery ▸ 'locked in an arms race' compares workers to nations vying to outdo each other in the possession of ever more powerful weapons; suggests a pointless, dangerous escalation of competitiveness which no one can ever win.
5		Read lines 40–45. Using your own words as far as possible, explain the thinking behind what the French government did in the 1990s. No marks for straight lifts from the passage. 2 marks may be awarded for detailed/insightful comment; 1 mark for more basic comment. (Marks may be awarded 2+1 or 1+1+1.)	3	Possible answers include: ▸ there is more to life than constant work ▸ serving the needs/demands of big business is not the most important thing in life ▸ making money has a place in society, but it should not dominate us ▸ precedence should be given to personal happiness ▸ what matters is having sufficient time to appreciate life.
6		Read lines 46–50. By referring to at least one example, analyse how sentence structure is used to clarify what the writer is saying. 2 marks may be awarded for detailed/insightful comment plus quotation/reference, 1 mark for more basic comment plus quotation/reference; 0 marks for quotation/reference alone. (Marks may be awarded 2 or 1+1.)	2	Possible answers include: ▸ the colon introduces an explanation of the metaphor 'arms treaty' ▸ 'we all stop, together, now, at the 35 hour mark' is structured to sound like a list of crisp, military instructions ▸ list of benefits ('became fitter … back to life') indicates the large number of benefits from the scheme ▸ 'But' introduces the idea that there was a downside, that the benefits weren't allowed to last ▸ the colon introduces an expansion of 'dismayed' and allows the paragraph to end on a simple statement of the people's feelings.

Question number	Question text	Marks available	Commentary, hints and tips
7	Read lines 51–52. Analyse how the writer's use of language creates a positive tone on which to conclude the passage. 2 marks may be awarded for detailed/insightful comment plus quotation/reference; 1 mark for more basic comment plus quotation/reference; 0 marks for quotation/reference alone. (Marks may be awarded 2 or 1+1.)	2	Possible answers include: ▶ 'a voice is calling' suggests an invocation of hope, a sort of mystical appeal ▶ 'happier, healthier' suggests the improvement in mental and physical health to be gained ▶ 'alternative' suggests there is another way, we do not have to accept the status quo ▶ 'great free spaces beyond' suggests openness, liberation, unspoiled terrain.

Passage 2

Question number	Question text	Marks available	Commentary, hints and tips
8	Look at both passages. Both writers express their views about work. Identify three key areas on which they agree. You should support the points by referring to important ideas in both passages. You may use bullet points in this final question, or write a number of linked statements. Evidence from the passage may include quotations, but these should be supported by explanations. The approach to marking is shown in the 'Commentary, hints and tips' column. Key areas of agreement are shown in the table below. Other answers are possible.	5	The mark for this question should reflect the quality of response in two areas: ▸ identification of the key areas of agreement in views ▸ the level of detail given in support. The following guidelines should be used: ▸ 5 marks – identification of three key areas of agreement with insightful use of supporting evidence ▸ 4 marks – identification of three key areas of agreement with appropriate use of supporting evidence ▸ 3 marks – identification of three key areas of agreement ▸ 2 marks – identification of two key areas of agreement ▸ 1 mark – identification of one key area of agreement ▸ 0 marks – failure to identify one key area of agreement and/or misunderstanding of task. **NB** If you identify only two key areas of agreement, you may be awarded up to a maximum of 4 marks, as follows: ▸ 2 marks for identification of two key areas of agreement plus either ▸ a further 1 mark for appropriate use of supporting evidence to a total of 3 marks or ▸ a further 2 marks for detailed/insightful use of supporting evidence to a total of 4 marks. If you identify only one key area of agreement, you may be awarded up to a maximum of 2 marks, as follows: ▸ 1 mark for identification of one key area of agreement ▸ a further 1 mark for use of supporting evidence to a total of 2 marks.

	Area of agreement	Passage 1	Passage 2
1	the role of work in our lives	we are locked into an outdated lifestyle dominated by work	work dominates the way we live; we work excessively long hours
2	there is more to life	leisure, culture, personal happiness should be encouraged	there are better, more fulfilling things to do (hobbies, family, culture, personal relationships)
3	effect on physical/mental health	increased incidence of stroke and heart attack	the prevalence of stress from overwork
4	past predictions about changes to work patterns	predictions of a three-day working week have proved wrong	predictions of a 15-hour working week have proved wrong
5	the power of big business	idea of 'serving corporations'; big business forced French government to withdraw the 35-hour maximum working week	our personal freedom is taken over by demands of 'bosses and employers'; we are 'in submission to them'
6	things are getting worse	the competitiveness which makes us need to seem to be working long hours	increase in pension age; more oppressive working patterns (zero-hours contracts, part-time work)
7	hope for the future	the schemes in Utah and in France demonstrate that change is possible and has many benefits	advances in technology should be exploited to reduce demands on humans' working lives

Critical Reading
Section 1 – Scottish Text – 20 marks
Part A – Scottish Text – Drama

Text 1 – Drama – *The Slab Boys* by John Byrne

Question number	Question text	Marks available	Commentary, hints and tips
1	Look at lines 1–27. By referring to at least two examples, analyse how dialogue and stage directions make the audience feel sympathy for Hector. 2 marks may be awarded for detailed/ insightful comment plus quotation/ reference; 1 mark for more basic comment plus quotation/reference; 0 marks for quotation/reference alone. (Marks may be awarded 2+2, 2+1+1 or 1+1+1+1.)	4	Possible answers include: **Dialogue:** ▶ Hector's pathetic enthusiasm: 'Will I go now and ask her? Will I?' ▶ 'I can do that after I've asked Lucille' – his determination to ask her makes the audience concerned he will be humiliated ▶ Hector's enthusiasm for 'swanking' and his belief that his clothes are 'up to date' when they are not again make the audience concerned for his humiliation ▶ Phil's justification for the balaclava ('it's draughty in Willie's room') verges on the insulting ▶ the glibness of Phil's invented story for him shows how much contempt he has for Hector, how much he enjoys manipulating him ▶ the 'Triple pneumonia … Double rupture …' knockabout might amuse Phil and Spanky, but it is further evidence of their having fun at someone else's expense ▶ Hector's 'I'll away along then' is pathetic in its simplicity and naivety ▶ 'Good man' and 'good luck son' – the insincerity of Phil and Spanky's good wishes. **Stage directions:** ▶ the fact that the attempt by Alan to warn him is thwarted by Phil's threat with the pen such that (even) Alan is obliged to lie to him ▶ 'Forces Hector's arms into sleeves' and 'pulls helmet over head', showing him as at the mercy of others ▶ the stage direction '*Slightly bamboozled*' paints him as a sad, put-upon figure ▶ 'shove him out the door' suggests desperation to get rid of him ▶ their bursting into uncontrollable laughter the moment he leaves.

Question number	Question text	Marks available	Commentary, hints and tips
2	Look at lines 28–30. Analyse how the playwright's use of language in these lines allows Phil and Spanky to make fun of Alan. 2 marks may be awarded for detailed/insightful comment plus quotation/reference; 1 mark for more basic comment plus quotation/reference; 0 marks for quotation/reference alone. (Marks may be awarded 2 or 1+1.)	2	Possible answers include: ▶ they make fun of Alan's rather public school turn of phrase 'a lousy trick' ▶ they echo it sneeringly in similar terms: 'by jove' and 'you cad' ▶ they mock Alan's (to them) posh way of speaking by pretending to speak in the same way.
3	Look at lines 31–39. By referring to at least two examples, analyse how the playwright emphasises the animosity between Alan and Phil. 2 marks may be awarded for detailed/insightful comment plus quotation/reference; 1 mark for more basic comment plus quotation/reference; 0 marks for quotation/reference alone. (Marks may be awarded 2+2, 2+1+1 or 1+1+1+1.)	4	Possible answers include: ▶ the quite aggressive, forceful tone of 'Hey, watch it! Chuckit!' ▶ Alan knows he's 'speaking out of turn', but is prepared this time to stand up to Phil ▶ (for Alan) the use of 'poor little bastard' shows how angry he is, trying to make Phil see how awful things are going to be for Hector ▶ he reels off what is going to happen to Hector ('thinking … he really does cut a dash … he'll probably stop off … doff the coat and hat') to paint a full scenario of Hector's humiliation as a result of Phil's behaviour ▶ the rather extreme 'she'll wet herself' shows just how disastrous he thinks Phil's behaviour is ▶ contempt in 'you and your crummy friend' ▶ Phil's response is couched in mock public school language, implying that the ethics of the public school don't operate here ▶ refers to Alan as 'Steerforth Minor', reducing Alan to a public school stereotype (with the added barb of 'Minor') ▶ throws Alan's words 'poor little bastard' back at him, as if to say 'don't you dare call him that' ▶ claims he and Spanky have some sort of right to humiliate Hector, as if there are situations Alan could never understand ▶ Alan has the staying power to come back with 'More than a bit', showing he doesn't accept Phil's argument.

Question number	Question text	Marks available	Commentary, hints and tips
4	By referring to this extract and to elsewhere in the play, discuss the importance of the conflict between Phil and Alan in exploring at least one theme in the play. You can answer in bullet points in this final question, or write a number of linked statements.	10	Up to 2 marks can be achieved for identifying elements of commonality as identified in the question, i.e. how conflict between Phil and Alan is important in exploring a theme. A further 2 marks can be achieved for reference to the extract given. 6 additional marks can be gained for discussion of similar references to at least one other part of the text by the author. In practice this means: Identification of commonality. (1+1) Phil and Alan conflict over class and work ethic and the bullying of other characters. (1) While Alan is usually fair and reasonable, Phil is temperamental. (1) From the extract: 2 marks for detailed/insightful comment plus quotation/reference; 1 mark for more basic comment plus quotation/reference; 0 marks for quotation/reference alone. 2 marks only for discussion of extract. In this extract the conflict between Phil and Alan demonstrates the different values they hold in terms of making a fool of (or bullying) other people. Alan thinks that Phil's behaviour towards Hector is unfair, whereas Phil sees it as amusing. (2) From at least one other part of the text as above for up to 6 marks. Possible references include: ▶ Alan is the butt of many of Phil's jokes and sarcasm, providing much of the humour of the play and helping to characterise Phil as a spokesman for rebellious youth ▶ Alan represents the successful, privileged middle class that Phil despises, is part of the class system which the play explores through Phil's sense of alienation and unfair treatment ▶ Alan is the antithesis of Phil in terms of work ethic, conventional manners, respect for 'superiors', often causing the audience to question the validity and sincerity of Phil's extreme opinions.

Question number	Question text	Marks available	Commentary, hints and tips
5	Look at lines 1–9. By referring to at least two aspects of character, explain what impressions are created of Jenny in these lines. 2 marks may be awarded for detailed/insightful comment plus quotation/reference; 1 mark for more basic comment plus quotation/reference; 0 marks for quotation/reference alone. (Marks may be awarded 2+1 or 1+1+1.)	3	Possible answers include: ▶ her appearance (make-up, clothing, hair) suggests someone rather brazen, shameless, unconcerned with appearances ▶ 'Leave me go' suggests defiance, aggression, no fear of father ▶ *shakes herself free* suggests independence, lack of respect for father ▶ *glaring at each other* suggests she is strong-willed, not intimidated by her father ▶ '… in front o ma friend' suggests concern for status, lack of concern for father's point of view, perhaps taunting him with unknown 'friend' ▶ 'nane o your business', 'Nane o your damned interferin business' suggest prepared to insult, defy her father, use provocative language ▶ 'I'm grown up noo' suggests she is assertive, tired of being treated like a child ▶ 'An I tellt ye!' suggests anger in her voice, standing up for herself.
6	Look at lines 11–21. By referring to at least two features, analyse how a dramatic conflict between John and Jenny is created. 2 marks may be awarded for detailed/insightful comment plus quotation/reference; 1 mark for more basic comment plus quotation/reference; 0 marks for quotation/reference alone. (Marks may be awarded 2+2, 2+1+1 or 1+1+1+1.)	4	Possible answers include: ▶ the fact that all the speeches in these lines are short and aggressive, frequently indicated by use of exclamation marks ▶ John grabs her – physical hostility ▶ the aggression in 'Where wis ye? Answer me!' – harsh question and command ▶ Jenny's sullen, minimal response 'At the pickshers' ▶ John's relentless demand for more information (to begin with he wanted to know where she was, now it's where she was after that) ▶ her behaviour when he lets her go – 'flops' suggesting lack of respect; *glaring sullenly* showing her antagonism; *rubbing her shoulder* to remind John (and the audience) of his manhandling of her ▶ John, with both questions answered, presses on with dismissive comment about her friend – 'yon' sounds contemptuous ▶ Jenny's provocative response 'That's a peety. I dae.' ▶ John resorts to insulting language: 'Ye impident little bitch!' ▶ the open threat of more violence: 'tak ma belt tae ye' ▶ Jenny's dismissive, sneering, challenging, defiant 'Jist you try it!'.

Question number	Question text	Marks available	Commentary, hints and tips
7	Look at lines 22–27. By referring to at least two examples, analyse how dialogue and/or stage directions are used to convey John's anger. 2 marks may be awarded for detailed/insightful comment plus quotation/reference; 1 mark for more basic comment plus quotation/reference; 0 marks for quotation/reference alone. (Marks may be awarded 2+1 or 1+1+1.)	3	Possible answers include: ▶ 'paint smeared' – he belittles her appearance, 'paint' instead of 'make-up' suggesting garish, unsophisticated; 'smeared' suggesting something messy, unattractive ▶ 'a ower yer face' – as if she has applied it randomly, made herself look hideous ▶ 'Look at yersel!' – antagonistic exclamation, implying she looks a mess ▶ *'drags … propels … holding … scrubs'* – violent, aggressive actions suggesting his temper ▶ 'There!' – a sort of triumphant declaration of his victory ▶ 'the colour God meant it tae be' – self-righteous, pompous moralising.
8	By referring to this extract and to elsewhere in the play, discuss the role of Jenny in *Men Should Weep*. You can answer in bullet points in this final question, or write a number of linked statements.	10	Up to 2 marks can be achieved for identifying elements of commonality as identified in the question, i.e. the role of Jenny in the play. A further 2 marks can be achieved for reference to the extract given. 6 additional marks can be gained for discussion of similar references to at least one other part of the text by the author. In practice this means: Identification of commonality. (1+1) Jenny is characterised as a rebel, an independent spirit (1), not prepared to put up with poverty and degradation. (1) From the extract: 2 marks for detailed/insightful comment plus quotation/reference; 1 mark for more basic comment plus quotation/reference; 0 marks for quotation/reference alone. 2 marks only for discussion of extract. In this extract we can see Jenny's independent spirit as she argues with her father that it is 'nane of (his) damned interferin business' where she has been. (1) We see Jenny does as she wants and is trying to make the most of her youth as she has been out late enjoying herself (we assume). (1) From at least one other part of the text as above for up to 6 marks.

Question number	Question text	Marks available	Commentary, hints and tips
8 (continued)			Possible references include: ▶ she is structurally important: her three appearances (arriving home late; leaving; returning with offer of money) are key moments in the play and in the development of John and Maggie's relationship ▶ she is prepared at an early stage to challenge her parents' authority ▶ her assertion of independence by giving up her job and then by leaving home is an important strand in the theme of the changing roles of men and women at the time ▶ she is the one who points out most forcefully the squalor in which they live ▶ her successful challenge to her father's refusal to accept tainted money at the end of the play is an important catalyst for Maggie's change of viewpoint ▶ the mixed emotions she brings out in John serve to show what a confused, weak character he is ▶ her capacity for kindness and decency at the end are part of the healing process in the family.

Part B – Scottish Text – Prose

Text 1 – Prose – *Mother and Son* by Iain Crichton Smith

Question number	Question text	Marks available	Commentary, hints and tips
9	Look at lines 1–7. By referring to at least two examples, analyse how the writer creates a hostile atmosphere. 2 marks may be awarded for detailed/ insightful comment plus quotation/ reference; 1 mark for more basic comment plus quotation/reference; 0 marks for quotation/reference alone. (Marks may be awarded 2+2, 2+1+1 or 1+1+1+1.)	4	Possible answers include: ▶ 'clothes were dripping' suggests he is completely drenched, in great discomfort ▶ 'streaming down his cheeks' suggests an extreme amount which he is unable to control ▶ 'reddened by the wind and the rain' suggests he has suffered at the hands of the weather ▶ 'in partial darkness' suggests gloomy, a little forbidding ▶ 'the daylight was hooded' suggests deliberate attempt to block out natural light ▶ 'shivered slightly' suggests discomfort, a hint of premonition ▶ 'a cold, dismal afternoon' suggests physical discomfort ▶ 'weather was extraordinarily bad' suggests extremes of unpleasant weather ▶ 'monotonous and uncomfortable' suggests tedious, unrewarding, disagreeable work.

Question number	Question text	Marks available	Commentary, hints and tips
10	Look at lines 8–17. Analyse how the writer's use of language shows two sides to the son's personality. For full marks, both sides need to be covered but not necessarily in equal measure. 2 marks may be awarded for detailed/insightful comment plus quotation/reference; 1 mark for more basic comment plus quotation/reference; 0 marks for quotation/reference alone. (Marks may be awarded 2+2, 2+1+1 or 1+1+1+1.)	4	Possible answers include: **Positive, gentle side:** ▸ 'handsome face' suggests physical attractiveness ▸ 'smooth' suggests gentle, appealing ▸ 'good-looking face' suggests warmth, appeal ▸ 'wide blue eyes' suggests openness, honesty ▸ 'deep and unquestioning' suggests calm and trusting, decent. **Negative, menacing side:** ▸ 'petulant' suggests moody, petty ▸ 'something childish about it' suggests undeveloped, lack of maturity, possibly irrational ▸ 'stolid' suggests impassive, slow-witted ▸ 'dangerous and irresponsible' suggests potential for reckless, damaging behaviour ▸ 'cursed' suggests roughness, anger ▸ 'impatiently' suggests irritability, hint of aggression.
11	Look at lines 18–22. Analyse how the writer creates a vivid impression of the room. 2 marks may be awarded for detailed/insightful comment plus quotation/reference; 1 mark for more basic comment plus quotation/reference; 0 marks for quotation/reference alone. (Marks may be awarded 2 or 1+1.)	2	Possible answers include: ▸ 'dull yellow' suggests gloomy, dismal ▸ repetition of 'numerous … numerous' suggests it is over-crowded, cluttered, untidy ▸ 'some whole, some broken' suggests disorder, lack of care ▸ 'dog … as if searching for crumbs' creates a rather melancholy, pathetic picture ▸ 'linoleum looked a bit worn' suggests either poverty or lack of care ▸ 'soiled pillows' suggests lack of hygiene, lack of care ▸ 'some dark, rough material' suggests plain, uncomfortable (unidentifiable other than as 'some').
12	By referring to this extract and to at least one other story by Iain Crichton Smith, discuss how he creates complex central characters in his stories. You can answer in bullet points in this final question, or write a number of linked statements.	10	Up to 2 marks can be achieved for identifying elements of commonality as identified in the question, i.e. how Crichton Smith creates complex central characters in his stories. A further 2 marks can be achieved for reference to the extract given. 6 additional marks can be gained for discussion of similar references to at least one other short story by the author. In practice this means: Identification of commonality. (1+1)

Question number	Question text	Marks available	Commentary, hints and tips
12 *(continued)*			Crichton Smith's characters tend to be stuck in situations that they want to escape from (1) and this makes them behave and react in complex ways. (1)
			From the extract: 2 marks for detailed/ insightful comment plus quotation/reference; 1 mark for more basic comment plus quotation/reference; 0 marks for quotation/ reference alone.
			2 marks only for discussion of extract.
			This extract reveals that although the son is downtrodden but has a sense of duty in being home, he is also possibly 'dangerous and irresponsible' as seen later in the story. (2)
			From at least one other short story as above for up to 6 marks.
			Possible references include:
			▸ *The Telegram* – fat woman: narrow-minded, insular, no ambition, dislike of thin woman's airs, capable of deep sympathy when it seems other woman will receive telegram; thin woman: sacrifices for her son, aspirational, contempt for other women in village
			▸ *The Red Door* – Murdo: conforms unquestioningly to expectations; begins to sense the dullness of his life and questions his quality of life, sees the red door as a symbol of change, associates it with Mary, makes bold decision to seek her out
			▸ *Home* – man: almost childish enthusiasm for revisiting former home; naive memories of the place and the people, attempts to fit in with current residents, realises he is out of place, at end is seen as comfortable among the well-off; woman: no interest in reliving the past, sees it differently from her husband, knows where 'home' is.

Text 2 – Prose – *The Eye of the Hurricane* by George Mackay Brown

Question number	Question text	Marks available	Commentary, hints and tips
13	By referring to the whole extract, analyse how the Captain tries to convince the narrator to buy him alcohol. 2 marks may be awarded for detailed/insightful comment plus quotation/reference; 1 mark for more basic comment plus quotation/reference; 0 marks for quotation/reference alone. (Marks may be awarded 2+2, 2+1+1 or 1+1+1+1.)	4	Possible answers include: ▸ very matter-of-fact opening ('Now, Barclay, about this cold of mine') tries to convince Barclay that he just needs alcohol for his cold ▸ 'That little bitch' disparages Miriam early on, an attempt to neutralise her influence on the narrator, to get him 'on-side' ▸ 'can't do a thing about it' tells narrator that his drinking is not something he can control, claims it's a natural phenomenon which has to be faced up to ▸ addresses him like teacher/pupil: 'Do you understand that, Barclay?' ▸ 'I thought writers were supposed to understand things' – flatters the narrator with a reference to his writing ▸ ingratiates himself with the narrator ('I like you. I'm very glad you're living in this house.') ▸ uses an elaborate seagoing metaphor to justify asking narrator to help ▸ 'I'm the skipper of this ship' – asserts his dominant role as 'skipper' ▸ tries to make it simple: 'And the first thing I want you to do …' ▸ 'next you will pay me four pounds – resorts to open threat of raising rent, evicting him.
14	Look at lines 18–21. By referring to at least two examples, analyse how the narrator uses imagery in these lines to explain his views on charity. 2 marks may be awarded for detailed/insightful comment plus quotation/reference; 1 mark for more basic comment plus quotation/reference; 0 marks for quotation/reference alone. (Marks may be awarded 2+2, 2+1+1 or 1+1+1+1.)	4	Possible answers include: ▸ 'Charity is no hard-minted currency … a shilling here and a sovereign there': it is not a simple matter of tangible coinage, cash to be handed out as and when you wish ▸ 'it is the oil and wine that drop uncertainly through the fingers': it is like liquid, not easily defined, not easily controlled ▸ 'the wounds of the world': the idea that suffering can happen at any time in any place ▸ 'wherever the roads of pity and suffering cross': compares pain and the compassion to alleviate it to roads which, when they intersect, allow 'charity' to be delivered.

Question number	Question text	Marks available	Commentary, hints and tips
15	Explain what the last paragraph (lines 26–27) suggests about the narrator's feelings for the Captain. 2 marks may be awarded for detailed/insightful comment plus quotation/reference; 1 mark for more basic comment plus quotation/reference; 0 marks for quotation/reference alone. (Marks may be awarded 2 or 1+1.)	2	Possible answers include: ▶ pity – sees him as a lonely, lost figure, caught up in his own fantasies ▶ concern – the constant pacing must be indicative of mental struggle.
16	By referring to this extract and to at least one other story by Mackay Brown, discuss how he creates confrontations between characters. You can answer in bullet points in this final question, or write a number of linked statements.	10	Up to 2 marks can be achieved for identifying elements of commonality as identified in the question, i.e. how Mackay Brown creates confrontations between characters. A further 2 marks can be achieved for reference to the extract given. 6 additional marks can be gained for discussion of similar references to at least one other short story by the author. In practice this means: Identification of commonality. (1+1) Characters in Mackay Brown's stories confront each other often, which adds tension to and/or explanation of the stories. (1) These confrontations can be from the past or the present and are sometimes with characters who are 'faceless' (i.e. the radio and Andrina). (1) From the extract: 2 marks for detailed/insightful comment plus quotation/reference; 1 mark for more basic comment plus quotation/reference; 0 marks for quotation/reference alone. 2 marks only for discussion of extract. Conflict is created in this extract between the Captain and Mr Barclay. The Captain uses a number of techniques to try to persuade Barclay to buy him alcohol: feigning illness, flattery and finally punishment. This shows the desperation the character has been driven to on the death of his wife. (2) From at least one other short story as above for up to 6 marks. Possible references include: ▶ *Andrina* – between Torvald and Sigrid in the past; Torvald is forced to confront his own past

Question number	Question text	Marks available	Commentary, hints and tips
16 (continued)			▸ *A Time To Keep* – Bill has confrontations with the factor, with Ingi's father, with the men from Two Waters ▸ *The Wireless Set* – Betsy 'confronts' Lord Haw-Haw

Text 3 – Prose – *Dr Jekyll and Mr Hyde* by Robert Louis Stevenson

Question number	Question text	Marks available	Commentary, hints and tips
17	Look at lines 1–6. Analyse how the writer's language presents a positive impression of Jekyll. 2 marks may be awarded for detailed/insightful comment plus quotation/reference; 1 mark for more basic comment plus quotation/reference; 0 marks for quotation/reference alone. (Marks may be awarded 2 or 1+1.)	2	Possible answers include: ▸ 'well-made' suggests a pleasing, regular appearance ▸ 'smooth-faced' suggests a gentle, mild appearance ▸ 'capacity and kindness' suggests he is accomplished, benevolent, caring ▸ 'cherished' suggests he looks favourably on the other man ▸ 'sincere' suggests he is open, free from any malice ▸ 'warm affection' suggests he is friendly and kind.
18	Look at lines 7–17. By referring to at least two examples, analyse how the tension between Utterson and Jekyll is conveyed. 2 marks may be awarded for detailed/insightful comment plus quotation/reference; 1 mark for more basic comment plus quotation/reference; 0 marks for quotation/reference alone. (Marks may be awarded 2+2, 2+1+1 or 1+1+1+1.)	4	Possible answers include: ▸ 'distasteful' suggests Jekyll reacts against Utterson's mention of the will ▸ the attempted humour of 'you are unfortunate in such a client' suggests he is trying to laugh it off, to defuse any animosity ▸ the comments on Lanyon suggest he is trying to deflect Utterson away from the will ▸ 'pursued … ruthlessly disregarding' shows that Utterson will not be deflected, is determined to make his point ▸ 'a trifle sharply' suggests Jekyll is irritated at Utterson's doggedness ▸ the tone of 'You have told me so' is a bit of a put-down, suggests annoyance at the repetition ▸ 'I tell you so again' suggests Utterson is determined to raise the subject anyway ▸ the change in Jekyll's expression ('grew pale … blackness about his eyes') suggests resentment at Utterson's mention of Hyde ▸ 'I do not care to hear more' is a firm attempt to close the subject ▸ 'I thought we had agreed to drop' is a direct challenge.

Question number	Question text	Marks available	Commentary, hints and tips
19	Look at lines 18–29. By referring to at least two examples, analyse how the writer reveals aspects of the relationship between Jekyll and Utterson. 2 marks may be awarded for detailed/insightful comment plus quotation/reference; 1 mark for more basic comment plus quotation/reference; 0 marks for quotation/reference alone. (Marks may be awarded 2+2, 2+1+1 or 1+1+1+1.)	4	Possible answers include: ▸ Utterson's desire to help his friend is shown by his being prepared to continue despite Jekyll's objections ▸ Jekyll's defence that 'You do not understand my position' appeals for understanding without the need to explain ▸ 'cannot be mended by talking' seems to imply that although they would normally discuss matters, this is now not possible ▸ Utterson appeals to the history of their friendship ('You know me …') and offers confidentiality ('I am a man to be trusted') suggesting he thinks there is a special relationship between them ▸ Utterson offers Jekyll the chance to solve the problem ('Make a clean breast … get you out of it') showing a depth of friendship ▸ Jekyll asserts his belief in his friend's decency ('downright good of you') ▸ Jekyll attempts to reassure Utterson that he is in control of the situation ('I can be rid of Mr Hyde') ▸ Jekyll pleads for trust from Utterson ('give you my hand') ▸ Jekyll hopes his friend will accept his word that it is a 'private matter' and asks for his discretion.
20	By referring to this extract and to elsewhere in the novel, discuss how Stevenson presents the character of Henry Jekyll. You can answer in bullet points in this final question, or write a number of linked statements.	10	Up to 2 marks can be achieved for identifying elements of commonality as identified in the question, i.e. how Stevenson presents the character of Henry Jekyll. A further 2 marks can be achieved for reference to the extract given. 6 additional marks can be gained for discussion of similar references to at least one other part of the text by the author. In practice this means: Identification of commonality. (1+1) Jekyll is a character torn between his 'good' and 'bad' sides. (1) Stevenson presents this by creating a character who attempts to split off the 'bad' but it is a disaster and Jekyll's sin becomes an addiction and the 'evil' side takes over. (1) From the extract: 2 marks for detailed/insightful comment plus quotation/reference; 1 mark for more basic comment plus quotation/reference; 0 marks for quotation/reference alone.

Question number	Question text	Marks available	Commentary, hints and tips
20 (continued)			2 marks only for discussion of extract. This extract presents the foolishness of Henry Jekyll's character. He thinks he has found a way round Hyde taking control by leaving him everything in his will, but claims at the end he can be 'rid of Hyde' whenever he chooses. Later in the novel we see this is not true. (2) From at least one other part of the text as above for up to 6 marks. Possible references include: ▶ born to a good family and well educated ▶ the wealthy and respectable doctor and experimental scientist ▶ a sociable person with a circle of friends from similar backgrounds ▶ appears to others as moral and decent, engaging in charity work and enjoying a reputation as a courteous and genial host ▶ thinks that as a youth he was perhaps too light-hearted, confesses to youthful indiscretions ▶ becomes interested in and then obsessed with the idea of 'duality' ▶ admits that Hyde emerged when he was feeling pride and arrogance ▶ comes to realise that Hyde possesses a force more powerful than he originally believed ▶ dies in despair, not knowing what his fate is.

Text 4 – Prose – *Sunset Song* by Lewis Grassic Gibbon

Question number	Question text	Marks available	Commentary, hints and tips
21	Look at lines 1–7. By referring to at least two examples, analyse how the writer conveys the strength of Rob's feelings about language. 2 marks may be awarded for detailed/insightful comment plus quotation/reference; 1 mark for more basic comment plus quotation/reference; 0 marks for quotation/reference alone. (Marks may be awarded 2+2, 2+1+1 or 1+1+1+1.)	4	Possible answers include: ▶ 'shame'/'shamed' suggests that non-users of Scots/Scotch are a source of dishonour, humiliation ▶ 'the split-tongued sourocks' suggests a contemptuous attitude, accusation of hypocrisy ▶ 'Every damned little narrow dowped rat' is all-inclusive condemnation of English-speakers ('Every'); contemptible ('damned'); insubstantial, lacking substance ('little', 'narrow dowped'); loathsome, to be looked down on ('rat') ▶ 'put on (the English)' suggests the use of English is forced, affected, pretentious ▶ 'thin bit scraichs' suggests he thinks of English as weak, anaemic, shrill, strident ▶ 'You can tell me, man …' Rob's tone is quite belligerent, challenging Gordon to dare to disagree.

Question number	Question text	Marks available	Commentary, hints and tips
22	Look at lines 8–14. Explain how the writer conveys in these lines the harshness of life working the land. 2 marks may be awarded for detailed/insightful comment plus quotation/reference; 1 mark for more basic comment plus quotation/reference; 0 marks for quotation/reference alone. (Marks may be awarded 2 or 1+1.)	2	Possible answers include: ▸ repetition ('coarse, coarse', 'work, work, work', and 'chave, chave, chave') stresses the amount of effort required, echoes the repetitive nature of the work ▸ 'from the blink of day till the fall of night' conveys the extreme length of the working day ▸ 'soss and sotter' – the alliteration/onomatopoeia emphasise the filth, unpleasantness of the work.
23	Look at lines 15–21. By referring to at least two examples, analyse how the writer's use of language conveys the conflicting views about 'scientific' farming methods. 2 marks may be awarded for detailed/insightful comment plus quotation/reference; 1 mark for more basic comment plus quotation/reference; 0 marks for quotation/reference alone. (Marks may be awarded 2+2, 2+1+1 or 1+1+1+1.)	4	Possible answers include: ▸ there are four different (reported) speakers involved: Cuddiestoun, banker's son, Chae, Long Rob; shows range of views being put forward ▸ sentence openers ('Syne … So … But … And') indicate different points of view being proposed ▸ 'childe' suggests contempt for banker's son, suggests naive, inexperienced ▸ 'clutter of machines' presents machinery as untidy, chaotic, not effective ▸ *the best friend of man* suggests human quality, of extreme usefulness ▸ Chae's forceful tone: *'Damn't, no …'* ▸ Rob's mocking, humorous tone: 'damned machine that would muck you a pigsty even though they all turned socialist to-morrow'.
24	By referring to this extract and to elsewhere in the novel, discuss how *Sunset Song* celebrates the traditional way of life. You can answer in bullet points in this final question, or write a number of linked statements.	10	Up to 2 marks can be achieved for identifying elements of commonality as identified in the question, i.e. how *Sunset Song* celebrates the traditional way of life. A further 2 marks can be achieved for reference to the extract given. 6 additional marks can be awarded for discussion of similar references to at least one other part of the text by the author. In practice this means: Identification of commonality. (1+1) *Sunset Song* explores how a traditional way of life can be celebrated through language, farming and community. (1) The challenge to these celebrations arrives in the name of progress and change. (1)

Question number	Question text	Marks available	Commentary, hints and tips
24 (continued)			From the extract: 2 marks for detailed/insightful comment plus quotation/reference; 1 mark for more basic comment plus quotation/reference; 0 marks for quotation/reference alone.
			2 marks only for discussion of extract.
			This extract examines the celebration of traditional Scottish language. (1) Rob claims people should be proud to speak, 'Scotch', as it has words that cannot be translated to English, such as 'gloaming'. (1)
			From at least one other part of the text as above for up to 6 marks.
			Possible references include:
			▶ the closeness of the community, providing mutual support (e.g. the fire at Peesie's Knapp, the funeral, the wedding, Hogmanay, the dedication of the war memorial)
			▶ the centrality of the land and the seasons
			▶ Chris's decision to stay on the farm; her attachment to the land
			▶ the importance of the Standing Stones as symbols of permanence
			▶ the impact of the War – on individuals (e.g. Ewan) and on the land (e.g. the stripping away of the forests).

Text 5 – Prose – *The Cone-Gatherers* by Robin Jenkins

Question number	Question text	Marks available	Commentary, hints and tips
25	Look at lines 1–7. Analyse how the sentence structure in these lines helps to convey how Calum is feeling. 2 marks may be awarded for detailed/insightful comment plus quotation/reference; 1 mark for more basic comment plus quotation/reference; 0 marks for quotation/reference alone. (Marks may be awarded 2 or 1+1.)	2	Possible answers include: ▶ the balancing around the semicolon helps to convey the idea that Calum has changed from being a beater to thinking of himself as a deer ▶ the sentence beginning 'He could not, however …' serves to introduce the contrast between the deer's agility and Calum's clumsiness ▶ the structure of the sentence beginning 'He fell and rose again …' imitates the frantic, headlong action it describes with a list of movements ('fell … rose … avoided … collide'); it also lists all the things Calum feels are ignoring him and the deer, so many that he feels completely cut off from help or sympathy.

Question number	Question text	Marks available	Commentary, hints and tips
26	Look at lines 8–21. By referring to at least two examples, analyse how the writer's use of language in these lines creates a sense of 'commotion' (line 10). 2 marks may be awarded for detailed/insightful comment plus quotation/reference; 1 mark for more basic comment plus quotation/reference; 0 marks for quotation/reference alone. (Marks may be awarded 2+2, 2+1+1 or 1+1+1+1.)	4	Possible answers include: ▸ 'barked fiercely' suggests harsh, loud, aggressive noise ▸ 'rush into the danger' suggests a reckless dash ▸ 'roared to him' suggests an impassioned, panicked cry ▸ 'resounded with their exultant shouts' suggests an echoing effect, all the calls mixing together ▸ 'bellowed' suggests loud, deep, fanatical ▸ 'bawled' suggests frantic, hysterical ▸ the list of adjectives, 'silent, desperate, and heroic', suggests the extent of their plight ▸ 'guns banged' suggests loud, aggressive noise, associated with death/violence ▸ 'wails of lament' suggests high-pitched exclamations of mourning ▸ 'dashed on at demented speed' suggests reckless speed, desperate, almost out of control ▸ 'shot out' suggests a sudden, dramatic appearance ▸ 'a deer screaming' suggests high-pitched, suffering, in pain ▸ 'scrabbling about' suggests agitated, distressed movement ▸ 'feverishly reloading' suggests excited, tense movement ▸ the rather paradoxical 'Screaming in sympathy' suggests the confusion at the scene ▸ the list of actions 'flung … clasped … tried to comfort' suggests a rush of actions ▸ 'flung' suggests acting with passion, no thought of consequences ▸ 'dragged him about with it in its mortal agony' suggests frantic movement back and forth at the moment of death.
27	Look at lines 22–30. By referring to at least two examples, analyse how the writer makes the reader aware in these lines of Duror's state of mind. 2 marks may be awarded for detailed/insightful comment plus quotation/reference; 1 mark for more basic comment plus quotation/reference; 0 marks for quotation/reference alone. (Marks may be awarded 2+2, 2+1+1 or 1+1+1+1.)	4	Possible answers include: ▸ the contrast between the immobility of Forgan, Roderick and Lady Runcie-Campbell, and Duror 'leaping out of the wood' like something possessed, emphasises Duror's disturbed state of mind ▸ the paradoxical 'berserk joy' depicts him as out of control, unaware of what his real emotions are ▸ the blunt abruptness of the simple sentence 'There was a knife in his hand' focuses attention on it and foreshadows the violent act he is about to carry out

Question number	Question text	Marks available	Commentary, hints and tips
27 (continued)			▸ 'he never heard' suggests he is switched off, so caught up in his emotions that he cannot process the sound of her words ▸ 'Rushing … he threw … with furious force, … seizing … cut its throat savagely' combine to depict someone in an uncontrolled, violent bloodlust, acting with tremendous strength and energy ▸ the ambiguity of his pose after the kill, not proud, but apparently grieving, suggests a confusion in his own mind ▸ clinging onto the knife suggests he is in shock, doesn't know what to do.
28	By referring to this extract and to elsewhere in the novel, discuss how the writer presents the character of Calum. You can answer in bullet points in this final question, or write a number of linked statements.	10	Up to 2 marks can be achieved for identifying elements of commonality as identified in the question, i.e. How Jenkins presents the character of Calum. A further 2 marks can be achieved for reference to the extract given. 6 additional marks can be gained for discussion of similar references to at least one other part of the text by the author. In practice this means: Identification of commonality. (1+1) Calum is the personification of innocence (1) and although he is physically deformed, he has inner beauty. (1) From the extract: 2 marks for detailed/insightful comment plus quotation/reference; 1 mark for more basic comment plus quotation/reference; 0 marks for quotation/reference alone. 2 marks only for discussion of extract. Calum is presented here as a very caring character as he tries to help the deer as it is dying. (1) This shows us Calum's innocence and empathy with the deer. It is as if he is blinded by the deer's pain and can see nothing else. (1) From at least one other part of the text as above for up to 6 marks. Possible references include: ▸ his identification/empathy with nature (the rabbit, the chaffinches) ▸ his agility in the trees and love of the freedom and the solitude there ▸ his trust in Neil

Question number	Question text	Marks available	Commentary, hints and tips
28 (continued)			▸ his lack of malice towards the upper classes (in contrast to Neil) ▸ his discomfort in company (the pub) ▸ his behaviour at the deer drive ▸ his childlike desires (the doll) ▸ his inability to comprehend Duror's malice ▸ his Christ-like death.

Part C – Scottish Text – Poetry

Text 1 – Poetry – *Tam o' Shanter* by Robert Burns

Question number	Question text	Marks available	Commentary, hints and tips
29	Look at lines 1–8. By referring to at least two examples, analyse how the extended simile in these lines creates a vivid picture of what is happening. 2 marks may be awarded for detailed/insightful comment plus quotation/reference; 1 mark for more basic comment plus quotation/reference; 0 marks for quotation/reference alone. (Marks may be awarded 2+2, 2+1+1 or 1+1+1+1.)	4	Possible answers include: ▸ 'As bees …' suggests a sense of outrage, a need to escape assault; idea of the small and vulnerable ('bees') being threatened by something larger ('herds') ▸ 'As open pussie's …' suggests a sudden ('pop') attack close at hand ('before their nose') which causes extreme alarm ▸ 'As eager …' suggests a concerted response to a rallying cry, one being chased by many.
30	Look at lines 9–26. By referring to at least two examples, analyse how Burns makes this part of the poem dramatic. 2 marks may be awarded for detailed/insightful comment plus quotation/reference; 1 mark for more basic comment plus quotation/reference; 0 marks for quotation/reference alone. (Marks may be awarded 2+2, 2+1+1 or 1+1+1+1.)	4	Possible answers include: ▸ the pause to lecture Tam creates tension by delaying the continuation of the story ▸ the direct address to Meg ('do thy speedy utmost') reminds reader of the urgency involved ▸ setting a sort of target for Meg/Tam ('There at them …') sets up the dramatic chase, creating uncertainty about their fate ▸ idea of Nannie being way out in front of the other witches creates fear that she will catch Tam ▸ referring to Maggie as 'noble' increases the sense of good versus evil in the chase ▸ the frantic efforts by Nannie ('flew at Tam wi' furious ettle') increase the tension ▸ 'But little wist she …' – a last-minute turn of fortune, the hero has a trick up his sleeve ▸ 'Ae spring' – a single leap, one last final effort ▸ 'But left behind …' – the sacrifice involved in saving her master.

Question number	Question text	Marks available	Commentary, hints and tips
31	Look at lines 27–32. Analyse how far these lines can be read as a warning to the reader. 2 marks may be awarded for detailed/insightful comment plus quotation/reference; 1 mark for more basic comment plus quotation/reference; 0 marks for quotation/reference alone. (Marks may be awarded 2 or 1+1.)	2	Possible answers include: ▶ not serious: it's just a conventional conclusion, with the expected element of moralising and instruction ('take heed … Think … Remember'); it can't really be a 'tale o' truth' so any resultant moral isn't convincing; it's just a bit of fun, developing the idea of men as in need of guidance, playing on superstitions of witchcraft; the way that 'tale' puns on 'tail' (line 24) can be seen as making light of the whole idea ▶ serious: it warns reasonably enough about over-indulgence (in drink or lascivious thoughts), of paying a high price for unwise behaviour; it is addressed only to men, the weaker sex as far as irresponsible behaviour is concerned.
32	Referring to this poem and at least one other poem by Burns, discuss the way his poetry passes judgement on people and/or institutions. You can answer in bullet points in this final question, or write a number of linked statements.	10	Up to 2 marks can be achieved for identifying elements of commonality as identified in the question, i.e. how Burns's poetry passes judgement on people and/or institutions. A further 2 marks can be achieved for reference to the extract given. 6 additional marks can be gained for discussion of similar references to at least one other poem by the author. In practice this means: Identification of commonality. (1+1) Burns's poetry, through themes of morality and men's carelessness (1), passes judgement on foolish characters and/or attitudes to religion and nature. (1) From the extract: 2 marks for detailed/insightful comment plus quotation/reference; 1 mark for more basic comment plus quotation/reference; 0 marks for quotation/reference alone. 2 marks only for discussion of extract. *Tam o' Shanter* – passes judgement on men in general (and Tam in particular) for their drunkenness, their foolhardy behaviour when drunk, their easy attraction to a pretty woman. The extract warns men to 'remember Tam o' Shanter's mare when considering drink and women'. (2) From at least one other poem as above for up to 6 marks.

Question number	Question text	Marks available	Commentary, hints and tips
32 (continued)			Possible references include: ▶ *To a Mouse* – passes judgement on mankind in general for its careless attitude to nature and for its self-absorption ▶ *Holy Willie's Prayer* – passes judgement on Hamilton, on Holy Willie himself, on the Kirk in general ▶ *To a Louse* – passes judgement on the social pretensions of the woman in the church ▶ *A Poet's Welcome to his Love-Begotten Daughter* – passes judgement on the Kirk, on all who criticise him for fathering a child out of wedlock and on those who think he is not a loving father ▶ *A Red, Red Rose* – Burns (perhaps) passes judgement on the strength of his love.

Text 2 – Poetry – *Valentine* by Carol Ann Duffy

Question number	Question text	Marks available	Commentary, hints and tips
33	Look at lines 1–5. By referring to at least two examples, analyse how the poet's language in these lines creates a dramatic opening to the poem. 2 marks may be awarded for detailed/insightful comment plus quotation/reference; 1 mark for more basic comment plus quotation/reference; 0 marks for quotation/reference alone. (Marks may be awarded 2+2, 2+1+1 or 1+1+1+1.)	4	Possible answers include: ▶ starting with a negative 'Not a …' ▶ the abruptness of the minor sentence, which constitutes not just a line on its own but a stanza/verse paragraph ▶ the feeling that it is part of an ongoing conversation ▶ the bizarre idea of 'an onion' as a substitute for the conventional 'red rose' or 'satin heart' ▶ the use of present tense makes it immediate, direct ▶ series of short sentences sounds staccato, breathless ▶ 'moon wrapped in brown paper' suggests a startling contradiction ▶ comparison of 'light' to 'the careful undressing of love' is hard to fathom.
34	Look at lines 6–17. By referring to at least two examples, analyse how the poet's language in these lines describes love in an unusual way. 2 marks may be awarded for detailed/insightful comment plus quotation/reference; 1 mark for more basic comment plus quotation/reference; 0 marks for quotation/reference alone. (Marks may be awarded 2+2, 2+1+1 or 1+1+1+1.)	4	Possible answers include: ▶ 'blind you with tears' suggests the power of love to cause unhappiness ▶ 'a wobbling photo of grief' suggests the distorted view a victim of love may have ▶ repetition of 'It will …' suggests a relentlessness in love's power to hurt ▶ 'I am trying to be truthful' sounds like an assertion to an unheard listener who is trying to reject the speaker's claims ▶ the alliteration in 'a cute card or a kissogram' seems to be suggesting/mocking the childishness of the traditional message

Question number	Question text	Marks available	Commentary, hints and tips
34 (continued)			► 'fierce kiss' suggests the lingering aftertaste of the onion – the difficulty of escaping a relationship ► 'possessive' suggests jealousy/the desire to control ► juxtaposition of 'possessive' and 'faithful' undermines the normally positive view of commitment.
35	Look at lines 18–23. Analyse how the poet's language in these lines creates an unsettling mood. 2 marks may be awarded for detailed/insightful comment plus quotation/reference; 1 mark for more basic comment plus quotation/reference; 0 marks for quotation/reference alone. (Marks may be awarded 2 or 1+1.)	2	Possible answers include: ► the imperative 'Take it' suggests the speaker is overbearing, domineering ► 'shrink' suggests the restrictive, claustrophobic nature of marriage ► the comparison of the inner rings of an onion to a wedding ring suggests the constraining nature of marriage ► the positioning of 'Lethal' in a line of its own suggests the dangerous nature of love ► repetition and/or word choice of 'cling' suggests the possessive nature of love ► 'knife' suggests a threatening, violent, dangerous aspect to love ► the juxtaposition of 'fingers' and 'knife' suggests that something which should be gentle and loving (as in the caressing of the skin) has violent, destructive connotations.
36	By referring to this poem and to at least one other poem by Duffy, discuss her use of striking imagery. You can answer in bullet points in this final question, or write a number of linked statements.	10	Up to 2 marks can be achieved for identifying elements of commonality as identified in the question, i.e. how Duffy makes use of striking imagery. A further 2 marks can be achieved for reference to the extract given. 6 additional marks can be gained for discussion of similar references to at least one other poem by the author. In practice this means: Identification of commonality. (1+1) Duffy uses striking imagery in her poems to emphasise her characters' experiences. (1) These images help the reader appreciate the poet's ideas on the themes of childhood and love. (1) From the extract: 2 marks for detailed/insightful comment plus quotation/reference; 1 mark for more basic comment plus quotation/reference; 0 marks for quotation/reference alone. 2 marks only for discussion of extract.

Question number	Question text	Marks available	Commentary, hints and tips
36 (continued)			*Valentine* – several bizarre images to describe the negative power of love: 'blind you with tears like a lover', 'a wobbling photo of grief', with explanation. (2)
			From at least one other poem as above for up to 6 marks.
			Possible references include:
			▸ *In Mrs Tilscher's Class* – imagery: 'skittle of milk', 'laugh of a bell', 'glowed like a sweet shop', 'a xylophone's nonsense', 'commas into exclamation marks'
			▸ *Originally* – imagery: 'anxiety stirred like a loose tooth' to convey niggling worry in her mind, 'tongue/shedding its skin like a snake' to describe the slow change in accent
			▸ *Mrs Midas* – imagery: 'unwrapping each other, rapidly/like presents' to convey the passion in their previous life, 'amber eyes/ holding their pupils like flies' to suggest the horror of the dream
			▸ *The Way My Mother Speaks* – imagery: 'shallows of my breath', 'browsing for the right sky', 'a green erotic pond'
			▸ *War Photographer* – religious imagery in opening lines.

Text 3 – Poetry – *The Bargain* by Liz Lochhead

Question number	Question text	Marks available	Commentary, hints and tips
37	Look at lines 1–19. By referring to at least two examples, analyse how the poet's language in these lines conveys the uneasy atmosphere between the couple. 2 marks may be awarded for detailed/ insightful comment plus quotation/ reference; 1 mark for more basic comment plus quotation/reference; 0 marks for quotation/reference alone. (Marks may be awarded 2+2, 2+1+1 or 1+1+1+1.)	4	Possible answers include: ▸ 'queue' has connotations of delay, annoyance ▸ 'blue haze of hot fat' suggests unhealthy, unpleasant, smothering, slightly dangerous ▸ 'grit/our teeth' – wordplay suggests tension, irritation in the relationship ▸ alliteration in 'grit … granules' suggests harsh, annoying ▸ 'I keep/losing you and finding you' – double meaning: literal at the market, metaphorically suggests a troubled, on-off relationship ▸ 'you thumb … I rub' suggests activities which, though similar, are separate ▸ the two items ('manuals for/primary teachers' and 'dusty Chinese saucer') seem to vie with each other for uselessness, suggesting that the looking is mostly a displacement activity ▸ 'till the gilt shows through' – image of getting to the reality of something + pun on 'guilt', suggesting her feelings

Question number	Question text	Marks available	Commentary, hints and tips
37 (continued)			▶ tone of 'Oh come on' suggests irritation, impatience ▶ 'trap' suggests being tricked, forced ▶ stallholder's comments seem to reflect on the couple's uneasiness, with mention of 'death' and 'doldrums', which could equally apply to the relationship.
38	Look at lines 20–29. By referring to at least two examples, analyse how the poet's language in these lines conveys the bleak mood of the speaker. 2 marks may be awarded for detailed/insightful comment plus quotation/reference; 1 mark for more basic comment plus quotation/reference; 0 marks for quotation/reference alone. (Marks may be awarded 2+2, 2+1+1 or 1+1+1+1.)	4	Possible answers include: ▶ 'packing up time' suggests something coming to an end; literally the stallholders are packing up, but the relationship seems to be also at that stage ▶ 'the dark coming early' is both literal and metaphorical – a symbolic darkness falling on the relationship, with 'early' suggesting she thinks it is coming prematurely ▶ 'beady bag' is a curiously vague and inelegant way to describe the bag, perhaps suggesting she feels foolish for buying it ▶ 'maybe rosewood' suggests it may not be of any value ▶ 'the inlaid butterfly' – a living creature depicted as inanimate, symbolic of the fading relationship ▶ 'broken catch' symbolic of the broken relationship, whatever should hold it together ('the catch') is broken ▶ 'waistcoat that needs a stitch' suggests something needing repair, as does the relationship ▶ 'it just won't get' is pessimistically certain that no mending will happen ▶ the rather enigmatic book title, *Enquire Within – Upon Everything*, suggests that solutions to all problems can be easily found – something she knows in her heart is not true.
39	Look at lines 30–33. Analyse how the poet's language in these lines creates a conclusion you find either optimistic or pessimistic. 2 marks may be awarded for detailed/insightful comment plus quotation/reference; 1 mark for more basic comment plus quotation/reference; 0 marks for quotation/reference alone. (Marks may be awarded 2 or 1+1.)	2	Possible answers include: ▶ pessimistic: physical discomfort of the cold getting even worse suggests no improvement ▶ pessimistic: the lack of communication is a reflection of the emptiness in the relationship and/or the fact that they are only too aware of the problems, no need or desire to discuss them ▶ optimistic: 'I wish …' could be seen to have a positive tone, hoping that they might 'learn' ▶ either: the strong rhyme at end ('say … away') could suggest a harmonious, tidy conclusion or a sense of finality, drawing a veil over matters.

Question number	Question text	Marks available	Commentary, hints and tips
40	By referring to this poem and to at least one other poem by Lochhead, discuss how she explores the tension that can arise in relationships. You can answer in bullet points in this final question, or write a number of linked statements.	10	Up to 2 marks can be achieved for identifying elements of commonality as identified in the question, i.e. how Lochhead explores the tension that can arise in a relationship. A further 2 marks can be achieved for reference to the extract given. 6 additional marks can be gained for discussion of similar references to at least one other poem by the author. In practice this means: Identification of commonality. (1+1) Lochhead uses tension in her poems as a device to increase conflict between characters. (1) This often relates to problems in romantic relationships, be it between partners or family relationships. (1) From the extract: 2 marks for detailed/insightful comment plus quotation/reference; 1 mark for more basic comment plus quotation/reference; 0 marks for quotation/reference alone. 2 marks only for discussion of extract. *The Bargain* – tension (implicit and explicit) between speaker and partner throughout: 'There doesn't seem to be a lot to say'; the projection of the disintegrating relationship onto the weather and surroundings ('dark coming early' … 'raw cold gets colder'). (2) From at least one other poem as above for up to 6 marks. Possible references include: ▸ *Last Supper* – tension in the relationship ('betrayal with a kiss') leading to the bitchy discussion of the break-up 'among friends', and the implied repetition: 'go hunting again' ▸ *Box Room* – tension between the speaker and the boyfriend's mother – disguised by superficial politeness from mother and reticence/nervousness from speaker; tension and uncertainty in speaker's feeling for boyfriend (e.g. her rather sneering description of the books and the egg collection)

Question number	Question text	Marks available	Commentary, hints and tips
40 (continued)			▸ *My Rival's House* – tension between the speaker and her prospective mother-in-law due to her overprotectiveness of her son 'this son she bore … never can escape', 'thinks she means me well', 'She won't/ give up' ▸ *Revelation* – tension between innocence and experience; between male and female ▸ *View of Scotland/Love Poem* – some tension between speaker and mother in opening recollection; tension between past and present; between childhood beliefs and adult understanding.

Text 4 – Poetry – *Assisi* by Norman MacCaig

Question number	Question text	Marks available	Commentary, hints and tips
41	Look at lines 1–4. Analyse how the poet's use of sound in these lines enhances the description of the beggar. 2 marks may be awarded for detailed/ insightful comment plus quotation/ reference; 1 mark for more basic comment plus quotation/reference; 0 marks for quotation/reference alone. (Marks may be awarded 2 or 1+1.)	2	Possible answers include: ▸ the sibilance in 'sat, slumped' suggests lethargy, discomfort ▸ the long vowel sounds in 'sat, slumped' suggest heaviness, tiredness ▸ the onomatopoeic effect in 'slumped' to suggest heaviness, defeat, echoes of 'lump', 'dumped' ▸ the alliteration in 'tiny twisted' draws attention to the unpleasantness, ugliness ▸ the line break between 'which' and 'sawdust' creates a small dramatic pause before the horror of the description.
42	Look at lines 5–17. By referring to at least two examples, analyse how the poet creates an ironic tone in these lines. 2 marks may be awarded for detailed/ insightful comment plus quotation/ reference; 1 mark for more basic comment plus quotation/reference; 0 marks for quotation/reference alone. (Marks may be awarded 2+2, 2+1+1 or 1+1+1+1.)	4	Possible answers include: ▸ juxtaposition of grand church ('three tiers') with St Francis's reputation ('brother/ of the poor') and/or his simple lifestyle ('talker with birds') ▸ sardonic observation that the dwarf has an 'advantage' over St Francis, but only that he is 'not … dead yet' ▸ 'A priest explained …' – what might seem at first to be praise for/approval of the priest is undermined by the realisation that the 'goodness/of God' is not evident in the 'suffering' of the dwarf ▸ presenting himself as the detached observer with mock admiration for the priest's 'cleverness' ▸ if 'I understood' is read with emphasis on 'I', it might suggest the tourists and/or the priest didn't understand.

Question number	Question text	Marks available	Commentary, hints and tips
43	Look at lines 20–27. ('It was they … St Francis.') By referring to at least two examples, analyse how the poet's language develops the idea of the beggar as a 'ruined temple'. 2 marks may be awarded for detailed/insightful comment plus quotation/reference; 1 mark for more basic comment plus quotation/reference; 0 marks for quotation/reference alone. (Marks may be awarded 2+2, 2+1+1 or 1+1+1+1.)	4	Possible answers include: ▶ 'ruined' in the sense that he is physically deformed, a distortion of a so-called normal human being ▶ 'eyes/wept pus' – not shedding tears in the conventional way, but leaking infected fluid ▶ ugly sound of word 'pus' ▶ heavy sound of three stressed syllables ▶ 'back … higher/than his head' – distortion of the normal ▶ a 'temple' in the sense of something with deep religious significance, often of immense beauty ▶ despite all the unpleasant surface appearances, the dwarf is polite ('Grazie') ▶ his voice is compared with that of a child (innocent) speaking to its mother (Madonna and child idea) ▶ compared with a bird (nature, innocence) speaking to St Francis (icon of compassion, humility).
44	By referring to this poem and to at least one other by MacCaig, discuss his use of wry humour in his poetry. You can answer in bullet points in this final question, or write a number of linked statements.	10	Up to 2 marks can be achieved for identifying elements of commonality as identified in the question, i.e. how MacCaig uses wry humour in his poetry. A further 2 marks can be achieved for reference to the extract given. 6 additional marks can be gained for discussion of similar references to at least one other poem by the author. In practice this means: Identification of commonality. (1+1) MacCaig uses wry humour in his poetry to make serious points in an amusing way. (1) Often serious themes such as violence and death are made more dramatic via this device. (1) From the extract: 2 marks for detailed/insightful comment plus quotation/reference; 1 mark for more basic comment plus quotation/reference; 0 marks for quotation/reference alone. 2 marks only for discussion of extract. *Assisi* – the tongue-in-cheek 'over whom/he had the advantage/of not being dead yet'; mockery of the tourists in 'clucking contentedly/fluttered'. (2) From at least one other poem as above for up to 6 marks.

Question number	Question text	Marks available	Commentary, hints and tips
44 (continued)			Possible references include: ▸ *Hotel room, 12th floor* – the reductive descriptions of the helicopter and the Empire State Building; the 'ups and acrosses' image of the buildings' lights; aspects of the Wild West comparisons ▸ *Brooklyn cop* – the idea that the cop is 'less timid' than a gorilla; the invention of 'Phoebe's Whamburger'; the surprising question at the end ▸ *Visiting hour* – the disembodied nostrils; the jokey confusion of 'here and up and down and there'; the vampire image reversed in 'not guzzling but giving' ▸ *Aunt Julia* – the observation about boots: 'when she wore any'; the list beginning 'She was buckets …' ▸ *Basking shark* – the parenthetical '(too often)' after 'once'; the description of the shark as a 'roomsized monster with a matchbox brain'; the unusual word 'shoggled'.

Text 5 – Poetry – *The Ferryman's Arms* by Don Paterson

Question number	Question text	Marks available	Commentary, hints and tips
45	Look at lines 1–10. By referring to at least two examples, analyse how the poet combines ordinary detail with suggestions of the unworldly in his description of the pool game. For full marks both the 'ordinary' and the 'unworldly' should be covered but not necessarily in equal measure. 2 marks may be awarded for detailed/insightful comment plus quotation/reference; 1 mark for more basic comment plus quotation/reference; 0 marks for quotation/reference alone. (Marks may be awarded 2+2, 2+1+1 or 1+1+1+1.)	4	Possible answers include: ▸ 'cue-ball … parched D … slate … nap' are recognisable, concrete details of the scene ▸ 'clacked' suggests both the known sound of ball on slate, but also a sound which is a little unusual, hollow, echoing ▸ 'globe' suggests something much larger than a simple pool ball, hints at the globe of the world ▸ 'physics … negotiable' contradicts the idea that the laws of physics are immutable ▸ 'miracles' hints at the supernatural ▸ 'immaculate' has religious, spiritual overtones ▸ 'wee dab of side' is a straightforward, familiar jargon term used in the game ▸ 'did the vanishing trick' suggests something uncanny, inexplicable ▸ 'as if nothing had happened' suggests normal rules are not applicable ▸ 'shouldering its way' personifies the ball, suggesting it has human powers to move the other balls (with hint of shouldering a coffin?).

Question number	Question text	Marks available	Commentary, hints and tips
46	Look at lines 11 ('The boat chugged …') to 16 ('…the shoreline.'). By referring to at least two examples, analyse how the poet creates a sinister atmosphere in these lines. 2 marks may be awarded for detailed/insightful comment plus quotation/reference; 1 mark for more basic comment plus quotation/reference; 0 marks for quotation/reference alone. (Marks may be awarded 2+2, 2+1+1 or 1+1+1+1.)	4	Possible answers include: ▶ 'chugged' suggests a quiet, determined, slightly menacing sound ▶ 'without breaking the skin of the water' suggests a ghostly, unnatural movement through the water ▶ 'black' suggests death ▶ 'somewhere unspeakable' suggests a vague, unknown origin, threatening and frightening ▶ the repeated 's' sound suggests a constant hissing, menacing noise ▶ the word 'mussitates' is disturbing in its very strangeness ▶ 'a nutter's persistence' suggests someone driven to madness by attempting to come to terms with the inevitability of death ▶ 'read and re-read' suggests a dogged determination to understand something that cannot be fully understood ▶ 'shoreline' suggests, perhaps, the dividing line between life and death.
47	Look at lines 16 ('I got aboard …') to 20 ('… for next time.'). Explain the significance of the term 'losing opponent' to the extract as a whole. 2 marks may be awarded for detailed/insightful comment plus quotation/reference; 1 mark for more basic comment plus quotation/reference; 0 marks for quotation/reference alone. (Marks may be awarded 2 or 1+1.)	2	Possible answers include: ▶ the idea of 'opponent' focuses on the concept of duality which runs through the poem (black and white balls, potted and unpotted balls, winner and loser, life and death) ▶ the uncertainty about who actually wins or loses creates an eerie, unnerving mood ▶ the idea that the ferry's departure for the loser is firmly fixed ('on the hour') suggests the inevitability of death ▶ the idea that the loser is left 'stuck in his tent of light … for the next time' suggests a repeated, inevitable process.
48	By referring to this extract and to at least one other poem by Paterson, discuss the effectiveness of the way he ends his poems. You can answer in bullet points in this final question, or write a number of linked statements.	10	Up to 2 marks can be achieved for identifying elements of commonality as identified in the question, i.e. the effectiveness of the way Paterson ends his poems. A further 2 marks can be achieved for reference to the extract given. 6 additional marks can be gained for discussion of similar references to at least one other poem by the author. In practice this means: Identification of commonality. (1+1) Paterson's poems often end summing up the central concerns of the poem such as the themes of love or death. (1) Other endings are ambiguous and leave the reader to make their own conclusions. (1)

Question number	Question text	Marks available	Commentary, hints and tips
48 (continued)			From the extract: 2 marks for detailed/insightful comment plus quotation/reference; 1 mark for more basic comment plus quotation/reference; 0 marks for quotation/reference alone.
			2 marks only for discussion of extract.
			The Ferryman's Arms – enigmatic, sinister conclusion with doubt cast on who is in fact the 'losing opponent'; creates idea of a constantly repeated game ('for next time'), alluding to the inevitability of death; leaves an impression of the doppelganger/duality idea which is central to the poem. (2)
			From at least one other poem as above for up to 6 marks.
			Possible references include:
			▶ *Baldovan 11.00* – ends on a mysterious note: the journey returns to 'the point we left off' but everything has changed ('voices sound funny and all the houses are gone'), time has shifted; the boys' journey, which started in a fixed recognisable world, has become a metaphorical one, presumably towards death or the unknown future
			▶ *Nil Nil* – the final stanza ('In short, this is where you get off, reader') jerks the reader away from the stories of the football team and the jet pilot, as if to make clear they are invention; yet he continues with themes of death and fading away ('failing light … steadily fades') which could refer to the relationship between poet and reader
			▶ *Waking with Russell* – the central image of the 'smile' is repeated, described as a powerful natural force ('poured through us like a river'); concludes on a note of extreme tenderness and unqualified love for his son ('kissed … pledged … forever'), summing up the idea of celebration for his new-found commitment
			▶ *Rain* – ends very enigmatically with the shift to italic print which introduces the idea of rain as superior to all other important liquids ('ink … milk … blood') and with power to cleanse and (re)generate; the final single line (*'none of this matters'*) can be interpreted in many ways
			▶ *The Circle* – returns to starting point of the boy's attempts at painting, but focuses now on the appearance of the water-jar in which the swirl of colour is elevated into a 'little avatar'; the tone of the ending is joyous and celebratory, with a sense of musicality in the repeated sounds of 'filling … ring … singing … everything'.

Revision notes

Revision notes

Acknowledgements

The Publishers would like to thank the following for permission to reproduce copyright material:

pp.1–2 The article 'It's a tough choice, of course, but maybe this is the one to read first' by Ben Macintyre, from *The Times* © The Times/News Syndication 28 February 2004.

p.3 The article 'Why I choose to have less choice' by Tim Lott, from *The Guardian*, 19 May 2015. Copyright Guardian News & Media Ltd 2019.

pp.4–5 The article 'If you want to save the world, veganism isn't the answer' by Isabella Tree from *The Guardian*, 25 Aug 2018. Copyright Guardian News & Media Ltd 2019.

pp.5–6 The article 'I make vegan cheese in Amsterdam. And no one here calls it faux' by Brad Vanstone from *The Guardian*, 6 March 2019. Copyright Guardian News & Media Ltd 2019.

pp.19–20, **56** and **77** extracts from *Men Should Weep* by Ena Lamont Stewart, published by Samuel French Ltd. Reprinted by permission of Samuel French Ltd (A Concord Theatrical Company) and Alan Brodie Representation.

pp.21–22, **61** and **82** extracts from *The Cone-Gatherers*, reprinted with permission of Canongate Books Ltd © Robin Jenkins 2004.

Carol Ann Duffy poems/extracts on **p 23** ('War Photographer'), **p.24** ('The Way My Mother Speaks') and **p.85** ('Valentine') from *New Selected Poems 1984–2004*, published by Picador 2011. Copyright © Carol Ann Duffy. Reproduced by permission of the author c/o Rogers, Coleridge & White Ltd., 20 Powis Mews, London W11 1JN.

pp.51–52 The article 'The sooner zoos become extinct the better' by Janice Turner, from *The Times* © The Times/News Syndication, 4 June 2016.

pp.52–53 Text adapted from PETA: www.peta.org.

pp.54–55 and **75–76** extracts from *The Slab Boys* © 1982 John Byrne. *The Slab Boys* was first performed at the Traverse Theatre, Edinburgh, on 6 April 1978. All rights whatsoever in this play are strictly reserved and application for performance etc. should be made to the Author's agent: Casarotto Ramsay & Associates Limited, Waverley House, 7–12 Noel Street, London W1F 8GQ (rights@casarotto.co.uk). No performance may be given unless a licence has been obtained.

p.57 extract from 'The Red Door' and **p.78** extract from 'Mother and Son' by Iain Crichton Smith, from *The Red Door: The Complete English Stories 1949–76*, published by Birlinn. Reproduced with permission of the Licensor through PLSClear.

George Mackay Brown extracts **p.58** extract from 'A Time to Keep' and **p.79** extract from 'The Eye of The Hurricane' by George Mackay Brown, from *A Time to Keep*, published by Polygon. Reproduced with permission of the Licensor through PLSClear.

p.59 and **p.80** extract from *Dr Jekyll and Mr Hyde* by Robert Louis Stevenson. Public domain.

pp.60 and **81** extracts from *Sunset Song* by Lewis Grassic Gibbon, published by Jarrold Publishing, 1932. Public domain.

p.62 'A Poet's Welcome to His Love-Begotten Daughter' by Robert Burns. Public domain.

p.64 'Mrs Midas' copyright © Carol Ann Duffy. Reproduced with permission of the Licensor through PLSClear.

Liz Lochhead extracts **pp.65** 'Revelation' and **p.86** 'The Bargain' from *A Choosing: Selected Poems*, published by Polygon (Birlinn). Reproduced with permission of the Licensor through PLSClear.

Norman MacCaig extracts **pp.67–68** 'Visiting Hour' and **p.88** 'Assisi' by from *The Poems of Norman MacCaig*, published by Polygon. Reproduced with permission of the Licensor through PLSClear.

Don Paterson extracts **p.69** 'Nil, Nil' and **p.89** 'The Ferryman's Arms' from *Nil, Nil by Don Paterson* published by Faber & Faber, 2004. Copyright © Don Paterson. Reproduced by permission of the author c/o Rogers, Coleridge & White Ltd., 20 Powis Mews, London W11 1JN.

pp.72–73 The article 'We don't need this culture of overwork' by Johann Hari, from *The Independent*, 8 January 2010 © The Independent.

pp.73–74 The article 'Retiring at 77? Surely we should strive to work less' by Owen Jones, from *The Guardian*, 3 March 2016. Copyright Guardian News & Media Ltd 2019.

p.83 extract from 'Tam o' Shanter' by Robert Burns. Public domain.